# Why the North Won the Vietnam War

# Why the North Won the Vietnam War

Edited by
Marc Jason Gilbert

palgrave

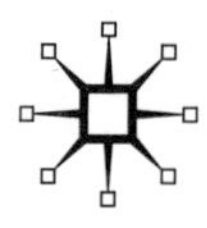

WHY THE NORTH WON THE VIETNAM WAR



First published 2002 by PALGRAVE™
175 Fifth Avenue, New York, N.Y.10010 and
Houndmills, Basingstoke, Hampshire RG21 6XS.
Companies and representatives throughout the world

PALGRAVE is the new global publishing imprint of St. Martin's Press LLC Scholarly and Reference Division and Palgrave Publishers Ltd (formerly Macmillan Press Ltd).

ISBN 0–312–29526-X hardback
ISBN 0–312–29527–8 paperback

**Library of Congress Cataloging-in-Publication Data**
Why the North won the Vietnam war / [edited] by Marc Jason Gilbert.
p. cm.
Includes bibliographical references and index.
ISBN 0–312–29526-X — ISBN 0–312–29527–8 (pbk.)
1. Vietnamese Conflict, 1961–1975. 2. Vietnamese Conflict, 1961–1975—Vietnam (Democratic Republic) I. Gilbert, Marc Jason.

DS557.7.H69 2002
959'.704'3—dc21 2001056135

A catalogue record for this book is available from the British Library.

Design by Letra Libre, Inc.

First edition: June 2002
10 9 8 7 6 5 4 3

Printed in the United States of America.

*In war, you must win!*

*—Senior General Vo Nguyen Giap*

# CONTENTS

# Abbreviations and Acronyms

| | |
|---|---|
| ARVN | Army of the Republic of Vietnam |
| ASD/ISA | Assistant Secretary of Defense for International Security Affairs |
| CAP | Combined Action Platoon |
| CCP | Chinese Communist Party |
| CIA | Central Intelligence Agency |
| CICV | Combined Intelligence Center Vietnam |
| CINPAC | Commander in Chief, Pacific |
| CIO | Central Intelligence Organization |
| CORDS | Civil Operations and Revolutionary Development Support |
| COSVN | Central Office for South Vietnam (Hanoi's field command in South Vietnam) |
| DIA | Defense Intelligence Agency |
| DMZ | Demilitarized Zone |
| DRV (DRVN) | The Democratic Republic of Vietnam |
| GVN | The Government of Vietnam |
| HES | Hamlet Evaluation Surveys |
| ICP | Indochinese Communist Party |
| IVS | International Voluntary Services |
| JCS | Joint Chiefs of Staff |
| MAAG | Military Assistance and Advisory Group |
| MACV | Military Assistance Command, Vietnam |
| NATO | North Atlantic Treaty Organization |
| NCRC | National Council of Reconciliation and Concord |
| NLF (NLFSV) | National Liberation Front (of South Vietnam) |
| NSA | National Security Agency |
| NVA | North Vietnamese Army (same as PAVN) |
| PAVN | People's Army of Vietnam |
| PLA | People's Liberation Army |
| PLAF | People's Liberation Armed Forces |
| PRG | Provisional Revolutionary Government |

| | |
|---|---|
| PROVN | Program for the Pacification and Long-term Development of South Vietnam |
| PRUs | Provincial Reconnaissance Units |
| RVN | Republic of Vietnam |
| RVNAF | Republic of Vietnam Armed Forces |
| SEATO | Southeast Asia Treaty Organization |
| VCI | Viet Cong infrastructure |
| Viet Cong | Insurgent forces in the Republic of Vietnam |
| VVAW | Vietnam Veterans against the War |
| VWP | Vietnam Workers' Party |

# ACKNOWLEDGMENTS

The editor wishes to recognize the unstinting support of the trustees of the U.S. Army War College, Colonel U.S. Army Reserve (ret.) John O'Shea of the Reserve Officers Association, and of Brigadier General USAF (ret.) Carl Reddel, Colonel USAF (ret.) Elliot Converse III, and Donna Quisenbury, all formerly of the Eisenhower Institute for World Affairs, which made possible the conference that facilitated the development of this volume. He is also grateful for the assistance of Deborah Gershonowitz, Kasey Moon, Jennifer Stais, and Meg Weaver of Palgrave-St. Martin's, who were instrumental in seeing this volume into print. Further, he acknowledges the support of North Georgia College and State University; the head of its Department of History, T. Christopher Jespersen; the Department's administrative assistant, Vicki Dowdy; and its student associate, Curtis Spiva, for their help in the preparation of the manuscript. Randee L. Head, who prepared the volume's index, richly deserves similar acknowledgment for her work.

Thanks are also due to a diverse group of scholars including Ambassador Bui Diem, John M. Carland of the Center for Military History; historians Timothy Castle and Arthur Dommen; anthropologists Dan Duffy and Donald Marshall, analyst-activist Daniel Ellsberg; Ted Gittinger of the Lyndon Baines Johnson Presidential Library; General Andrew Goodpaster; Richard Hunt, formerly of the Center for Military History; William Head, Chief Historian, Robins Air Force Base; Douglas Pike and James Reckner of the Center for the Study of Vietnam, Texas Tech University; David Shreve of the Presidential Recordings Project, The Miller Center of Public Affairs, University of Virginia; Walt W. Rostow; and the late Admiral Elmo R. Zumwalt, who were kind enough to facilitate the editor's work and/or his own research, though what he has made of their assistance is his construction alone.

The editor also wishes to extend a long-overdue thanks to Dr. Gerald Shure and Dr. Robert Meeker of System Development Corporation's Conflict Resolution Study Team who, from 1966–1969, gave this one-time very smallest cog in the American military industrial complex what he turned into his own little corner in the war without windows. In a sense, this volume began there, for ever since it was first set in motion in one of this

RAND Corporation spin-off's all-metal part-time staff assistant cubicles, that little cog has been turning in an effort to understand why some of the best minds of what is now called the "Greatest Generation" and some of the stoutest hearts of his own found themselves in "a terrible jam, way down yonder in Vietnam," rubbing elbows with the ghosts of generations of Chinese, Mongols, and French that preceded them there. Whether this volume furthers that understanding will be for the reader to decide. As for the volume's other contributors, it must be said that rarely have so many scholars attempted to engage the American War in Vietnam with so passionate a commitment to a fair and open consideration of so controversial an aspect of that "conflict" as why it was won or lost. For that commitment, the editor is grateful beyond words.

# Preface

## Earl H. Tilford, Jr.

Who won or lost the Vietnam War? For more than a quarter century, this question has plagued Americans, but few others. Most of the rest of the world, especially the Vietnamese, understood immediately the meaning of the Viet Cong flag raised above the Presidential Palace in Saigon on April 25, 1975. Many Americans, still unsure as to whether the war was lost—or, worse, self-deluded into thinking they won—have yet to ask the better questions: Why did the world's leading military and economic power lose? And why does it still matter?

Americans have a peculiar notion of war. With more or less friendly countries to the north and south and fish to the east and west, for the nation's first two centuries, we picked and chose our wars to satisfy the better angels of our nature, on whose side we wanted to fight. In wars from 1776 to 1945, good triumphed. The children of the American Revolution won its first great crusade, the American Civil War. Their grandchildren, the generation dubbed by reporter Tom Brokaw as the "Greatest Generation," fought and won the last crusade, World War II. Their children—this generation—fought but do not yet understand their war, a war that history, if it is kind, still may name a "lost crusade." Even then, the emphasis will be on the word "lost."

In 1962, with the leading edge of what would be known as the Vietnam Generation foundering in a paradigm shift between Elvis and the Kingston Trio, at the fringes of our awareness Bob Dylan, in a song entitled "With God on Our Side," mused with a voice that rolled like gravel down a chute, "The reasons for fightin' I never did know." The words continue to irritate, like an annoying stone in our jogging shoe, the presence of which makes it impossible to run comfortably, but which also means we must stop, lose the rhythm of our pace, untie the shoe, expose and remove the stone. For many of us who gathered at Gettysburg College in October 2000 to address the question "Why the North Won the Vietnam War," that was what we were doing. The title of the conference rankled some but not most of those who made the trip to Gettysburg.

Carl von Clausewitz, on page 1, Book One, of *On War* (1832) wrote, "War is thus an act of force to compel the enemy to do our will." Straightforward enough; it's the stuff of clearly defined objectives and missions. But at the bottom of the page lies the qualifier: "The maximum use of force is in no way incompatible with the simultaneous use of the intellect." Before anything else and after all is done, war is an intellectual exercise, albeit one with potentially catastrophic physical ramifications. Winning or losing is a matter of perception—of will. The winner's will triumphs, the loser's breaks. The scope of death and destruction will depend on the value attached to the outcome by each of the warring parties.

For most of the world, the Vietnam War was decided over a quarter century ago. The Viet Cong and their North Vietnamese allies, after more than 10,000 days of fighting, watched from the grounds of Saigon's Presidential Palace as the last American helicopter departed the roof of the U.S. Embassy. For those Americans aboard the last helicopter, that was reality after fifteen years of fighting, $200 billion in resources, 8 million tons of mostly wasted aerial ordnance dumped on ill-defined and largely irrelevant targets, and more than 58,000 lives lost. The victors paid far more dearly than the vanquished, more than a million dead, the cost of forcibly reunifying a country after nearly a hundred years of division.

What was America's war in Vietnam? It was a war that both defined and altered a generation. Those of us who listened to Bob Dylan groan, "The reasons for fightin' I never did know" are, like him, a long way down life's jogging trail. Having long passed the midpoint in our run, we rankle at the stone in the shoe. We wonder if we can finish the run without stopping to remove the stone. Our mind tells us we can, but not comfortably. The same questions remain: How? Why? And why does it still matter?

*Earl H. Tilford, Jr., Ph.D.*
*Professor of History*
*Grove City College*
*Grove City, Pennsylvania*

# Introduction

MARC JASON GILBERT

In the aftermath of the American Civil War, a gathering of former Confederate officers voiced their conviction that a multitude of errors made by their own political and military leaders had doomed the Southern cause to defeat, particularly at the pivotal Battle of Gettysburg. Some grumbled about General Robert E. Lee's lack of strategic vision, while others blamed Generals Longstreet and Ewell for making critical errors on the field of their greatest battle. Only the most distinguished of those present, General George Pickett, remained aloof from this orgy of self-criticism. A reporter, intrigued by the Gettysburg veteran's silence, asked him to share with the group his view of why the South had lost the battle that all but decided the War Between the States. Thus prompted, Pickett replied dryly, "Gentlemen, I have always thought that the Yankees had something to do with it."

In keeping with Pickett's notion, in 1958, with the United States on the verge of a centennial celebration of its Civil War, Professor David Herbert Donald of Columbia University sponsored another gathering, this time of scholars, on the campus of Gettysburg College so near to the battlefield upon which Picket's division established the albeit brief high watermark of the Confederacy. Their collective task was to examine the international, strategic, economic, and social factors that led to victory for the Union and defeat for the Confederacy. During that conference, Norman A. Graebner of the University of Virginia called attention to the impact of France and England's lack of support for the rebellion; T. Harry Williams of Louisiana State University illuminated the deficiencies of the Southern military strategy; David M. Potter judged the South's political leadership to have been grossly incompetent; Richard N. Current of the University of Wisconsin stressed the importance of the economic superiority of the North; while Donald himself argued that the excessive emphasis on individual freedom, characteristic of Southern culture, fatally undermined military discipline. Their presentations, as edited by

Donald, later appeared as *Why the North Won the Civil War* (1960). This work, whose 1996 edition includes a historiographical essay on the causes of the South's defeat by Henry Steele Commager, has earned a respected place in American military history.[1]

In the spirit of the 1958 Gettysburg conference, on October 26–28, 2000, the Army War College Foundation, the Eisenhower World Affairs Institute and the Reserve Officers Association sponsored a conference at which a body of scholars again gathered at Gettysburg College to address a parallel theme, "Why the North Won the Vietnam War." The conference was designed and moderated by this writer and by Dr. Earl H. Tilford, Jr., then of the Army War College. Like its predecessor, it addressed the diplomatic, political, military, economic, and social factors that led to the defeat of the United States and its allies in what is best described as the Second Indochina War, but which is known to scholars in this country as the American War in Vietnam and to the American public as the Vietnam War. The deliberate reference in its title to Prof. Donald's conference and its resulting book was not only intended to lend perspective to this meeting, but also to signal that the scholars gathered at Gettysburg fully shared Pickett's ability to think outside of the box. Their presentations focused as much on Vietnamese in the "South"—the National Liberation Front (NLF) and the Republic of Vietnam (RVN)—as they did on Vietnamese in the "North" (the Democratic Republic of Vietnam or DRV), and as much on Vietnamese of all allegiances as on the United States. None of these presenters believe the so-called "North" won the war on its own, nor did they place much value on the idea that the U.S. intervention in Vietnam failed to achieve its goals solely due to its own mistakes, in part because they believe that the enemy often paid dearly to force its American opponents to make these errors. They attribute to the Vietnamese, communist and noncommunist, a primary role in the outcome of a struggle over the direction of Vietnam's quest for modernization and development that predated that intervention and has continued until this day. They do so, in part, to rectify one of the great ironies of the war. Thousands of American lives were destroyed and millions more were touched by the fire of the war ostensibly fought in aid of the Vietnamese people. Yet the Vietnamese themselves, their sacrifices and their aspirations, rarely appear in American postmortems on that war. The Vietnamese and, for that matter, Laotians, Cambodians, and Thais were major factors in the wars in Indochina. To see them as merely faceless victims of an American failure to defeat and/or save them is to deprive them of their own history.

This present volume was planned prior to the conference. The presentations made at Gettysburg were viewed as a means of improving the authors' work via a collegial exchange of ideas among the presenters themselves, and between them and a select audience that ranged from serving military officers to representatives of veterans groups and historians as diverse as Herbert Y. Schandler (a veteran of two tours of duty in Vietnam and author of *The Unmaking of a President: Lyndon Johnson and Vietnam,* 1983) and Barbara Tischler (whose interest in the place of Vietnam in American Studies is reflected in *Sights on the Sixties,* 1992). The run-up to the conference and its proceedings led to some changes in the project, but it did not move far beyond the bounds of its predecessor. It was decided that, howsoever persistent the notion that the news media lost the Vietnam War, the work of Daniel Hallin (*"The Uncensored War": The Media and Vietnam,* 1986), William Hammond (*The U.S. Army and Vietnam: The Military and the Media, 1962–1968,* 1989), and Clarence Wyatt (*Paper Soldiers: The American Press and the Vietnam War,* 1993) has satisfied most students of the war that its role in that defeat was marginal at best. It was thus not addressed extensively in this volume. When planned presentations by Vietnamese on the war and by scholars of American wartime decision making along the lines of H. R. MacMaster's *Dereliction of Duty* (1997) and Brian VanDeMark's *Into the Quagmire* (1995) failed to materialize, the other contributors expanded their treatment of these dimensions of the war so that the volume would be as comprehensive and thus as useful as possible, while still following many of the topics and the general plan laid out by David Donald and his colleagues. That plan served to keep this work's focus chiefly on the "whys" rather than the war's related "lessons," which have received exhaustive treatment elsewhere.

Donald's volume eventually came to feature an essay on the way historians have come to view the causes of the American defeat in Vietnam. It was decided to offer one here, so constructed as to provide the setting for and tie together the chapters comprising this work. Its focus is one aspect of the conflict in Indochina that clearly sets apart the analysis of America's most divisive foreign war from its own internal strife of the 1860s. While arguments about who "won" or "lost" these wars and how these ends were achieved is characteristic of the postmortems of each of them, the debate over how the Second Indochina War ended in defeat for the United States occurred in a far different social context. That unique context helped shape the variety of interpretations of why America failed to achieve its key stated objective in Southeast Asia: the maintenance of a non-communist Republic of Vietnam. The following discussion of these interpretations assumes that no single truth or perspective can "explain" this failure. Thus it will not satisfy those whose view of the war requires such an explanation or who are unwilling to admit that there is any truth to be found in the arguments of those students of the war with whom they disagree. To the extent to which this survey appears, howsoever unintentionally, discomfiting, it will have served an important secondary purpose: Exposing some of the intellectual tripwires that have for so long frustrated the achievement of historical consensus over the war, thus helping succeeding generations to better avoid the fate of so many investigators of the Vietnam generation who have fallen victim to friendly as well as hostile fire in the culture wars of the late twentieth century.

## Facing Defeat

In the wake of their defeat in the American Civil War, Southerners were overwhelmed by the devastation of their land and their way of life. Their government, based on a conception of states rights, had been overthrown. The lynchpin of the South's economic system, slavery, which the Southern theory of states rights had been evoked to defend, was abolished, at least in law. Its leaders were deprived of their civil liberties, and the land itself lay under the hand of an army of occupation. The blow to the values of the antebellum South was so severe that the wounds to the psyches of those who held them dear have been transferred to generation after generation of their descendents. In the 1980s, a departing Japanese consul based in Atlanta remarked that the rigors of his tour of duty in the South had been eased as he had been working among a people whose attitude toward life was dominated by the same event. "We both," he said, "know what it is like to be defeated in war."

The immediate damage done by the American War in Vietnam to America's political, social, and economic fabric, as great as it was, was light in comparison to the rents made by its domestic debacle in the previous century. Public confidence in American political leaders and institutions had been seriously eroded by the war, but had not been destroyed: Voters in great numbers gave their support to candidates who served in the war, opposed it, or, as in the cases of successful senatorial candidates John Kerry and Al Gore, did both. The economy had been damaged, but its extent only became clear in the mid-1980s: In the aftermath of the war, an Arab oil embargo and disco fever held the nation's attention, not debates over whether the economy was weakening due to wartime deficit spending. The "Vietnam Syndrome," a general postwar unwillingness by the United States to commit its troops abroad, was lamented by some, but kept the nation from direct intervention in both Iran and Nicaragua, perhaps sparing it from the crushing domestic and foreign policy debacle that the Soviet Union experienced as a result of its Afghan adventure.[2]

Domestically, the termination of the American War in Vietnam (if not the wars in Indochina) had, at least momentarily, a cleansing effect. The American left, having seen the end of what it considered an American imperialist war, moved on to battles such as environmental protection and the expansion of the rights of women and racial minorities. Once American troops had left Vietnam, the region's fate generally passed beyond their political horizon, even when Vietnamese gulags and the genocide in Cambodia rose above it.[3]

The American right suffered a catastrophic failure of leadership that sealed the fate of the Republic of Vietnam, but it wished to put the war behind it so quickly that it may have tried to cover up the mishandling of its last hurrah in Indochina: the *Mayaguez* incident.[4] After a decent interval, it declared the war a noble cause and moved on to battles aimed at securing the triumph of the free market and creating a balanced national budget, even at the cost of reducing the benefits and care offered to the warriors who fought for that noble cause.[5] The vast majority of Americans regarded the war as a misadventure best forgotten. If there was a consensus on the war among the general public, it was that the United States should never refight the Vietnam War: never again gradually deploy American conventional forces in pursuit of a limited war in Asian jungles occupied by communist rebels who fuel the guerrilla phase of their struggle with resources drawn from anticolonialist poverty-stricken farmers having difficulty identifying with their elitist noncommunist authoritarian government, i.e., no more Vietnams, literally.

## The Standard Interpretation Emerges

It was in this context, a mood of resigned acceptance for most of the country, that what here will be called the standard (or orthodox school) interpretation[6] of the causes of the American defeat in Vietnam began to emerge. This interpretation was neither monolithic nor static. It initially drew on the work of writers such as George Ball (*The Past has Another Pattern,* 1982), Chester Cooper (*The Lost Crusade,* 1970), and David Halberstam (*The Making of a Quagmire,* 1964; *The Best and the Brightest,* 1972) that was rooted in their authors' evolving wartime views as to why America was headed for defeat, views that helped shape some of the public's initial perceptions of the causes of that defeat. However, the sources of the standard interpretation eventually grew beyond this circle of disaffected Washington insiders to include the vast majority of professional scholars in the United States, including marine-turned-historian David Marr (*Vietnam, 1945,* 1995) and wartime civilian analysts William Duiker (*The Communist Road to Power,* 1981) and Neil Jameson (*Understanding Vietnam,* 1995). Its overall assessment grew so popular that its acceptance eventually crossed political lines from the left of center (Marilyn Young, *The Vietnam Wars,* 1991) to right of center (Robert Shulzinger, *A Time for War,* 1997).

According to this interpretation, the war was lost due to a combination of American and allied Vietnamese weaknesses and their Vietnamese foe's strengths or, rather, the asymmetrical relationships between the strengths and weaknesses of all combatants: the enemy was strongest in the very areas where forces allied to the United States were weakest, and the enemy's weaknesses could not easily be exploited by allied strengths. Chief among the

Vietnamese foe's strengths was its ability to project itself as the champions of Vietnam's independence and its pursuit of a plan of campaign possessed of unity of direction and political cohesion that, while imperfect, survived the vicissitudes of war with the greatest power on earth. Whereas these Vietnamese were fighting to reunify their country and possibly assert their precolonial regional dominance, their American foe was fighting to preserve old colonial territorial and ideological divisions among Vietnamese in a theater distant from both its own shores and also its national interests. The Vietnamese leadership America fought in Vietnam was willing and able to sacrifice their population in a total war for their aims. Yet, the Vietnamese regime that fought alongside the United States could not even politically afford to draft college students until after the pivotal Tet Offensive of 1968, while the United States assumed a limited war posture it regarded as appropriate for its more limited purpose: halting the spread of communism in a region that represented an indirect threat to the security of its ally Japan and no direct threat to the United States itself.

Even the most ardent communist internationalists among the Vietnamese foe had to deal with the knowledge that most Vietnamese regarded communist ideology as, at best, a means to an end, and that their Cold War allies, China and the Soviet Union, were intent on using Vietnam to advance their own hegemonic designs. However, the power inherent both in revolutionary communism and traditional Vietnamese statecraft rendered the obstacles the DRV/NLF faced minor compared with those faced by its American opponent. These were misguided idealism, a failure to understand Vietnamese history, a misinterpretation of world communism, and an American war-making machine that was hampered by paradigm paralysis. That war machine also suffered from civilian-military relations so dysfunctional as to render both soldiers and politicians unable to tell the truth about the war to each other, let alone to the American public. These misperceptions and self-deceptions collectively drew American officials, step by incremental step, into a "quagmire" from which it proved hard to extricate itself with honor. American leaders, political and military, soon saw that they could not win in Vietnam at a politically acceptable level of commitment (or achieve a victory worth its geo-political, human and material cost). But they also could not afford the stigma of defeat, given the unforgiving Cold War political atmosphere a generation of war managers and politicians in both major parties had themselves created. And so they, or those brave souls they led into such dubious battle, soldiered on, until the United States withdrew from Vietnam on terms that were identified at the beginning of the war as well below the minimum outcome that could be described as "victory."

According to Daniel Ellsberg (*Papers on the War*, 1972), the fear of being the first to "lose" a war to the communists since the "fall" of China led to the "minimum candor" and outright lying by civilian and military authorities that fatally undermined the American war effort. Ellsberg together with Leslie Gelb and Richard Betts (*The Irony of Vietnam,* 1972) suggest in a corollary to the standard interpretation that American authorities, trapped in a war they knew they could not win, may have sought out a strategy that prioritized an achievable stalemate over an unobtainable victory. Whether so designed or not, the policy of limited war they adopted successfully spared eight presidential administrations from paying the full bill each had feared would come due for "losing" Indochina. Lyndon Johnson paid a high, but personal, price, while his vice president, Hubert Humphrey, failed to succeed him by only a hairsbreadth, largely due to the perception that his rival, Richard M. Nixon, had a better exit strategy. According to one of his most charitable biographers, Joan Hoff, President Nixon disengaged the United States from the war in 1973 "on only marginally better terms" than those that had been judged unacceptable in 1969, a poor return, she concludes, for the "additional 20,000 American lives lost during this three-year period." Yet, Nixon has largely escaped the criticism such loss of life should warrant.[7] His successor, Gerald Ford, washed his hands of the whole matter as opposing Vietnamese forces rolled into the capital of the Republic of Vietnam, but even his presidency was not forfeited as a result of "losing Vietnam." Whether these results are seen as ironic or tragic, the stalemate system, if such it was, worked.

A further key to the orthodox school was its valuation of the war's international, domestic, and war-fighting environment. As mentioned above, it contends that to win on the ground short of engaging in a global war, the United States had to preserve in Vietnam a political division of a people with a strong common identity while defending a weak regime in the South beset by an internal rebellion supported by a Vietnamese regime in the North that was the legatee of a recent anticolonial struggle. The opponents of American intervention within and without the southern regime were riding a rising tide of decolonization, not propping up colonialism's last vestiges, as the United States did by supporting the French in the First Indochina War (1945–1954). Domestically, the Democratic Republic of Vietnam benefited from the fullest support on the home front enjoyed by any nation at war in the modern period. The United States, on the other hand, faced turmoil at home it fueled by its inability to justify its war policy (or the war itself) in terms that could garner and hold the degree of public support its chief Vietnamese opponent enjoyed.

The orthodox school views the Republic of Vietnam as facing even more internal difficulties than its American ally. It was what some American leaders charitably called a nation with "no tradition of . . . national government"[8] and what the less charitable among them called a "government-that-is-not-a-government." It was led by an urban landholding and commercial elite that was reluctant to introduce political and economic reforms that could come only at its own expense. It was also too closely tied to the former colonial regime to convince key constituencies of its worth unless it enacted such reforms. Gabriel Kolko (*Anatomy of a War,* 1985) suggests that the problems of the RVN lay in part in the manner in which the French discouraged the emergence of a middle class from which possibly more legitimate noncommunist national leadership might emerge. The weakness of the Saigon regime that Americans often attributed to individual leaders was thus endemic and virtually beyond resolution. In the end, RVN proved too much of an autocracy to court public support and not enough of a dictatorship even to attempt to command it. It survived numerous coups but faced domestic opposition from within its own ruling circle and could manage antiwar protests only by imprisoning its political opponents under conditions so deplorable that it would ultimately undermine American support. As even American policymakers conceded, the Democratic Republic of Vietnam and the National Liberation Front executed those it labeled as exploiters of the people and made an effort to observe the Maoist precept that revolutionaries should respect the property of the masses. Meanwhile, the Republic of Vietnam sold offices of state, and its army was forced to live off the people in a manner that was more random and often more brutal than the levies of Viet Cong tax collectors. Under a prohibition from its American ally against launching a "march North"[9] it could never sustain, and occupied by foreign troops, it could not compete with its rival's claim to represent the goal of independence and reunification that all Vietnamese sought. Even some Americans among the foreign troops viewed with contempt the regime they were defending, believing that their own commander in the field was using them "to impose upon the Vietnamese a government that he would have fought to the death to prevent being imposed on us."[10]

This interpretation of the war argues that the strategic steps taken to prop up the Saigon regime while avoiding a wider war led to a limited war characterized by a gradualist policy that America's foremost systems analyst and later lion of American conservatism, Albert Wohlstetter (*On Vietnam and Bureaucracy,* 1968), called "mini brute force," i.e., "a slow application of brute force in the hope of achieving quickly objectives that could be achieved, if at all, only by a rapid use of such force." By "if at all," Wohlstetter meant not that the United States could not mount a full-scale invasion of the DRV, but that such a step seemed to be ill suited to American strategic goals. In a speech given in 1968 before an audience that included policymakers such as Henry Kissinger, Wohlstetter argued that, while the United States strove to align its war aims with the appropriate application of force, it had never been able to do so. "The bombing of the North Vietnam, for example, was wrong even on its own terms—it was poorly adapted for reducing the number of North Vietnamese in South Vietnam." Nor was the bombing and artillery usage in the South calculated to serve its intended ends there as "they exacted much too high a toll in bystanders and friendly forces." Wohlstetter noted in frustration that so long as a gap existed between policy and the means employed to achieve it, no victory in Vietnam was possible. After the war, some of America's wartime military leaders and analysts decried the application of mini brute force, but their critiques failed to answer Wohlstetter's most pressing question: how would more rapid and brutal use of force against the DRV directly produce the political stability in the South required for victory? As Robert Buzzanco (*Masters of War,* 1996) has observed, although these military leaders had during the war understood the need to match force structure to strategic goals, none risked their careers to stop what they later claimed was America's fatal error in failing to take corrective steps to restore this balance. The stalemate machine hummed along in the Pentagon as well as at the White House.

The orthodox school holds that the Vietnamese pursued military operations based on nostrums that were deeply rooted in Vietnamese history. They employed a protracted war to defeat foreigners fighting far from home—a strategy whose utility was proven by America's own Revolutionary War as well as Vietnam's own centuries'-long wars with China. As in those wars, when the enemy's troops were demoralized and isolated by protracted conflict, Vietnam's leaders shifted to a conventional strategy better suited to destroy what forces remained to be faced. U.S. forces were not destroyed in Vietnam, they withdrew—leaving their Vietnamese ally vulnerable—but this was another contingency the Vietnamese had mastered almost 500 years earlier.[11] It was based on the idea that wars have interlacing dual tracts, political and military. National fighting spirit, the international context, and the home front were as much a part of warfare as military operations. This posture was made more effective by the manner in which the American foe was trapped by or sought out of political necessity to either isolate or marginalize these dimensions of the conflict.

The U.S. military strategy, according to the orthodox school, also was rooted in its history. Yet it pursed operations governed by analogies to those past American wars, particularly the Korean War, that, according to Wohlstetter and, later, Yuen Foong Khong (*Analogies at War,* 1992) had so little in common with the struggle in Indochina that their application was judged a major reason for the U.S. defeat. The U.S. limited war and fighting in cold blood posture, while frustrating, was, according to wartime Secretary of the Army Stanley Resor, adopted in the belief that it best served the situation it faced[12] and was an option in tune with the prevailing global and historical context.[13] But a major problem in fighting a limited war in coalition with and within a weak "host" country was that the prospects of success were only as great as the strength of that country. The Republic of Vietnam was never more than marginally viable, and no combination of battlefield strategies could, in the orthodox view, alter that truth.

Whether contemplating a limited or "all-out" strategy, U.S. policymakers exaggerated the importance of military power in settling what even many military advisors, including the U.S. Army Chief of Staff, General Harold Johnson, knew ultimately to be a political problem in Vietnam.[14] It was slow to abandon the model of conventional warfare that it had long mastered, even though its vaunted superiority in mobility and superior firepower was so neutralized by the enemy that it was able to control when and where it fought the vast majority of the time.[15] As early as 1958, a charter member of the orthodox school and one of America's foremost philosophers of history, Reinhold Neibuhr, warned that it was this "undue reliance on purely military power" that would prove America's undoing in Southeast Asia, for military power alone could not "reverse the injustices of Vietnam's decaying feudalism and the inequalities of its recent colonial past." It was this pursuit of a military solution to the perceived political threat that the Vietnamese revolution posed to American interests that would, he argued, ultimately frustrate American policy.[16]

Sadly, according to the orthodox school, even as U.S. forces withdrew, they taught their failing model of conventional warfare to the forces of the Republic of Vietnam, which pursued it to the very bitter end against an even better prepared and armed foe. Whereas the Democratic Republic of Vietnam was able to cadge advanced weapons from the Soviet Union even after the latter lost faith in Vietnam's loyalty, the Republic of Vietnam's unquestioned loyalty to the American cause—it was, after all, its own—was not enough to gain matching support. As the Vietnamese ambassador to the United States, Bui Diem, noted in his memoirs (*The Jaws of History*, 1987), the U.S. Congress, responding to what became widespread criticism of the war not only among activists and social elites but from its vaunted heartland, came to regard the RVN as too incompetent, too corrupt, and too undemocratic to warrant American largess long after its troops had been withdrawn.

The U.S. Congress could make such a decision because its nation's commitment to the independence of the Republic of Vietnam—which might have justified indefinite American support or even "going to the brink"—had never been as great as its commitment to the Republic of Korea or even possibly to Thailand.[17] The problem was that the American people never perceived Vietnam as vital to America's national interests. U.S. leaders understood this from the outset. They knew that if the degree of commitment required to secure the continued existence of an independent Republic of Vietnam demanded the level of public support comparable to that needed to match a direct threat to their country's existence, the U.S. effort would fail. They nonetheless pursued the war, partly out of confidence in their country's ability to meet any challenge—even that of a limited war—and partly out of their fear of failure to sustain America's image as the defender of the free world. It was thus that the American intervention in Vietnam came to violate the prime directive of philosophers of the military art from Sun Tzu to Carl von Clausewitz: War is so terrible and risky that it can be embarked on only when a state's interests are so clearly imperiled that only victory in war can ensure its survival (and thus justify the mobilization and sacrifice of its human and material resources). In Vietnam, the United States was not fighting a battle for its survival; the enemy was (Hanoi's war aims versus the United States were limited, but their ultimate aim was total: the reunification of the country). Scholars of the orthodox school realize that it is better that a nation should go all out to win or not fight all. They recognize, however, that the politics and policies of the Cold War—and war is always the extension of policies with other means—prevented the United States from heeding this dictum. The enemy suffered no such difficulties.

The orthodox school also recognized that internecine conflict between politicians and the military was endemic in the two Vietnams and in the United States. However, so their argument runs, while the commanders of the forces deployed in the field by all sides complained of micromanagement by politicians that often had dire tactical results, these results were not decisive in determining the course of the war.[18] General Bruce Palmer, no friend of the orthodox school, notes that at no time did the Joint Chiefs of Staff tell the White House that its restrictions on targeting and other forms of political intervention were inhibiting the achievement of victory in Vietnam.[19] The Politburo in the North often harassed and eventually demoted its military chief, Senior General Vo Nguyen Giap, largely for ideological reasons, but even this had little impact on the war's ultimate outcome.

What was catastrophic was the inability of American leaders, civilian and military, to look over the horizon when adopting their overall strategy. Paradigm paralysis brought on by Cold War myopia led to even so well-established a nostrum as "No land wars in Asia" being blithely dismissed in the councils of war on Vietnam. Before committing U.S. combat troops to assume offensive operations in Vietnam, U.S. policymakers argued that the Vietnamese would be loath to call on too many Chinese reinforcements for fear of having their country taken over by their traditional enemy.[20] They even hoped that Vietnamese nationalism "might someday assert itself against China."[21] However, such was the power of the Cold War mentality that this awareness could not then be imported into American global strategic thinking. As Sidney Blumenthal has remarked about the controversies over America's strategy in Vietnam, "If there had been any strategy, the United States ought to have built up Vietnam to play as a counter to its historic adversary, just as [its] recognition of China played a part in containing the Soviet Union." As shocking as this view may be to some, it is virtually current U.S. policy, one approved of by Hanoi Hilton survivor Senator John McCain (R-AZ), who recently remarked that as Vietnam was a historical enemy of China's, it was America's best bulwark against Chinese expansionism in Southeast Asia.[22] Keith W. Taylor, one of America's foremost scholars of Vietnamese culture and a participant in the war, concluded that, in the long run, the American interventionist crusade against communism in Indochina has always been its worst enemy and Communist China's best ally, from its support of the French against the Vietminh to its long postwar boycott of Vietnam.[23]

Finally, the orthodox school does not believe that even a combination of the above mentioned factors doomed the United States to certain defeat in Vietnam. Many are aware of fresh documentation allegedly originating in Hanoi that suggests that at the end, its forces were more hard-pressed and closer to exhaustion than heretofore assumed. This documentation remains as yet unpublished, perhaps with good reason. Vietnam-era intelligence officers who have seen them dismiss them as forgeries. On their face, the documents appear to be nothing more than efforts by PAVN to justify a larger share of the national budget through arguing that the war was almost lost due to a lack of resources. Veteran Pentagon watchers are familiar enough with such ploys to know them when they see them. Yet, most orthodox writers would not be shocked to learn that, like the Napoleonic wars that ended at Waterloo, the final victory in Vietnam was a "near-run thing." They would, however, argue that victories seemingly achieved on narrow margins have more behind them than mere luck: in Wellington's "near-run thing," the British commander had bigger battalions, powerful allies, the British navy, and England's massive fiscal advantage over Napoleon's Continental System all behind him, while Napoleon did not even have time on his side. If Hanoi and its allies won by holding on one day, one platoon or even one bullet longer than their opponent, that victory would be just as sure and doubtlessly owed to long gestating underlying factors, particularly in a protracted war such as that fought in Vietnam.

In brief, the standard interpretation focuses on the macrohistorical or impersonal forces (decolonization, world communism, the political culture of the two Vietnams) at work in Indochina. It emphasizes the way in which Cold War politics forced America's Cold Warriors into a conflict where their strengths could be turned into weaknesses. It also emphasizes the war fighting capacity of their foe. Such an interpretation of the causes of America's defeat was particularly well suited to the immediate postwar period. Its macrohistorical focus suited those seeking respite from the narrow personal and rigid ideological fingering pointing that characterized the war years. Its respect for the enemy was also in tune with the seeming victory of the "heroic guerrilla" over a seemingly overextended hegemonic power.

Nonetheless, a reexamination of the orthodox school's premises became necessary when it was apparent that most of Vietnam's heroic guerrillas were being pushed aside by authoritarian socialist apparatchiks in postwar Vietnam. Ho Chi Minh may or may not have been a pragmatic socialist who would have made a better ally than enemy, but the needs and violent course of a thirty-year-war had guaranteed the supremacy of the most dogmatic communists in Vietnam. To be sure, as one Vietnamese official remarked, "War is easy, peace is hard," but it was inevitable, given postwar events there, that some of the earliest writings of the orthodox school about the course of Vietnamese communism would appear naïve. In retrospect, some writers within the orthodox school, such as James Harrison (*Endless War,* 1982), may have exaggerated the enemy's skills and resources. Some also appeared too ready to blame the war's chief political victim, the Republic of Vietnam, for the war's failure, and were uncritical in their acceptance of hagiographic accounts of enemy behavior offered by far from disinterested Western observers, such as Wilfred Burchett (*Vietnam-Inside Story of a Guerilla War,* 1965).

Yet the orthodox school's basic assumptions, well-established within five years after the war's end, were continually validated by evidence drawn from congressional hearings during and after the war, postwar interviews with war managers, the close study of the Department of Defense's in-house history of the war (*The Pentagon Papers,* 1971) and the steady post-war stream of declassified official documentation on the war. Remarkably, the most compelling part of this ever-growing record was that left by those within the U.S. government who had anticipated an American defeat in Vietnam or who gave close consideration to the failing strategies employed there when the ultimate outcome was still in doubt.

The *Pentagon Papers* and other documentation at the heart of the standard interpretation of the American defeat make clear that, beginning in the early 1950s, when France's waning fortunes in Vietnam suggested the possibility of a greater American presence in Southeast Asia, a number of the best minds ever to serve the American military profession agitated against any escalation of American involvement in the region. Generals James Gavin, Matthew Ridgway, and David Shoup argued with increasing intensity that the "true struggle" in Vietnam would, indeed, be "waged on a political basis" and that the political advantage in Vietnam was held by the anticolonialist Ho Chi Minh and his communist and noncommunist supporters. They believed that the French triumph in their conquest of Indochina ultimately doomed both French colonialism and also direct American intervention. That conquest revealed the bankruptcy of the old Vietnamese order so clearly that the brightest among the Vietnamese intelligencia came to believe that only a revolutionary movement could restore Vietnamese unity and independence. Also, by successfully crushing all noncommunist revolutionary movements in the 1930s except the Communists (although not for lack of trying), the French cleared the way for Ho Chi Minh to defeat them under a nationalist mantle and develop a formula attuned to peasant aspirations. The fruits of this victory were apparent to General William DePuy, while he served as Assistant Chief of Staff for Operations at Military Assistance Command, Vietnam (MACV). He noted in 1964 that America's allies in Vietnam would be largely members of a feudal elite who had allied themselves with France or not taken part in the struggles against European colonialism. On the other hand, the Vietminh/Viet Cong had fought the French and had been "recruited from the common clay." America's likely foe in Vietnam thus possessed credibility as defenders of the nation that no American money or arms could buy for its clients. Due to these considerations, DePuy judged that any visible support tendered to a pro-American regime in the South would be the "kiss of death" for that government in the minds of most Vietnamese. Generals Gavin Ridgway, and Shoup later railed against the American-backed government in Saigon as corrupt and dictatorial and condemned the commitment of U.S. combat forces when the weaknesses of that regime in meeting mostly local insurgents required such intervention in 1965. They later publicly opposed the war of attrition adopted by U.S. forces as having little potential for achieving victory as defined by the U.S. government: a Republic of Vietnam able to defend itself and not hostile to American interests.[24]

The orthodox school notes that close consideration was given by these and other senior American leaders to the possibility of breaking out of a possible quagmire in Vietnam by invading the DRV directly or by closing the DRV's lines of supply to the South by an allied occupation of central Laos and the southern province(s) of the DRV. However, as early as 1954 several generals, including Ridgway (then Army Chief of Staff) and Gavin (then Army Plans Chief), judged that this might lead to a war with China and that, even if China did not intervene, the cost of a wider war in Indochina in terms of manpower and logistical support would result in a loss of resources so acute that it would prevent the deployment of effective and reliable allied forces elsewhere. In Ridgway's opinion, the use of any American forces in Vietnam "aside from any local success they might achieve, would constitute a dangerous strategic diversion of limited U.S. military capabilities and commit our armed forces in a non-decisive theatre to the attainment of non-decisive local objectives."[25] Subsequently, much of the opportunity for this alternative wider war scenario was closed off before the very earliest decisions were made to commit American combat troops in Southeast Asia due to events in Laos.

There is general agreement that the U.S. image of monolithic communism blinded its own leaders to divisions between China and the Soviet Union over Indochinese as well as global affairs. In the early 1960s, this led the United States into committing itself to the defense of Laos by means which provoked a great power confrontation in that country. The American resolution of this Laotian crisis, a sham neutralization of Laos and Cambodia, shifted the struggle to Vietnam, where the United States could better utilize the logistic multipliers inherent in its long sea frontier. Unfortunately, it also created sanctuaries in which the enemy in Vietnam could operate safely. After the Laos Accords were signed in 1962, some saw in the Pathet Lao and DRV controlled lands along the Ho Chi Minh Trail a debacle in the making: The enemy would exploit these to the point that U.S. military might demand an invasion of these countries, leading to the very war the "neutralization" of Laos was designed to avoid—it was that or a humiliating withdrawal. It did not matter that the Vietnamese were permitted by their allies to violate the Accords. The United States could not afford to disregard them on this or any other grounds, as this would restart the great power crisis the Laos Accords were meant to resolve. Since the United States could not go back to the status quo ante, it bent the Accords as far as it could, but, unlike the Vietnamese, it could never afford to break them. Further, as the results of the eventual Cambodian incursion in 1970 may suggest, an advance across Laos would have placed enormous pressure on Laos and, eventually, on Thailand. Since all Laotian political parties would have resisted any American "request" to occupy its territory, the United States would have its hands full with local, as well as international, resistance to this step. Finding itself between a rock and a hard place, U.S. military strategy in Indochina floundered, pushed by events into a decision-making process that, even if it did not seek a stalemate for political reasons, may have been capable only of staving off defeat.[26]

This did not mean that the perceived need for an "El Paso" (the code word for Westmoreland's personal version of a Laos incursion scenario) quietly faded away. Many in the military, out of the force of traditional military logic or frustration with the demands of a limited war posture raised the idea despite President Johnson and Robert McNamara's resistance to it. General Andrew Goodpaster included ground operations in Laos and in the southern DRV as a matter of course in the mission statement he prepared for President Johnson in 1965. As National Security Adviser, Walt Rostow also championed this step.[27] But even if the Laos Accords could be safely broken without initiating Armageddon, Ridgway and others had long since established that any major American military operation that was perceived by China as a violation of the territorial integrity its former tributary states, Laos or Vietnam, would trigger a Chinese intervention. China could ill-afford to do so given its own internal problems, but that was true before its Korean incursion. And China was then locked into a death-struggle with the Soviet Union over who would wear the mantle of leader of world revolution. Those pressing Johnson to adopt a wider war were thus up against formidable obstacles.

Chief among them, as is apparent from documents released after the war, was that the wider war's advocates ignored the impact of the American experience in Korea that had traumatized a generation of American politicians. The Chinese had then warned the United States that they would intervene in the face of American activity on their frontier with Korea. Truman had accepted the military's assurances that this would not happen and their further assurances that if it did happen, they could easily meet it. Yet, China did intervene at enormous cost to the American people. President Johnson, who received a similar warning from China over Vietnam, was determined that he would not be victimized like Truman. Nonetheless, the military made no effort to find a vocabulary that could assuage his fears. They were even, to some degree, oblivious to them. When President Johnson asked his own army chief of staff what would happen if China responded militarily to the wider war scenario he favored, the answer was the famous retort that this would mean "a whole new ball game." Johnson was shocked that his military advisors were so far removed from the realities of global war. The opponents of a wider war were far more pragmatic and thus more persuasive. In November 1964 one of the President's most trusted military advisors, former army chief of staff and ambassador to Saigon, General Maxwell Taylor, rejected an advance into what became called the enemy's Cambodian and Laotian "sanctuaries" on the most practical of grounds. "We don't often catch the fleeing VC in the heart of SVN [South Vietnam], Taylor lamented. "I see little likelihood of catching them in Cambodia."[28]

Taylor's concerns were mirrored by General James Gavin's testimony before the Senate Foreign Relations committee in 1966. Gavin, repeating tactics successfully employed by Ridgway in the 1950s to block massive U.S. military intervention in Indochina,[29] told the committee that he was willing to consider the creation of a line blocking infiltration into the RVN drawn from Thailand across Laos to central Vietnam, if it would serve America's strategic purposes "but to me these [steps] appear to be terribly costly in our manpower and national wealth, and I use the word wealth to include material resources." Gavin also followed Ridgway's lead in offering that if America actually wished to defeat Communism in Asia by force of arms, it should be attacking China in Manchuria, not thinking of an opened-ended commitment in the jungles of Southeast Asia. Any effort to expand the war there could lead to a global conflict where American forces would be fighting thousands of miles from their homeland and on the doorstep of an enemy who could largely dictate the pace and course of the engagement. Gavin would not risk one American soldier's life in such a campaign.[30]

When, not long after, word leaked that General Westmoreland was considering an Indochinese cordon sanitaire, the concept was pilloried by retired General Maxwell Johnson, a former planning officer for the Joint Chiefs of

Staff. Johnson concluded that such operations were not only impractical, but also strategically unsound. If General Westmoreland thought he could secure the South by holding off infiltration from the North with U.S. forces in the Laotian panhandle and leaving "pacification" duties to the Army of the Republic of South Vietnam, he had a much lower opinion of the Viet Cong/PAVN's ability to harass the force in Laos and a much higher opinion of the Army of the Republic of Vietnam's ability to defeat the Viet Cong in the south than their respective histories warranted.[31]

This ever-widening circle of inner establishment "wider war" war critics included the father of containment, George F. Kennan, whose views on this issue, like Gavin's, were made public during early congressional hearings on the war. The chief architect of the Vietnam conflict, Robert McNamara, also came to oppose this alternative strategy, though he kept his views from the public in order, he later claimed, to further his efforts within the Johnson administration to secure a negotiated settlement. Both Kennan and McNamara accepted that President Lyndon Johnson had entered into a limited war in Vietnam in keeping with a long established, conservative imperative: halting the march of communism in Asia. But after 1965, they began warning him against honoring this commitment via a counterproductive wider war or by any means that might weaken American power where and when its direct national interests were challenged. By 1967, both Kennan and McNamara believed that the cost of "winning" the war by more aggressive military means would violate these terms of engagement. They were particularly opposed to an invasion of Laos or the DRV. Anticipating one of the most frequently evoked "lessons" of Vietnam for future wars—the importance of coalition warfare—they were convinced that if extreme measures were taken against the DRV, the United States would lose whatever international support remained for its Vietnam policy, without which victory would be even more remote. Such operations, moreover, not only could "bring the Chinese in at some point," but, as Ridgway and Shoup had argued, even if successful in a military sense, they would sacrifice vital American foreign policy assets and interests elsewhere for a meaningless victory in "a remote and secondary theater."[32] They recommended that instead of expanding the war, the United States should abandon its commitment, judging it to have been made on the basis of gross misconceptions of Vietnamese society and world communism.[33]

Between late 1965 and 1967, McNamara and Kennan specifically sought to undercut the chief claim of those who then favored the geographic expansion of the war. This claim was that such action, in the absence of Chinese intervention, would lead to an immediate battlefield victory. In November of 1965, barely four months after playing a major role in the commitment to send over a hundred thousand additional combat troops to Vietnam by the end of that year, McNamara determined that the enemy would not rush to its defeat after the first main force battle between regular People's Army of Vietnam (PAVN) and U.S. troops in the Ia Drang Valley, as many of Johnson's civilian and military advisors, including Westmoreland, predicted they would. They had, instead, simply shifted to a variety of strategies focused upon "keeping us busy and waiting us out."[34] This was, in his opinion, as likely to be true after an invasion of Laos or the southernmost districts of the DRV designed to cut the Ho Chi Minh Trail, an event he hoped to forestall by his now much derided "electronic fence" which would obviate the presence of U.S. ground troops in Laos.[35] Kennan argued that such operations would also be both costly and ineffective. He told America's leaders that "fidelity to the communist tradition would dictate that if really pressed to extremity on a military level, these people should disappear entirely from the open scene and fall back on an underground political and military existence" and that "insofar as a total rooting out of the Viet Cong" was concerned, this "could only be achieved at a degree of damage to civilian life and of civilian suffering, generally, for which I would not like to see this country responsible."[36] Kennan went further, arguing that more aggressive prosecution of the war was no longer necessary to win the Cold War in Asia and that the United States could, as well as should, withdraw its forces as soon as practicable. He pointed out that in view of the failure of communism in India and Indonesia (by late 1965), the dangers of the "so-called domino effect seems to me to be considerably less than it was when the main decisions were taken that have led to our present involvement . . . [therefore] I should think that it should be our government's aim to liquidate this involvement just as soon as this can be done."[37] In that same year, John T. McNaughton, McNamara's chief deputy on Vietnam policy, abandoned his conviction that a communist Vietnam would threaten U.S. interests in Asia and discarded applicability of the domino theory to Vietnam, whose "fall" would, he had come to believe, have no serious consequences for U.S. interests, but whose survival might come at an unacceptable price: "[the] 'occupation' of South Vietnam, the 'quarantine' of Indo-China, pressures to invade North Vietnam, war costs at a rate equal to 10–20 times the GNP of the people being fought for, etc." Subsequently, McNaughton echoed Kennan's view that the war had already been won. In a memo he wrote that appeared under McNamara's name (and incidentally angered the military in part for its frank acceptance of the negative psychological impact of limited war on U.S. troops), McNaughton posited that "to the extent that our original intervention and existing actions in Vietnam were motivated by the perceived need to draw the line against Chinese expansionism in Asia, our objective has already been attained. . . ."[38] In September 1967, the Director of the Central Intelligence Agency (CIA), Richard Helms, attempted to aid this disengagement effort with a wartime finding that the impact of the "fall" of Vietnam would not have the dire effects that had been feared by a succession of American presidents.[39]

It thus appears that a large number of experienced and influential Cold Warriors believed that even if the war in Southeast Asia could have been advanced by more aggressive military means, this so-called progress would come at a very high price in American moral, political and human capital and still not eliminate the threat to American interests in Vietnam. The war would continue, but by different means. This point has since been made by both by the most famous Vietnamese Communist defector, Colonel Bui Tin, and also Douglas Pike, a wartime State Department expert on the enemy's forces.[40] They may, of course, all have been wrong and an invasion of the DRV or the adoption of an advance into Cambodia, Laos and/or the DRV was the way to victory. But the record left by many of America's most astute military and civilian leaders indicates that President Johnson had good reason to oppose a greater application of American power in Vietnam, particularly the insertion of American combat troops into Laos or the southern provinces of the Democratic Republic of Vietnam. At the same time, conservative Cold War dogma (and political pressure), America's long record of military success under adverse conditions, and perhaps also what his friend William Fulbright would later call "the arrogance of power" gave Lyndon Johnson little reason to conclude that without the isolation of the battlefield, America was doomed to defeat. Any American military failure in Vietnam would thus seem to be rooted not in strategic opportunities lost to ignorant, meddling or weak-willed politicians, but in the capacity of the Joint Chiefs of Staff to hold so tightly to a chimerical vision of victory by all-out war as to be incapable of properly managing—or effectively vocalizing their concerns regarding—the limited war the president set before them. This failure was compounded by Robert McNamara's inability to achieve a meeting of the minds between the warriors and their commander-in-chief, which it was his job to do.

The views of military men of the stature of Gavin, Ridgway, and Shoup and the dissent of Washington insiders such as Kennan, McNamara, and McNaughton as revealed in the *Pentagon Papers* and other contemporary records strengthened the orthodox school's central critique developed during that conflict. The war seemed more than ever a mistake, an ill-informed attempt by the United States to sacrifice whatever remained of the legitimate revolutionary aspirations of the people of the two Vietnams on the altar of the Cold War via a commitment of containment theory so total as to blind the United States to the realities of its own history, the limits of its own power and the primacy of its interests elsewhere. The enemy enjoyed superior political cohesion and a favorable local and international environment, while the United States sought in firepower the solution to what was a political problem. The combination of such factors produced a conflict that, for the United States, was seemingly unwinnable. Three of the war's chief architects, Robert McNamara, McGeorge Bundy and William Bundy, made statements in the 1990s that suggest that they arrived at a similar conclusion.[41] They certainly anticipated each of these developments at the war's most critical juncture, when making the choice to Americanize the war in July of 1965:

> For 10 years every step we have taken has been based on a previous failure. All we have done has failed and caused us to take another step which failed. . . . Also, we have made excessive claims we haven't been able to realize. After 20 years of warnings about war in Asia, we are now doing what McArthur and others have warned against. We are fighting a war we can't fight and win, as the country we are trying to help is quitting [while we are failing] on our own to fully realize what guerrilla war is like. We are [also] sending conventional troops to do an unconventional job. . . . Aren't we talking about a military solution when the solution is political?[42]

Yet they dismissed these concerns due to their confidence in America's war-fighting capacity and a Munich-driven[43] fear of surrendering without a fight to what they saw as global communist aggression. In the end, they helped convince the president that the risks of disengagement—of immediate defeat—were greater than the risks of sending American combat forces into what they all recognized would be a new war, an American war, in Vietnam.[44] Only in retrospect did they realize they had miscalculated the strength of the enemy's resolve and their own error in raising the stakes in Vietnam to an international test of will American interests did not later appear to justify.

While many Americans saw their post-war mea culpa as self-serving, McNamara and the Bundys at least were acknowledging the macrohistorical forces the orthodox school emphasized and which their colleague Undersecretary of State George Ball most feared. Ball was one of the first high-ranking wartime civilian American officials to see clearly the ultimate fate of the course America was taking in Vietnam. In June-July of 1965, the president's advisors had faced the ultimate dilemma of the war: the contradictions in strategy between meeting the enemy in the field and providing the local security necessary for propping up the RVN. Robert McNamara was confident that the United States could meet any contingency. Ball disagreed. The effort to do so, he told the president, would be overwhelmed by the flow and interplay of larger issues, such as the legacies of the Vietnamese anticolonial struggle, one of which was the weak anticommunist regime it had produced in the South. Ball knew the president loved to win and hated losers. He sought to gentle the old Texas war-horse into accepting that no man, ally, or the American people expected him to defy the burdens of recent Vietnamese history and that it was all right to plan for a withdrawal in the face of it. "It is no one's fault," Ball advised President Johnson. "It is in the nature of the struggle."[45] If the American War in Vietnam is to be considered a tragedy, it is because, deep in his heart, Lyndon Johnson may have thought Ball was right, as has been suggested by the contents of President Johnson's just released telephone tapes.[46]

## The Revisionist Challenge

Despite the orthodox school's widespread acceptance, its strong evidentiary base, and its Taoist appeal, it has not gone unchallenged. No sooner had it found its seeming confirmation in the documentary record of the war and also experienced something approaching an early scholarly apotheosis (in George Herring's *America's Longest War,* 1979) than powerful forces arrayed themselves against it. The need of social conservatives to offer a reply to the liberal gains of 1960s and, ultimately, the success of conservative political ideology reflected in the collapse of communism in the Soviet Union and Eastern Europe led to a revival of traditional American patriotism and a reassertion of America's status as without rival as a world power. Many translated this belief into a campaign meant to revive America's self-image as the dominant society of the twentieth century. In these circumstances, it was inevitable that some would come to assert that, such was America's moral and martial superiority, the war in Vietnam could have been lost only if it had been betrayed from within. Even some of those conservatives such as Norman Podhoretz (*Why Were We in Vietnam,* 1982) who felt the war should never have been fought and possibly could not have been be won, believed it had been lost at home. The most common targets of the earliest and best known efforts to "revise" the standard interpretation of the American defeat in Vietnam (and here referred to as "revisionist" only in the commonly accepted use of the term) were thus the familiar targets of wartime prowar intellectuals: liberals in the government, the media, and the antiwar movement. Nixon, Ford, and conservatives who opposed the war were not part of this indictment and remain so.

This stab-in-the-back thesis is familiar to most historians as the method successfully employed by German leaders to restore the patriotic fervor of their people a decade after their defeat in the Great War. Coincidentally—it is not suggested here that it was anything else—the first revisionist writings after Vietnam followed the pattern of the German experience. They were based on the postwar exculpatory writings of the commanders who presided over their nation's defeat in war. These officers employed the same tactics as those that characterized the German effort: the rewriting of history in willing ignorance, if not also defiance, of much of the historical record.[47] In

1969 Westmoreland told an interviewer that he enjoyed a "carte blanche," that President Johnson had "never tried to tell me how to run the war" and "let me run the war as I . . . saw fit."[48] Only much later did he tell postwar listeners that the president made him fight with one hand tied behind his back.[49] Admiral U.S. Grant Sharpe (*Strategy for Defeat,* 1978) also focused on the wartime restrictions placed on the military by Washington, but, like Westmoreland, he dismissed rather than analyzed the policy concerns that lay behind them. We were prevented from taking certain actions, they argued, actions that, if taken, would have led to a military victory. Both assume this victory would be complete and suit America's best interests. They thus find it unnecessary to seriously consider information provided by the *Pentagon Papers* and other sources that suggests that these actions—more aerial bombardment of the DRV in Sharp's case—may not have been physically possible or may have had counterproductive results. What few sources they do cite, such as Brigadier General Douglas Kinnard's survey of the opinions on the war by holders of command rank in Vietnam (*The War Managers: American Generals Reflect on Vietnam,* 1977), are referred to in a manner that violates any canon of reasoned argument, let alone research.

Revisionists argue that the testimony of America's war managers that Kinnard gathered supports Sharpe's contention that civilian micromanagement of military operations lost the war. Such may be the case. However, what they choose to ignore was that Kinnard himself did not draw this conclusion from the data he collected. Kinnard found that much of the military's complaints about micromanagement were directed at the military command structure's interference in their actions, not at politicians in Washington. He concluded that the military's micromanagement of the war, its emphasis on bureaucratic needs over that of the mission, actually may have been as damaging as civilian interference, but that neither was necessarily decisive. He also concluded that, whatever its failings, civilian oversight and its imposition of limits on the military was both an American tradition and vital to its survival as a nation, as he contends was proven in Vietnam. Kinnard goes so far as to state that given the tactical and strategic restraints of limited war accepted by the American military, not only was civilian intervention correct, but there should have been more of it, not less, as this would have given the war management better focus, without the risks of a conflagration the military was ready to entertain. His final words are that had the civilians not restrained the military, America may itself have perished.[50]

Kinnard's conclusions stand as a pillar of the standard interpretation rather than its kryptonite, but that did not deter critics of the standard interpretation from pursuing the we-were-not-allowed-to-win corollary of the micromanagement issue, most clearly stated in General Dave Richard Palmer's *Summons of the Trumpet* (1978). Many of the war's civilian leaders and subsequent analysts have expressed dismay over the popularity of this thesis, which they hold is belied by the military's actual record of operations. They know that many in the military chafed under restrictions affecting cross-border operations and the targeting of enemy installations. They note, however, that the military that supposedly fought with one hand tied behind its back killed more than 10 percent of the entire Vietnamese population and that the bombs dropped during the most politically "restricted" air campaign of the war, Operation Rolling Thunder, were alone greater than the total tonnage of bombs dropped on the entire Pacific theater in World War II, including both the conventional and nuclear bombing of Japan. Robert McNamara noted in 1968 that, in the DRV, "We are dropping more ordinance at a higher rate than in the last year of WWII in Europe." It is little wonder that George Ball, who earlier in his public career contributed to the writing of the official analysis of America's strategic bombing campaign in World War II, rejected with great disdain the claim that the American War in Vietnam was lost by restrictions civilians had placed on military operations.[51]

One of the clearest examples of the decisive "political" restrictions cited by those seeking to revise the standard interpretation of the cause of America's defeat in Vietnam is the case of Linebacker II. Revisionists continually assert that this relatively unrestricted strategic bombing campaign against the DRV in 1972 to coerce it to sign what became the Paris Accords of 1973 would have won the war on terms more favorable to the United States if initiated in 1965. However, it has been some time since Dr. Earl H. Tilford, Jr. (*Crosswinds: The Air Force's Setup in Vietnam,* 1993), who served as an intelligence officer working on the air campaigns in Laos and is a respected air force historian, demonstrated convincingly that the Linebacker II campaign was initiated under entirely different circumstances in terms of foreign affairs. He noted that such a campaign may have led to Chinese intervention if initiated in 1965–1969, but Nixon's subsequent visit to China ensured that there was no such danger in 1972. More important, the Paris Accords signed by Hanoi in 1973 under the duress of Linebacker II still placed victory within Hanoi's grasp, hence its willingness to sign. That agreement also differed little from the terms offered and rejected earlier in October 1972, proving that the coercive force of Linebacker II was aimed at and achieved only modest gains. Whereas revisionists tout Linebacker II as proof of the war-winning strength of American air power, Tilford shows that this unquestionably successful application of air power was attributable largely to its limited political, strategic, and tactical objectives. Nonetheless, Linebacker II is still touted as a "war-winning weapon" in revisionist writing that ignores not only Tilford's analysis, but also the published work of air power historian Mark Clodfelter (*The Limits of Air Power,* 1989) and many other United States Air Force officers who support their analysis. This debate is significant because it tests the height of the bar demarcating reasoned argument about the past. Admiral Sharpe has contended that the United States could have won the war in 1965 if it had unleashed the full force of its strategic airpower, but Air Force historians, if not Admiral Sharpe, know that it was not until the "big-belly" version of the B-52 became available in 1967 that the campaign he imagined was even possible, and even then the Air Force feared the impact on their service, as well America's global strategic posture, if its pillar in the triad of American nuclear deterrence was diverted to Vietnam.[52] The outcome of the Vietnam War may not have been determined by such factors as the availability of appropriate military technologies, inter-service rivalry, and America's larger defense interests. However, to discuss alternative timetables, strategies, and outcomes in the absence of these considerations is to take the "coulda, shoulda, woulda" elements of the debate over the war to a place where reasoned scholarly discourse is not possible.

Most early revisionist writers, in fact, rarely engaged scholarly works on the war, especially those written by participants in the war, such as Tilford, which did not reflect their views. They also had a tendency to focus on "missed opportunities" as if historical cause and effect did not exist, or could easily be voided, though the more self-aware of such writers recognize that such argumentation "is akin to Monday morning quarterbacking and probably has as much validity."[53] Some orthodox writers suffer from the same faults, but revisionists tend to drift deeper into these errors, particularly when excluding entire categories of research. So strong is their contention that America defeated itself that the initial wave of revisionist narratives rarely included the Vietnamese themselves, save for the uncritically accepted testimony of Vietnamese expatriates who share their beliefs.[54] Just as rare are references to Vietnamese sources, even as only a possible check against the accuracy of questionable American estimates, such as the largely invented numbers used to tally the cost to the Viet Cong of the Tet Offensive.[55] Moreover, when writing about operations involving still-living insurgents, researchers are expected to interview a great many of them or at least seek sources for their voices outside those produced by their American enemy. Instead, revisionist writers evoke the wartime findings of the often-questionable measures developed by Americans to show how effective their effort was at silencing these insurgents. These measures include Hamlet Evaluation Surveys (HES), whose own compliers often believed them to be useless in determining enemy strength,[56] and those RAND Corporation field studies whose conclusions—if not their contents—might be tailored to suit RAND's clients, the failing American war machine.[57] Major RAND studies indicating that strategies favored by revisionists were failing or fatally misconceived are never referenced.[58]

Few revisionist studies are based on postwar research in Vietnam. Of course, this in itself is no guarantee of accurate scholarship, but even a little fieldwork might have helped improve conservative political pundit Michael Lind's recent book, *The Necessary War* (1999), which is already a mainstay of the revisionist school. Lind ignores the issue of Vietnamese nationalism or anticolonialism as a factor in American's defeat. Had he merely spent a little time in Ho Chi Minh City visiting its museums, he could have at least seen a guillotine of the type the French used to slaughter Vietnamese rebels. He also could have walked through an accurate reconstruction of the Tiger Cages on Con Son Island (Puolo Condore), which the French used to torture Vietnamese opponents like the late premier Pham Van Dong. Revisionists may be correct in arguing that some writers of the orthodox school, such as Francis Fitzgerald (*Fire in the Lake,* 1972), overemphasize the importance of Vietnamese nationalism and anticolonialism in determining the nature and outcome of the American War. It is quite another thing, however, to pretend that Vietnamese nationalism and anticolonialism were not factors in the war, particularly when arguing, as Lind does, that a more astute American counterinsurgency policy (which would have to overcome these factors) could have won it.

In sum, revisionist writing on how America lost its war in Vietnam has sought to shift the focus away from the Vietnamese and the larger historical forces that are favored by the orthodox school. Revisionist writers echo President Richard M. Nixon's wartime assessment that only Americans can defeat Americans. They see the failure to adopt unfettered and more effective military strategies—either a wider, more aggressive conventional war or a more effective counterinsurgency policy—as the key to this defeat, and hold liberal politicians alone liable for it. If the orthodox view of the war reflects concerns raised to little effect within and without the American war-making machine during the war, many revisionist writers, especially those who served in the military during the war, see in the revisionist thesis a means of redeeming the sacrifices made in what was to them truly a noble cause that was correct in conception, if flawed in execution. Thus, much of the writing in both schools reflects their authors' experience of the war and are, accordingly, subject to the same passions and vulnerable to the same resulting errors.

Yet, howsoever valid the early major revisionist assessments may have been, due to both the relative and the absolute weakness of the evidence offered in their support, most scholars of all political stripes (many of whom are Vietnam veterans) saw them as a rehash of wartime partisan hawkish polemics cast in terms the American public might find more convincing now that the war is a distant memory. These scholars are thus not taken aback by Lind's substitution of the term "bandwagoning" for the fading and, in orthodox circles, discredited "domino theory." Such obfuscation ("incursion" for "invasion," etc.) was a major part of the wartime political culture. That Lind may now seek by these means to win the battle for how the war is to be remembered is not surprising: *la guerre ideologique continué.* However, what has come as a surprise is how far revisionists are willing to go beyond stab-in-the-back theories or plays on words to secure that victory.

General William C. Westmoreland and others closely identified with the revisionist critique have recently argued that the appearance of *doi moi* (the economic liberalization of the Vietnamese economy) and the postwar freedoms enjoyed by Pacific Rim nations proves that the United States had won, not lost, the war. On close examination, this proposition may do violence to key elements of the larger revisionist argument and question the very necessity for the war itself.[59] It is, however, the disingenuousness of and irony inherent in this pronouncement that requires close attention here. It is disingenuous because the titular American objective in Vietnam was to sustain an independent Republic of Vietnam under a political regime that would pursue policies not inconsistent with U.S. interests in the region. In 1975 Vietnamese opposed to the American intervention occupied the capital of that Republic, accepted its surrender, absorbed it into the DRV and, when its efforts to normalize relations with the United States failed, rented one of its best ports to the naval forces of America's then archenemy, the Soviet Union.

These events fit no definition of victory in the Second Indochina War advanced by the United States. The logic employed by Westmoreland thus defies the customary means of attributing success or failure in war by measuring them against a combatant's own war aims. It also has rather disturbing ramifications for assessing the outcome of the Pacific War, fought from 1941 to 1945. Japan launched that conflict to ensure its continuing status as a major world power and to gain economic dominance over East Asia. Since Japan has achieved these goals in the postwar period, the logic of Westmoreland's observation leads inexorably to the conclusion that Japan won World War II. This conclusion is, in fact, popular among some American right-wing extremists, but not among most of the surviving members of the "greatest generation" who fought and assume they won that war. It is one thing to claim that the United States lost a major battle in the Cold War, Vietnam, but won the war. It is quite another to equate the outcome of the lost battle with the outcome of the war, particularly without seriously addressing whether that battle was, in fact, even necessary to help secure the larger victory (many Japanese believe that superior management, not empire, was always the key to their global position and consider the Pacific War to have thus been avoidable). More to the point, the United States did not respond militarily to the Hungarian or Czechoslovakian crises during the Cold War and economic liberalism has still triumphed there. Other events may have thus determined the outcome of the Cold War besides the American decision to intervene militarily or not, whether in Eastern Europe or Vietnam.

## Harry G. Summers, Jr. and the Revisionist First Wave

The weaknesses of the logic as well as the supporting evidence found in much revisionist writing are most apparent in what remains that school's seminal study, the late Harry G. Summers, Jr.'s *On Strategy* (1982). Summers' politically informed writing and embarrassingly selective research is legendary among his many friends as well as his critics.[60] His work also exhibits the near-universal tendency among early revisionist writers to employ a bankrupt form of counterfactual reasoning. For example, Summers advanced the now familiar proposition that if the United States had adopted a different military strategy, it would have won. Yet this supposition is offered without any attempt to account for any corresponding changes the enemy may have made to its strategy to frustrate this alternative American strategy. Summers did not do this because, as he himself confessed, he had little idea of and less interest in determining what the enemy's strategy was. This posture so troubled Douglas Pike that, when given a chance to confront Summers on this issue, he asked, "Harry, how can you write a book on strategy in Vietnam and not have one chapter in which you talk about the enemy?" Summers answered, "Well, that is very hard to do, hard to understand. Anyway, [the book] is about American strategy." Pike could only reply, "Well, would you write a book about fighting Rommel in the desert and not go into what Rommel was doing and thinking? Doesn't that escape you? The logic of it."[61] It matters to Pike, because he has attributed America's defeat in Vietnam to such logic, which he deemed "vincible ignorance." This, according to Pike, describes the process by which Americans were ignorant about Vietnam, knew that they knew nothing about the country, but were convinced that such ignorance did not matter. Pike distrusts interpretive schools of any kind, but he stands close to the orthodox school in arguing that the war was lost, in part, because of an American failure to value knowledge of the human terrain on which the war was fought.

Summers will, nonetheless, always be a significant and, it is hoped, a positive figure in the debate over the war for at least the following three reasons. First, Summers joined with those few revisionists who have entirely rejected the central elements of its stab-in-the-back thesis. He held U.S. civilian and military authorities jointly responsible for America's defeat. He frequently alluded to two factors that most historians of the war hold to be the chief evidence of wartime military misconduct: the failure of military leaders to act on their knowledge that every effort to strengthen the Republic of Vietnam actually weakened and discredited that regime and their failure to publicly protest or tender their resignations over the conduct of the war they now claim they knew they could not win. Summers has declared that the fact that

President Johnson might have been loath to listen to the military's warnings after committing America to the war "made it even more imperative that his military advisors should have told him what he did not want to hear. They did their commander in chief, their nation, and the servicemen and women whose lives and interests they had sworn to protect no favors by not speaking up." Summers, like the "academics" many revisionists openly despise,[62] believed that civilians such as Robert McNamara were the war's biggest villains, but he holds that in any victory lost in Vietnam, the military authorities were as culpable as any politician.[63]

Second, Summers shared the view of every serious scholar within and without the military that the American response to the Tet Offensive was shaped by panic that began in the military, not manufactured by the media, which spread to the White House through the instrument not of Walter Cronkite but by Generals Harold Johnson and Earle Wheeler, who initially discredited Westmoreland's claim of victory on the battlefield.[64] Summers had nothing but contempt for the media. But he was adamant that news reporting "did not lose the Vietnam War." Nor, in his view, did television, though, he noted, "There are those like [revisionists] George F. Will and William Westmoreland who would have it otherwise."[65]

Summers thus draws attention to other misrepresentations of this aspect of the revisionist line. The work of newsmen Peter Braestrup (*Big Story,* 1977) and Don Oberdorfer (*Tet!,* 1971) have been cited by revisionists as the major sources of support for their belief that the press lost the war. Yet neither Oberdorfer nor Braestrup, whose books are quite critical of certain aspects of wartime press coverage, have expressed this view. Braestrup refuted this revisionist contention in the clearest of terms, as has Oberdorfer whose views were seconded at a recent conference on the media and war by a panel he chaired composed of military photojournalists, Le Van (the wartime Vietnamese-language officer of the Voice of America), and Joe Galloway (co-author of *We Were Soldiers Once . . . And Young,* 1993), the only civilian war correspondent to receive a military medal for valor.[66] The previously mentioned works of Daniel Hallin, William Hammond, and Clarence Wyatt have seemingly both demolished the revisionist idea that the media created opposition to the war and also demonstrated that the media was made to serve as a scapegoat (and successfully so) by the military for their failing policies.

Lastly, Summers inspired many junior officers by his willingness to openly criticize the American military's performance in the war from within the military establishment and on theoretical as well as practical grounds. In this regard, even defenders of the standard interpretation, like Earl Tilford, gratefully acknowledge their debt to him. Summers argued that the United States might have been more successful if it had employed from the outset a more classical or Clausewitzian conventional war-fighting strategy aimed directly against the Democratic Republic of Vietnam and Laos. Instead, he argues, the United States favored the search-and-destroy operations Westmoreland conducted in the Republic of Vietnam that, Summers believed, overemphasized counterinsurgency. Summers writes as if U.S. war managers never considered the wider-war option and therefore does not address why these steps, rightly or wrongly, were continually rejected by many in the military as well as the civilian establishment. He also references none of the rich documentary evidence regarding this issue available in *The Pentagon Papers* and elsewhere. In addition, his views were challenged by the late William Colby (*Lost Victory*, 1989) and others[67] who claim in a revision of Summers's revisionism that the war could have been won if Westmoreland actually had done what Summers claims he did—fight a primarily counterinsurgent war—but, they allege, he did not. (This debate receives close treatment in chapter 6.) Still, Summers helped move discussion over the war somewhat closer toward the realm of legitimate historical discourse. Subsequent works, such as General Bruce Palmer's *Twenty-Five Year War: America's Military Role in Vietnam* (1984), Mark Moyar's *Phoenix and the Birds of Prey* (1997), and, in particular, Lewis Sorley's *A Better War* (1999), have moved the debate over the war further in this direction.

## Moving Toward a New Synthesis

As thus refocused, adherents of the orthodox and revisionist schools were able to engage each other more profitably later in the 1980s and 1990s. At the center of Lind's *Necessary War* is the validation of the standard interpretation's long-standing position regarding limited wars. The standard interpretation contends that, while it is easy to say that, once committed to war in Indochina, the United States should have used unlimited force quickly, a limited war strategy was and is likely to remain the most common form of modern warfare, howsoever difficult it is to wage. Lind agrees, pointing not merely to Korea and Vietnam but to Bosnia as examples of how America has fought to defend its interests via limited war. For their part, orthodox critics of revisionists who believe that more effective counterinsurgent warfare could have altered the war's outcome have become much more sophisticated in their understanding of that subject. Eric Bergerud's *Dynamics of Defeat: The War in Hau Nghia Province* (1993) offers no roseate picture of Viet Cong tactics, while still stressing their ultimate resilience and triumph on the battlefield. The revisionist challenge has also helped keep the orthodox school's macro-historical approach from slipping into determinism: international constraints, economic culture and social and political cohesion were factors in America's defeat in Vietnam, but leadership (Giap versus Westmoreland, Ho Chi Minh versus the American presidency), events on the battlefield and what Clausewitz called the "fog of war" (the Gulf of Tonkin Incident, the panic at Tet) made victory or defeat for either side far from inevitable.

As a result, some advocates of the standard interpretation of the American defeat in Vietnam have shifted to what has been called a "postrevisionist" posture. They no longer dismiss out of hand the revisionist contention that the war was "winnable." They still maintain, however, that the means most likely required to secure such an end could not guarantee victory "in any meaningful sense of the term."[68] These means included an invasion of the DRV along the lines of McArthur's assault at Inchon, the possible occupation of much of Indochina (certainly the Laotian panhandle and eastern Cambodia), and the long-term maintenance of a repressive non-communist regime in the South.[69] They argue that these measures would have risked every American's future and that of their children in a region they could not locate on a map at a cost in moral capital, blood and treasure beyond that which "they would—or should—have found acceptable."[70]

This movement toward consensus may seem small to some, but it is already bearing fruit, as can be seen in William Duiker's *Sacred War: Nationalism and Revolution in a Divided Vietnam* (1995). Duiker is a respected senior scholar of modern Vietnam who has long been known for his distaste of political cant. In *Sacred War,* he rejects the revisionist argument that the war could have been won by more aggressive American military means. However, he also finds the class-based analysis of the Vietnamese revolution offered by Gabriel Kolko inadequate. He concludes that the American defeat in Vietnam can be comprehended only in terms of the lack of vital interests at stake there and the manner in which traditional Vietnamese values underlay the communist appeal. Duiker thus captures what is central to the revisionist bible, *On Strategy:* the Clausewitzian notion that a nation should not put its blood and treasure in jeopardy unless vital interests are at stake. He also captures what is central to the concerns of the standard interpretation: the danger of underestimating the indigenous political dimensions of all conflicts. He thus is advancing an explanatory thesis governing the failure of American intervention in Southeast Asia that all fair-minded students of the war will find useful.

The chapters that comprise this volume reflect Duiker's hope for movement toward greater consensus on the war. It is thus appropriate that he is the author of the first of its offerings. In keeping with the intent of this work to follow David Donald's Civil War study as much as possible (while avoiding its own possibly deterministic flaws[71]), the first two of this volume's contributions focus on the international dimensions of the war. Duiker's subject is how the Vietnamese won the war by sustaining a superior diplomatic offensive against the world's most admired and powerful nation. Duiker believes that one of the keys to that victory was the ability of communist leaders in Hanoi to manipulate the international environment to their advantage. Their ability to obtain significant diplomatic and military assistance from both Moscow and Beijing—even during the bitterest stages of the Sino-Soviet dispute—helped to deter the United States from using its technological superiority to seek a total victory in the conflict in Indochina. At the same time, Hanoi's adroit handling of the issue of peace negotiations served to isolate the United States in the court of public opinion and win broad support throughout the world for the insurgent movement in South Vietnam and the cause of Vietnamese reunification. Duiker traces the historical origins of the Vietnamese communist approach to international diplomacy and how that historical experience was put to the test in formulating communist strategy and tactics during the Vietnam War.

Chapter 2 by George Herring complements Duiker's work by offering an analysis of how the United States found itself diplomatically outmaneuvered and isolated by its tiny Asian opponent. It assesses the reasons why America's allies refused to support, or supported only tepidly, America's military intervention in Vietnam, and the significance of this absence of support in terms of the course the war took and its eventual outcome. It also explores United States handling of its relations with major Cold War adversaries, the Soviet Union and China. Ironically, the United States counted on the help of these adversaries, especially the Soviet Union, in securing a settlement of the war. Regarding China, the Johnson administration, in particular, feared a repetition of Chinese military intervention, as in the Korean War. Herring argues neither the Soviet Union nor China had the means to bring North Vietnam to the conference table as desired by the United States, even when each had the inclination. And while the United States focused on preventing a wider war with China and the Soviet Union, it was Chinese and Soviet military aid that helped North Vietnam survive American escalation and eventually win the war. Although probably not decisive, international factors thus played a vital role in the outcome of the war.

The next four chapters analyze the role of American and Vietnamese military performance. The greatest flaw in American strategy in the war was its faith in "mini brute force," which was never wholly abandoned even in the face of overwhelming evidence of its failure. In chapter 3, Jeff Record explores why the United States failed to acknowledge this problem until it was too late to make an effective recovery. He further argues that conventional wisdom on the causes of U.S. defeat in the Vietnam War tends to ignore deficient professional U.S. military performance *within* the political limitations imposed by civilian authority on the application of force. According to Record, these deficiencies included: failure to provide timely and useful military advice to civilian authority; unwillingness to subordinate interservice rivalry to the demands of wartime military effectiveness; pursuit of a firepower-attrition strategy based on palpably false premises; misuses of available military manpower; and failure to recognize the limits of air power in Indochina's strategic and operational setting. While Record does not conclude that these deficiencies were, in themselves, decisive in the U.S. defeat, he demonstrates that they aided and abetted North Vietnam's ultimately victorious strategy.

In chapter 4, Robert Brigham's ultimate objective is to show how the U.S. manipulation of nomenclature, a major aspect of the war, distorted not only who its enemy was—a fatal error in any theater of war, according to Clausewitz—but the enormous disparity in the fighting capacity that existed between the People's Army of Vietnam, the National Liberation Front, and the Army of the Republic of Vietnam forces that was visible to American advisors and "grunts" alike. He argues that Vietnam's Communist Party defeated the United States and its Saigon ally in Vietnam using a protracted war strategy that borrowed equally from Mao Zedong's people's war strategy and Vietnamese traditions. He reminds us, however, as does each of this volume's contributors, that to ask why the "North" won the war is to miss the point entirely. The "North" refers only to a geographical location, not a political entity with long-standing cultural or historic precedent. The Communist party was a unified, nationwide party that had strong support throughout Vietnam. Utilizing the latest Vietnamese-language sources, Brigham argues that it was southern communists and their noncommunist supporters in the National Liberation Front who defeated the Saigon government and its American backers through the combination of the political, military, and diplomatic struggle movements. Furthermore, he demonstrates that the Army of the Republic of Vietnam was, ironically, at a distinct cultural disadvantage in the battle over the political future of Vietnam south of the seventeenth parallel. Brigham concludes that, while there were sharp differences of opinion within Vietnam over how the war should be fought, at every turn southerners shaped strategy and tactics.

One of the reasons Record ascribes to the poor strategic performance of the U.S. military in Vietnam is that, despite the best advice to the contrary, America's military leaders were forever looking for a magic bullet that would lead to triumph in Indochina. John Prados suggests in chapter 5 that the misadventures in American intelligence collection and analysis that may have contributed to its defeat were due, at least in part, to the delusion that intelligence might constitute the hoped-for panacea. He assesses intelligence apparati of the two Vietnams and compares them to American intelligence operations. Prados believes the most serious flaw in American thinking was that it little understood the asymmetry between its own intelligence difficulties as the counterinsurgent side and those of the insurgents. The United

States also refused to learn from the French in intelligence and other tactics and tended to denigrate the Vietnamese intelligence-gathering capacity, which inhibited its understanding of the war. Prados shows how American intelligence-gathering and analysis suffered from: a production orientation; the political impact of the estimates; the slow development of the organizations, on both the United States and South Vietnamese sides; the difficulties of collection; and a conflict between intelligence collection and operations. Prados notes that despite this, most major operations of all combatants were known to its opponents in advance. He concludes that, unfortunately for the United States, this proved more damaging to it than to its adversaries. Although these problems and the flaws in the U.S. intelligence operations were not beyond remediation, progress, when it came, arrived too little, too late.

Chapter 6, by this writer, addresses the central nature of the so-called "Other War," the struggle to win the hearts and minds of the people of the Republic of Vietnam. It argues that the proper appreciation of this dimension of the conflict can help resolve much of the debate over the manner in which the war could have been "won" and why it was lost. It contends that the manner in which the United States lost the "other war" largely determined the ultimate outcome on the battlefield for, in losing the insurgent war through a failed war of attrition resting on an inadequately democratic local base, America and its Vietnamese allies paved the way for Hanoi's more conventional offensive campaigns of 1972 and 1975. This chapter focuses on the period between 1965 and 1970, which the competing revisionist interpretations regard as the time when a "winning" American strategy could have been adopted. It concludes that neither a heightened conventional war nor a heightened war of pacification was possible given cultural and political forces at work in Vietnam and in the United States, none of which can be wished away by counterfactual reasoning and all of which was influenced by what, as Jeff Record reminds us, Richard M. Nixon called a war's running clock, whose iron hands bind those of every general who has ever taken the field.

President Eisenhower's reference to the need for securing for the West the commercial resources of Vietnam when asking for aid for a fledgling Republic of Vietnam and Presidential Advisor Walt Rostow's oft-repeated remark that Indochina was like a thumb pressing down on the pulse of the world's Asian trade routes has ensured that economics plays a prominent place in the debate over the war. However, in chapter 7, Andrew Rotter largely avoids the well-known arguments over the degree to which global trade and Cold War economic rivalry lay behind American intervention in Indochina's affairs. He does so as these issues are more closely related to the alleged causes of the conflict rather than its outcome. His focus is on how economic ideas influenced the American failure to achieve its goals. Rotter begins with the premise that the American War in Vietnam was shaped by a culture of economics that is, by definition, a network of significance people invent to give meaning to the process of exchange, to money, and to the production and consumption of goods and services. In this sense, the war was profoundly economic in nature. Among the most fundamental differences between Americans and Vietnamese was their understanding of economics. The images and stereotypes Americans formed of their Vietnamese allies and enemies were frequently the product of American economic culture. The vocabulary used by Americans and Vietnamese to describe their war was often economic in its origin. Economic culture strongly influenced the way each side made war: The Americans relied heavily on technology, machinery, and ordnance, while the National Liberation Front and the Vietnamese in the North mobilized people to work and fight together for the common causes of nationalism and socialism. Rotter concludes that, in these terms, the economic assumptions each side brought to the war had much to do with determining its outcome.

No aspect of the American War in Vietnam is more controversial than the role of the American home front. Yet it is little understood. The antiwar movement often is represented as a product of 1960s' excess, led by youth primarily on college campuses under the covert control of international communism. Yet its roots were in the previous decade; its leaders were middle-aged and as likely to be working mothers as college activists. The Central Intelligence Agency, moreover, found that the movement was too diverse and too suspicious of international communism to ever fall under its control. Thus far postmortems have focused on what impact the antiwar movement had on specific steps taken (or not taken) during the war and on its outcome. However, studies by scholars indicate that decision makers often were influenced as much by a fear of general public opinion as by any concern for the movement's possible reaction. Some studies go further, suggesting that the stakes of the allegedly "inhibited actions" seem less high in retrospect than hawk or dove would like to admit and may well have not been decisive. Other studies disagree with these assessments. What is missed in this process, however, is something so pregnant with meaning that it is mentioned in every list of "lessons" drawn from this conflict. During the American War in Vietnam, the United States government viewed antiwar opinion as an opponent to be manipulated or even as an ally of its battlefield foe: Johnson hoped the latter was true; Nixon needed desperately to believe it was. As a result, the United States was unable to build what is now deemed to have been essential for victory in Vietnam—domestic consensus behind the war—or was forced to try to do so with one hand tied behind its back.

Marilyn Young, in chapter 8, engages each of these controversies while placing the antiwar movement in the larger context of late 1950s early 1960s social protest. She also compares the American response to the Korean and

Vietnam wars, demonstrating how the former influenced the latter and how the context of war protest shifted between these wars in a way that legitimized, or at least destigmatized, antiwar sentiment. She illuminates the ongoing importance of the civil rights movement on antiwar protest and briefly discusses the social composition of the movement and its relationship to other aspects of social and cultural upheaval in the 1960s (the counterculture, antiwar protests of Vietnam veterans, the student movement). She also devotes considerable attention as to why both the movement's advocates and critics wish to believe that the war was lost not on the field of battle but in the streets of America.

The volume concludes with chapter 9, a commentary by Lloyd C. Gardner. He offers some reflections on the aspirations and contents of the chapters herein and on the continuing enterprise of gaining a better understanding of both Vietnam's struggle for independence and reunification and America's longest war. His comments focus on the self-delusions that plagued wartime American conceptions of diplomacy and warfare.

That focus is particularly appropriate at the time of this writing, September 11, 2001. On this day, another that will surely live in infamy, some veterans and others touched by the American War in Vietnam saw a terrible lesson unlearned. During that war, America's leaders expected their foe to act exactly as they would under similar circumstances, even though (or because) they knew nothing of the enemy's mindset. They also pursued their enemy with the same high-technology and firepower strategies that had succeeded in World Wars I and II and were expected to contribute to winning a World War III against the Soviet Union. These strategies failed in the "brushfire" war in Indochina, but with the Soviet Union still on the horizon, the United States rebuilt its traditional conventional and nuclear forces until they were more than the match for its similarly force-structured Soviet opponent. However, with the collapse of the Soviet Union and the emergence of terrorist threats, the American war machine again fell victim to paradigm paralysis, unable to see its new enemy in any other terms than its old one, the Soviet version of what they saw in their own mirror. The solution to terrorism was a missile shield against a "rogue" nuclear assault. The United States had missiles; the Soviets had missiles; the terrorists would too. But the new century's terrorists were like the guerrillas in Vietnam who employed those weapons that they could obtain most easily. Also like the Viet Cong, they made up in human resources—commitment and self-sacrifice—what they lacked in advanced weaponry. Vietnam was not only a guerrilla war, and today's terrorists may come to employ the most sophisticated of weapons. But philosophers of war, from Carl von Clausewitz to Sun Tzu, insist that victory goes to the combatants who know the enemy as well as they know themselves. Mastery of this precept is also both the best means of reducing or preventing human conflict and, the contributors to this volume believe, the surest means of making sense of the results of our failures to do so.

## Notes

1. David Donald, ed., *Why the North Won the Civil War* (New York: Collier Books, 1960; Simon and Schuster, 1996). More than 100,000 copies of this work in 26 editions have been sold. The 1996 edition includes a historiographical overview of the collapse of the Confederacy by Henry Steele Commanger.
2. President George Herbert Walker Bush later vowed that Operation Desert Storm/Desert Shield would bury the memory of Vietnam under the sands of Arabia but was careful to heed its chief lessons, that the insertion of troops abroad can stimulate local resistance, increase the risk of becoming mired in a conflict with ever-upward spiraling costs, exhaust the patience of allied nations, and possibly widen the war into neighboring countries. The costs of the failure of the allied forces to occupy Iraq and extirpate Saddam Hussein's regime have been high, but even had it been attempted, isolationist sentiment expressed within Bush's own party over subsequent U.S. operations in Bosnia make it clear that even they would not have supported such operations in Iraq had they been costly or prolonged.
3. David Hunt, "The Antiwar Movement After the War," in Jayne S. Werner and Luu Doan Huynh, *The Vietnam War: Vietnamese and American Perspectives* (Armonk, NY: E. Sharpe, 1992), 258–270.
4. See Ralph Wetterhahn, *The Last Battle: The* Mayaguez *Incident and the End of the Vietnam War* (New York: Carroll & Graf, 2001).
5. See Marc Jason Gilbert, "Lost Warriors: Viet Nam Veterans Among the Homeless," in Robert M. Slabey, *The United States and Vietnam from War to Peace* (Jefferson, N.C.: McFarland, 1996), 91–112.
6. There is little utility in employing here the practice by which some Vietnam War scholars, on both the political left and right, use the terms "orthodox" and "revisionist" schools as employed in Marxist-Leninist theory when discussing ideological purity. Discourse about the war is sufficiently convoluted without this additional complication.
7. Joan Hoff, "Nixon, Vietnam and the American Homefront," in Dennis Showalter and John G. Albert, *An American Dilemma, Vietnam, 1974–1973* (Chicago: Imprint Publications, 1993), 188.
8. "There is no tradition of a national government in Saigon. There are no roots in the country. Not until there is tranquility can you have any stability. I don't think we ought to take this government seriously. There is no one who can do anything. We have to do what we think we ought to do regardless of what the Saigon government." Henry Cabot Lodge, quoted in Notes of Meeting, July 21, 1965, The Lyndon Baines Johnson Presidential Library [hereafter referred to as Johnson Library], Meeting Notes File, Box 1, in *Foreign Relations of the United States, 1964–1968, Volume III, Vietnam June-December 1965,* no. 71,

*www.state.gov/ www/ about_state/ history/vol_iii/070.html;* and Horace Busby, Memorandum From the President's Special Assistant to President Johnson, July 21, 1965, Johnson Library, Office Files of Horace Busby, Vietnam, Box 3, Secret. 1965, in *Foreign Relations of the United States, 1964–1968, Volume III, Vietnam June-December 1965,* no. 75, *www.state.gov/www/about_state/history/vol_iii/070.html.*

9. One of the consequences of knowing so little about Vietnamese history was that U.S. officials merely scoffed at the term, which referenced the ancient Viet people's "March South" that led to their conquest of what in the 1960s were the lands of the Republic of Vietnam, then the lands of Cham and Khmer peoples. It evoked a powerful sentiment among all Vietnamese akin to the westward movement in American history.
10. Alfred S. Bradford, *Some Even Volunteered: The First Wolfhounds Pacify Vietnam* (Westport, CT: Praeger, 1994), 189. The "commander" Bradford refers to is General William Westmoreland. Bradford, a Wolfhound himself, is eclectic in his views, but the following places him in the orthodox camp: "This is not to say that we thought Hanoi would be better than Saigon, but only that it would be equally bad in a different way. We had our solutions [cleaning out ARVN battalions of corrupt and incompetent officers, but these were] impractical because we would have given the boot to members of the class with which our leaders identified."
11. Le Loi, founder of the Le dynasty, employed protracted war against Chinese troops until they were demoralized. Only then did he shift to conventional operations, forcing the Chinese to withdraw under conditions of a treaty in 1427 that secured peace between Vietnam and China for hundreds of years. Ho Chi Minh referred to Le Loi's victory when in France attempting to secure a withdrawal of French forces from Vietnam in the aftermath of World War II.
12. See Michael Getler, "Resor Still Unsure on Vietnam War," *Washington Post,* May 27, 1971, sec. A, 20.
13. One of America's premier military strategists and consultants, Edward L. Luttwak, has written that the era of mass warfare ushered in by Napoleon, with its Clausewitzian rallying of public opinion in pursuit of war until victory or national annihilation, had given way by the late twentieth century to a new age of limited wars with limited objectives, requiring patience rather than "hot blood," as exemplified by Korea and Vietnam. See Edward Luttwak, "Post-Heroic Military Policy." *Foreign Affairs* 75, no. 4 (July/August 1996): 33–44.
14. General Harold Johnson, Notes of Meeting, July 22, 1965, Johnson Library, Meeting Notes, File Box 1, in *Foreign Relations of the United States, 1964–1968, Volume III, Vietnam June-December 1965,* no. 76, *www.state.gov/www/about_state/ history/vol_iii/070.html.*
15. John M. Carland, *Stemming the Tide: May 1965 to October 1966* (Washington: Center for Military History, 2000), 356–357.
16. Reinhold Neibuhr, "The Anatomy of American Nationalism," in Ernest W. Lefever, ed., *The World Crisis and American Responsibility* (New York: Associated Press, 1958), 61–63.

17. See Ball to Rusk, McNamara, McGeorge Bundy, William Bundy, McNamara, McNaughton, and Unger, June 29, 1965, in The Senator Gravel Edition, *The Pentagon Papers* (New York: McGraw-Hill, abridged ed., 1993), vol. 4, 609–610, and George Ball, Memorandum for the President, July 1, 1965, in The Senator Gravel Edition, *The Pentagon Papers,* vol. 4, 615–617. Ball went so far as to argue that those who wished to use the Southeast Asian Treaty Organization alliance as a justification for an American commitment were merely twisting it to suit their interventionist purpose. It did not require an American defense of Vietnam. See George Ball, Memorandum From the Under Secretary of State to President Johnson, June 23, 1965 attached in McGeorge Bundy, Memorandum From the President's Special Assistant for National Security Affairs to President Johnson, June 27, 1965, Johnson Library, National Security File, Memos to the President, McGeorge Bundy, Vol. XI. Secret, in *Foreign Relations of the United States, 1964–1968, Volume III, Vietnam June-December 1965,* no. 24, *www.state.gov/www/about_ state/history/vol_iii/020.html.* Bundy sent this memo to the president with the observation that "George [Ball] asked me to say that he himself does not think the legal arguments about support for Vietnam are decisive. The commitment is primarily political and any decision to enlarge or reduce it will be political. My own further view is that if and when we wish to shift our course and cut our losses in Vietnam we should do so because of a finding that the Vietnamese themselves are not meeting their obligations to themselves or to us. This is the course we started on with Diem, and if we got a wholly ineffective or anti-American government we could do the same thing again. With a 'neutralist' government it would be quite possible to move in this direction."
18. See George W. Ball, "Block That Vietnam Myth," *The New York Times,* May 19, 1985, sec. E, 21, and John Prados, *The Hidden History of the Vietnam War* (Chicago: Ivan R. Dee, 1995), 192.
19. See Bruce Palmer, *The Twenty-Five Year War: America's Military Role in Vietnam* (New York: Simon & Schuster, 1984).
20. General Earle Wheeler told the President Johnson in response to his concern that China could send thousands of "volunteers" to help the DRV, "the one thing all NVN fear is Chinese. For them to invite Chinese volunteers is to invite China's taking over NVN." See Notes of Meeting, July 22, 1965, Johnson Library, Meeting Notes File Box 1, in *Foreign Relations of the United States, 1964–1968, Volume III, Vietnam June-December 1965,* no. 76, *www.state.gov/www/about_ state/history/vol_iii/070.html.*
21. Memorandum From the Legal Advisor (Meeker) to Secretary of State Rusk, December 25, 1965, Department of State, Central Files, POL 27 VIET S. Secret, in *Foreign Relations of the United States, 1964–1968, Volume III, Vietnam June-December 1965,* no. 244, *www.state.gov//www/about_state/history/vol_iii/240.html.*
22. For McCain's comments see "Good Morning Vietnam," *Time,* July 24, 1995, 50. See also comments by Winston Lord in "A New Anti-China Club," *Newsweek,* July 17, 1995, 30–34.

23. See Keith W. Taylor, "China and Vietnam: Looking for a New Version of an Old Relationship," in Werner and Doan Huynh, eds., *The Vietnam War,* 279–284. The orthodox school contends that, whether Ho could have been an Asian Tito or not, the United States was not very astute when it rejected out of hand the Vietnamese leader's appeals for normal relations in 1945 and 1947 and in its support for a continuation of French dominance in Indochina after World War II. See Mark Bradley, "An Improbable Opportunity: America and the Democratic Republic of Vietnam's 1947 initiative," in Werner and Doan Huynh, eds., *The Vietnam War,* 3–23.
24. The record of these dissents has been collected in Robert Buzzanco, "Division, Dilemma and Dissent: Military Recognition of the Peril of War in Viet Nam," in Dan Duffy, ed., *Informed Dissent: Three Generals and the Viet Nam War* (Westport, CT.: Vietnam Generation/Burning Cities Press, 1992), 24–28. See also Stephen Pelz, "Alibi Alley: Vietnam as History," *Reviews in American History,* 8, no.1 (1980): 139–141.
25. See Memorandum of the Chief of Staff, Army, dated 6 April 1954 quoted, and discussed in Ronald H. Spector, *Advice and Support: The Early Years of the U.S. Army in Vietnam, 1941–1960* (New York: The Free Press, 1985), 208–209.
26. See Memorandum From the Assistant Secretary of Defense for International Security Affairs, (John McNaughton) to Secretary of Defense McNamara, November 9, 1965, Johnson Library, National Security File, Country File, Vietnam, Vol. XLII, Memos (A), in *Foreign Relations of the United States, 1964–1968, Volume III, Vietnam June-December 1965,* no. 194, *www.state.gov/ www/about_state/history/vol_iii/190.html.* See also Norman B. Hannah, The Key to Failure: Laos and the Vietnam War (Lanham, MD : Madison Books, 1987).
27. General Goodpaster drew the author's attention to the study completed by a committee he chaired, dated July 14,1965, which advocated "barrier" operations. It is entitled "Intensification of the Military Operations in Vietnam: Concept and Appraisal—Report of an Ad Hoc Study Group" which was attached to the Memorandum from Richard C. Bowman of the National Security Staff to the President's Special Assistant for National Security Affairs (Bundy), July 21, 1965, Johnson Library, National Security File, Vietnam, Volume XXXVII, in *Foreign Relations of the United States, 1964–1968, Volume III, Vietnam June-December 1965,* no. 69, *www.state.gov/www/about_ state/history/vol_iii/060.html.* Walt Rostow's proposal to "invade the southern part of North Vietnam in order to block infiltration routes" can be found in W. W. Rostow, *The Diffusion of Power: An Essay in Recent History* (New York: Macmillan, 1972), 513. He was also kind enough to share his views with this writer at the Johnson Library on April 20, 2001 and later supply him with a draft of the Vietnam chapter of his forthcoming memoirs. At that time, his response to hearing the title of this then proposed volume was to ask, "You know, of course, how we could have won the war?" When this writer replied, "An occupation of the Laotian panhandle and the southern districts of the DRV?" Rostow said, "That's right!"

28. For General Johnson's remarks, see General Harold Johnson, Notes of Meeting, July 22, 1965, Meeting Notes, File Box 1, Johnson Library, in the *Foreign Relations of the United States, 1964–1968, Volume III, Vietnam June-December 1965,* no. 76, *www.state.gov/www/about_state/ history/vol_iii/070.html.* For Taylor's observations, see Buzzanco "Division, Dilemma and Dissent," 17.
29. Buzzanco, "Division, Dilemma and Dissent," 17.
30. See Gavin's testimony in J. William Fulbright, *United States Congress, Senate Committee on the Vietnam Hearings* [hereafter referred to as *Vietnam Hearings*] (New York: Random House, 1966), 66–106.
31. Buzzanco, "Division, Dilemma and Dissent," 17.
32. See George F. Kennan's testimony in *The Vietnam Hearings,* 107–166. See also Robert S. McNamara, Draft Memorandum for the President, October 14, 1966, in George Herring, ed., *The Pentagon Papers* (New York: McGraw-Hill, abridged ed., 1993), 162.
33. Ibid.
34. Robert S. McNamara, Memoranda for the President, 7 November and 7 December 1965, and Draft Memoranda for the President, 14 October, 1966, in George Herring, ed., *The Pentagon Papers,* 134, 136, 159.
35. Even the famous memorandum provided to McNamara suggesting an "anti-infiltration barrier" specified a "leasing" of Laotian territory. See Ibid., 142.
36. See George F. Kennan's testimony before the Senate Foreign Relations Committee, February 10, 1966 in *Vietnam Hearings,* 110
37. George Kennan quoted in *Vietnam Hearings,* 108–110.
38. See Memorandum From the Assistant Secretary of Defense for International Security Affairs, (John McNaughton) to Secretary of Defense McNamara, November 9, 1965, Johnson Library, National Security File, Country File, Vietnam, Vol. XLII, Memos (A), in *Foreign Relations of the United States, 1964–1968, Volume III, Vietnam June-December 1965,* no. 194, *www.state.gov/ www/about_state/history/vol_iii/190.html* and The Senator Gravel Edition, *The Pentagon Papers,* Vol. IV, 169–175.
39. Memorandum by Richard Helms, dated September 12, 1967 cited in Robert S. McNamara with Brian VanDeMark, *In Retrospect: The Tragedy and Lessons of Vietnam* (New York: Random House, 1995), 292–293.
40. Author interview with Bui Tin, April 16,1995. When asked what the result of an invasion of the Laotian panhandle would have had on the war, Bui Tin remarked, "We were always surprised that you never attempted it." As for its impact, he noted, "It could have halted major offensive operations in the South." When asked if this meant that the war would end, Bui Tin laughed heartily and then replied, "Of course not, it would continue by other means." This is also the opinion of Douglas Pike, a major wartime authority on the Viet Cong/PAVN. See Douglas Pike, "The Other Side," Peter Braestrup, ed. *Vietnam As History: Ten Years After the Paris Peace Accords* (Washington D.C.: University Press of America: 1984), 77 fn.1.
41. See McNamara, with VanDeMark, *In Retrospect,* passim. See also the televised interview and discussion session moderated by William Lehre of the

Public Broadcasting System on April 18, 1995 during which McGeorge Bundy offered his own terse mea culpa. McGeorge Bundy's brother and fellow war leader, William Bundy, opened his address at a conference on the war at the United States Air Force Academy, October 17–19, 1990, with the confession that he was as much responsible for the war as anybody. "Please forgive me," he said. "I am truly sorry." Two other war hawks, the late Secretary of State Dean Rusk and Walt Rostow, President Johnson's eternally optimistic National Security Adviser (he thought the war would end in an American victory long before the Tet Offensive), never doubted the war's value and purpose.

42. William Bundy, Notes of Meeting, July 22, 1965, Johnson Library, Meeting Notes File, Box 1, in *Foreign Relations of the United States, 1964–1968, Volume III, Vietnam June-December 1965,* no. 76, *www.state.gov/www/about_state/history/vol_iii/070.html.* Bundy, of course, was here summarizing what others were likely to say about the decision to commitment troops to Vietnam. However, as these notes indicate, such views were vocalized by the many in the decision-making loop, and not merely George Ball. President Johnson himself pondered over them in this document to the point of expressing his own doubts that the United States could win the war under the circumstances he saw likely to evolve in Vietnam,
43. During the final debates over the decision to commit troops, Henry Cabot Lodge remarked, "There is a greater threat to World War III if we don't go in. Similarity to our indolence at Munich." See Notes on Meeting, July 21, 1965, Johnson Library, Meeting Notes File, Box 1, in *The Foreign Relations of the United States, 1964–1968, Volume III, Vietnam June-December 1965,* no. 71, *www.state.gov/www/about_state/history/vol_iii/070.html.*
44. Johnson concluded that "Right now I feel it would more dangerous for us to lose this now, than endanger a greater number of troops." Notes of a Meeting, July 21, 1965, *Foreign Relations of the United States, 1964–1968, Volume III, Vietnam June-December 1965,* no. 71, *www.state.gov/www/about_state/history/ about_state/history/vol_iii/070.html.*
45. George Ball, Memorandum From the Under Secretary of State to President Johnson, June 18, 1965, Johnson Library, National Security File, Country File, Vietnam, Vol. XXXV, Memos (D), Top Secret, in the *Foreign Relations of the United States, 1964–1968, Volume III, Vietnam June-December 1965,* no. 7, *www.state.gov/www/about_state/history/vol_iii/001.html.*
46. See the conversation between President Johnson and Robert McNamara, June 21, 1965, 12:15 p.m., Tape WH6506.05, PNO 8168, Recordings of Telephone Conversations—White House Series, Recordings and Transcripts of Conversations and Meetings, Lyndon B. Johnson Library. LBJ told McNamara, "I think that in time, it's going to be like this Yale Professor said . . . that it's going to be very difficult for us to very long prosecute effectively a war that far away from home with the divisions that we have here—and, particularly, the potential divisions. That's really had me concerned for a month, and I'm very depressed about it because I see no program from either Defense

or State that gives me much hope of doing anything except just praying and gasping to hold on during the monsoon, and hope they'll quit. I don't believe they're ever going to quit. I don't see how . . . that we have any way of . . . either a plan for victory militarily or diplomatically." The author is indebted to Professor David Shreve, deputy director, Presidential Recordings Project, The Miller Center of Public Affairs, for providing him with the transcript of this tape. The publication of the corpus of the Johnson phone tape transcriptions is forthcoming.

47. Germany's leaders had expected a quick victory in that war and initially had accepted (or were forced to accept) responsibility for the ensuing protracted war of attrition they had not anticipated. By the 1930s, in the midst of a conservative revival, a new set of leaders paraded before the German public heroes of World War I willing to tell them that the German war machine would have secured victory had not liberal politicians sold it out by agreeing to an armistice. Left unmentioned was that the German army in France had long before the armistice refused to go on offensive operations and were "fragging" specialized units whose espirit de corps prevented other units from surrendering quickly to the advancing allied armies. Also unmentioned was the mutiny of the sailors of the German High Seas Fleet that prohibited all operations against the British in the North Sea.
48. See Carland, *Stemming the Tide,* 363.
49. See the comments of Westmoreland and General Bruce Palmer in Ted Gettinger, *The Johnson Years: A Vietnam Roundtable* (Austin, TX: Lyndon Baines Johnson Library, 1993), 76–77, 100–101, 159–161.
50. Douglas Kinnard, *The War Mangers* (Hanover, NH: University of New England, 1977), 161–162, 192.
51. George W. Ball, "Block That Vietnam Myth," *New York Times,* May 19, 1985, sec. E, 21.
52. See William Head, *Plotting A True Course: Strategic Bombing Theory and Doctrine Since World War II* (Westport, CT: Greenwood, forthcoming, 2002).
53. Lieutant General Bernard William Rogers, *Cedar-Falls-Junction City: A Turning Point* (Washington, D.C.: Departmentof the Army, 1974), p. 159.
54. See Steve Vlastos, "America's Enemy: The Absent Presence in Revisionist Vietnam War History," in John Carlos Rowe and Rick Berg, *The Vietnam War and American Culture* (New York: Columbia University Press 1991), 72.
55. See Ngo Vinh Long, "The Tet Offensive and Its Aftermath," in Marc Jason Gilbert and William Head, eds., *The Tet Offensive* (Westport, CT: Praeger, 1996), 89–123.
56. Although HES staff were "very committed people . . . [HES] wasn't very accurate. I mean, hell, you have companies and battalions switching positions in areas that would never show up in [the HES]. There were [also] social conditions that were very fundamental [and not addressed by the HES]." Author interview with Mike Chilton, one of the four HES coordinators (Chilton was the II Corps coordinator), July 22, 1997, International Voluntary Services Indochina Oral History Project, (transcript available at Stewart

Library, North Georgia College and State University, Dahlonega, Georgia, 30597).

57. RAND field staff tasked with studying Viet Cong morale rarely found dramatic evidence favoring the American war effort. As a result, on one occasion, a senior RAND executive was sent to Vietnam to ask them to put a brighter spin on their conclusions. Joseph Zasloff and other senior analysts, however, rarely pulled any punches. By 1967 few RAND personnel working on the war, including one of the corporation's founders, Bernard Brodie, believed it would have any positive outcome. See Daniel Ellsberg, *Papers on the War* (New York: Simon and Schuster, 1972), 159.
58. See, for example, Victoria Pohle, *The Viet Cong in Saigon: Tactics and Objectives during the Tet Offensive* (Santa Monica, CA: RAND Corporation, 1969), which warns against any attempt at "Vietnamization."
59. Westmoreland's contention that the war could have been won by expanding it forms the basis of most revisionist writing. However, Westmoreland now thinks that current conditions in Indochina warrant his crediting President Johnson "for not allowing the war to expand geographically . . . because our strategic objectives have been reached. You may disagree with me on this, but you cannot argue with the facts." Cited in Ted Gittinger, ed., *The Johnson Years: A Vietnam Roundtable* (Austin, TX: Lyndon Baines Johnson School of Public Affairs, University of Texas at Austin, 1993), 77. Harry G. Summers, Jr., goes further. Summers said that it is "sad" that so many Vietnamese had to die in a "people's war" when, after the war, the designers of that war showed their true Stalinist colors and abandoned them. He gloried in the fact that the pressure in Vietnam in support of *doi moi* and other forms of economic reconstruction have given new meaning to the revolutionary slogan "all power to the People." He wrote, "People brought down the communist tyranny in East Europe. And people will eventually bring it down in East Asia as well." (See Harry G. Summers, Jr., review of Morley Safer's *Flashbacks: On Returning to Vietnam, The Washington Monthly,* no. 3, 22 (April, 1990): 61) The irony embodied in Summers' thinking is that when communist regimes in East Europe and East Asia do pass into history by dint of the efforts of their own people, they will have demonstrated the United States' error in thinking that communism could be checked or destroyed only by interventionist American military might. The people within these regimes, as Summers now boasts, would do the job in time without the presence of American combat troops. If Summers wished to employ his own favorite method of judging the past events by their outcomes—the Clausewitzian "judgment by results," the defenders of the standard historical interpretation of the Vietnam War could argue that the American moral anticommunist crusade in Vietnam could have spared the lives of millions (or at least more than 58,000 Americans lives) if, in their interpretation of containment theory, the leaders of this crusade had given as much thought to the power of the people before the war as they have done after it.

60. Lieutenant General Dewitt C. Smith, in his somewhat caustic introduction to Summers' original edition of his study of the war, found fault with much of Summers' book. He discerned that while *On Strategy* trumpets the need for unity among the American military, the people, and their government, it makes no mention of "the enormous force, depth, and consequence of the moral judgment which many good Americans made against the war itself even when they were sensitive to the decency, valor and commitment of most who fought in Vietnam." Summers sought an officer friendlier to his ideas for the subsequent editions of his work. See Harry G. Summers Jr., *On Strategy: A Critical Analysis of the Vietnam War* (Carlisle Barracks, PA: Strategic Studies Institute, 1981), viii.
61. Douglas Pike, quoted in Kim Willenson, *The Bad War: An Oral History of the Vietnam War* (New York: New American Library, 1987), 22.
62. "Somebody has got to talk back to these professors," General William Westmoreland roared at a conference in 1995, despite the fact that the conference was hosted by a conservative academic group led by Peter Rollins, a Professor of English and a Westmoreland booster. See Marc Leepson, "At a Conference on McNamara's book, *In Retrospect,* Military Heavyweights lined up to "Knife the Mac," in *Vietnam Magazine,* 9 (December 1996), 62, 70–74.
63. Harry G. Summers Jr., "The Last Years of the War," in Jane Errington and B. J. C. McKercher, eds., *The Vietnam War and History* (New York: Praeger, 1990), 174.
64. See Willenson, *The Bad War,* 95–97; Buzzanco, "Division, Dilemma, and Dissent," 22–23.
65. Harry G. Summers Jr., review of Morley Safer's *Flashbacks: On Returning to Vietnam, The Washington Monthly,* no. 3, 22 (April, 1990): 61.
66. See Peter Braestrup, "The News Media and the War in Vietnam: Myths and Realities," in Leslie J. Cullen, ed., *Selected Papers on Teaching the Vietnam War: Occasional Paper No. 1* (Lubbock, TX: The Vietnam Center at Texas Tech University, 1998), 5–14. Kim Willenson asked Oberdorfer whether revisionists were correct in using his own and Braestrup's works to prove that the "press did the country a disservice." His reply is that it did not, but that Johnson and Westmoreland did in misrepresenting the war to the public. See Willenson, *The Bad War,* 194–195. Don Oberdorfer's panel on journalism was entitled "Reporting on the War," was convened and video recorded on February 27, 2000, at the Atlanta History Center, Atlanta, Georgia.
67. See also Guenter Lewy, *America in Vietnam* (New York: Oxford, 1978), and Andrew Krepinevich, *The Army in Vietnam* (Baltimore, MD: The Johns Hopkins University Press, 1986).
68. George C. Herring, *America's Longest War: The United States and Vietnam, 1950–1975* (New York: 3rd edition, McGraw-Hill, 1996), xi-xii.
69. See Clark Clifford's remarks in Kim Willenson, *The Bad War,* 92–94.
70. Herring, *America's Longest War,* xii.
71. See Gabor Boritt, ed., *Why the Confederacy Lost* (New York: Oxford University Press, 1992). In this work, historian James McPherson and others

argue that an over-emphasis on larger forces, such as population, economics, and dissent, has blinded some scholars to the primacy of the battlefield in securing the North's ultimate victory. The Union army, through key victories at key moments, achieved victory in a struggle whose outcome was far from inevitable.

## Chapter One

# Victory by Other Means

## The Foreign Policy of the Democratic Republic of Vietnam

William J. Duiker

Why did the communists win the Vietnam War? That question has tormented many Americans—and undoubtedly many Vietnamese as well—for over a quarter of a century. As a general rule, the answer usually has focused on the alleged mistakes committed by U.S. policymakers in prosecuting the war, such as a lack of political will or a faulty military strategy. It is past time to recognize that, whatever the errors committed in Washington or Saigon, the communist victory in Vietnam was a stunning achievement and a testimony to the strategic and tactical genius of the war planners of the Hanoi regime (formally known as the Democratic Republic of Vietnam, or DRV) as well as to the patience and self-sacrifice of millions of their followers throughout the country.

There are undoubtedly a number of explanations for the outcome of the war. Some are rooted in Vietnamese history and culture, while others are more subjective in nature, among which were the superior organizational ability of the communist leadership, its imaginative program and strategy, and the charismatic quality of the revolutionary movement's great leader, Ho Chi Minh. Yet there is little doubt that Hanoi's ability to manipulate the international and diplomatic environment to its own advantage was a key factor in its success. For two decades, North Vietnamese leaders were able to maneuver successfully through the shoals of a complex international situation—including a bitter dispute between their two major allies and a worldwide diplomatic offensive by the United States—in such a manner as to outwit their adversaries, win the often-reluctant support of their squabbling allies, and earn the sympathy and support of peoples on continents throughout the world.

How could a government that for many years was virtually isolated from the international community (and even in the mid-1960s possessed only limited experience in the diplomatic arena) manage to outwit and outmaneuver the statesmen who enacted official policy in the great capital cities of the world? As with so many aspects of the Vietnam conflict, the explanation must be sought in events that took place long before the first U.S. combat troops landed on Vietnamese soil in the spring of 1965. The diplomatic strategy that was applied by DRV leaders during the Vietnam War had been devised over an extended period of time that dates back to the first stages of the Indochina conflict before the end of World War II. Only by studying the experience of Ho Chi Minh and his colleagues during and immediately after the Pacific war will we be able to understand how and why they applied the lessons of that experience with such success in the decades that followed.

## Seeking the Moment of Opportunity

Up until the beginning of the Pacific war, the Vietnamese revolution had been only marginally affected by the international situation. It was not, however, for lack of trying. Early in the twentieth century, shortly after the consolidation of French colonial authority throughout Indochina, anticolonialist firebrands had turned their eyes to Japan in the hope that the imperial government in Tokyo, which had just won a stunning victory over tsarist Russia at Port Arthur, would provide assistance to emerging nationalist movements in Southeast Asia. After that gambit failed, their attention rapidly shifted to China, where in 1911 revolutionary forces under Sun Yat-sen had brought about the collapse of the decrepit Manchu empire. Those hopes, too, proved abortive when Sun's party was forced to cede power to the warlord general Yuan Shikai. But Vietnamese nationalists, perhaps influenced by the long tributary relationship between the two countries, did not despair of future Chinese support, and during the next few years hundreds of Vietnamese revolutionary activists fled across the northern border to seek Chinese assistance in the liberation of their country from foreign rule.[1]

The fascination of early Vietnamese nationalists with the chimera of foreign assistance was carried on after the formation of the Vietnamese Communist Party in 1930. The founder of the organization, Ho Chi Minh, had become convinced as a young man that his country could be liberated from the clutches of French imperialism only with help from abroad. Shortly after settling in Paris at the end of World War I, he became attracted to the ideas of the Bolshevik leader Vladimir Lenin, whose revolutionary program envisaged a global revolt by the oppressed peoples of the world against their colonial masters. After joining the French Communist Party in 1920, Ho received training as a communist agent in Moscow, and then went on to South China, where he established the Revolutionary Youth League, the first Marxist-Leninist revolutionary organization in colonial Indochina. Five years later it was transformed into the Indochinese Communist Party (ICP). But although the new party received training and other forms of assistance from local members of the Chinese Communist Party (CCP), the relationship was short-lived. When in the late 1920s CCP activities were suppressed by the Nationalist government of Chiang Kai-shek, ICP units operating in South China were forced into hiding. For the next decade, the Vietnamese revolutionary movement was essentially isolated from the outside world and reduced to a sheer struggle for survival.[2]

The coming of World War II, however, brought help from an unexpected source when, in the fall of 1940, Japanese military forces occupied Indochina in preparation for a future advance throughout Southeast Asia. Although the French colonial administration, which had just fallen under the control of the pro-Axis Vichy French, was left in place, French authority was significantly weakened, thus providing ICP leaders with the opportunity to build up their forces for an uprising to evict the French after the end of the Pacific war.

Ho Chi Minh, who had sharpened his understanding of international politics during nearly two decades as an agent of Lenin's revolutionary outreach organization, the Communist International, was well aware that his party's grasp for power would face better odds for success if it had support and recognition from the international community. Unfortunately, he could expect little help from the Soviet Union, since Moscow's interest in the Vietnamese revolution was obviously minimal. But if the wartime "Grand Alliance" that had been established among the Soviet Union, the United States, and other antifascist countries could be exploited, broad public support from the United States—and perhaps from Nationalist China and other allied countries as well—might be expected for the liberation of his country from French colonial rule after the expected Allied victory. Ho had carefully noted public remarks by U.S. President Franklin D. Roosevelt that the French should not be permitted to return to Indochina after the end of the Pacific war.

Recognition of the revolutionary movement as the legitimate voice of Vietnamese national aspirations by the victorious Allies—and by moderate elements within Vietnamese society itself—could be anticipated, however, only if the communist character of its leadership as carefully disguised. As a consequence, in the spring of 1941 Ho had set the stage by forming a broad multiparty alliance called the League for the Independence of Vietnam, popularly known as the Vietminh Front. The ICP was listed as a component of the front, but its leading role in the organization was not generally known. Ho Chi Minh then set out to win recognition and support for the movement from the Nationalist government in China and from the United States.

Ho's initial attempts to link the Vietminh Front with the Allied cause were derailed in August 1942, when he was arrested by Chinese authorities under suspicion of being a Japanese agent. But after his release a year later he resumed his efforts, and during the last months of the war he was able to establish an amicable working relationship with Chinese Nationalist commanders in South China as well as with U.S. military intelligence operatives in the area, who agreed to provide the Vietminh with limited technical assistance in return for their cooperation in providing intelligence information on Indochina to the Allies.[3]

At the end of the war, Vietminh forces occupied Hanoi and Ho Chi Minh declared the formation of a new independent republic, with himself as provisional president. But he was less successful in seeking international recognition for his new government as the legitimate representative of the Vietnamese people. Despite his tireless efforts to portray himself as a moderate nationalist and a fervent admirer of American democratic principles (primed with his offers for possible future U.S. economic and military concessions in the DRV), Ho's letters to Roosevelt's successor, Harry S. Truman, went unanswered. Similar appeals to London and Moscow also went without response.[4]

## Opportunity Lost?

In later years, Ho Chi Minh's appeal for support from the United States was cited by many observers as a lost opportunity for Washington to woo him from his allegiance to Moscow and transform him into an "Asian Tito." In retrospect, the Truman administration might indeed have been advised to test the willingness of the new Vietnamese state to embark on an independent course in world affairs. At that time, it had few true friends in the international arena and might have been sorely tempted to tailor its policies to those of any generous benefactor. On the other hand, there are ample grounds for skepticism that Ho Chi Minh (who was quite adept at flattering would-be allies or adversaries) was entirely sincere in his overtures to the United States. As a longtime practitioner of the Leninist strategy of the united front, Ho was quite willing to make tactical alliances with potential adversaries in the full understanding that such arrangements might be only temporary in character.

Ho Chi Minh's actual motives in seeking U.S. support were perhaps best disclosed in a speech on the international political environment that he presented to colleagues at the close of the Pacific war. In comments remarkable for their prescience, Ho analyzed the fluidity of the postwar international situation as well as the contradictions that might be turned to the advantage of the new Vietnamese government. If the wartime alliance between Moscow and Washington survived into the postwar era, he noted, the United States (and Nationalist China as well) might decide to oppose the European colonial powers and throw its support to the cause of Vietnamese independence. But if tensions erupted between the United States and the Soviet Union, the former probably would decide to support the French in Indochina in order to prevent the spread of communism in Asia. To limit the impact of such a possible contingency, which would virtually isolate the new Vietnamese state on the world's stage, Ho stressed the importance of placating the Americans and the Chinese as much as possible in order to use them against the French.[5]

Ho Chi Minh thus appeared to have little confidence that the anticolonialist sentiments expressed by President Roosevelt during World War II would continue into the postwar era, when the fundamentally imperialist nature of U.S. foreign policy would presumably be reasserted. Ho hinted as much in a letter that he wrote to Charles Fenn, a U.S. military intelligence officer whom he had met in South China earlier in 1945. "The war is finished," he remarked, but the upcoming departure of the Americans from the region "means that relations between you and us will be more difficult." In the end, he predicted, the Vietnamese would have to fight in order to earn their share in "the victory of freedom and democracy."[6]

As it turned out, Ho Chi Minh's attempt to apply the tactics of the united front on the world stage had only limited success. As tensions between Moscow and Washington increased in Europe, the Truman administration (as he had feared) reluctantly decided to support the restoration of French sovereignty in Indochina. The Nationalist government in China was still hoping to force the French out of Southeast Asia, but—like Washington—it was suspicious of Ho's communist leanings and, through the actions of its military representatives in northern Indochina, lent its support to his noncommunist rivals. The Soviet Union, the ICP's natural ally, was of no use at all, as Soviet leader Joseph Stalin, like Harry Truman, hoped to curry favor with Paris, where upcoming national elections might bring the communists to power in France.

By midsummer of 1946, Ho Chi Minh's worst premonitions had become reality. During peace talks at Fontainebleau, French representatives rejected his proposal for a compromise solution to the Indochina dispute. Lacking any visible support on the international scene, Ho reluctantly signed a modus vivendi to postpone additional peace talks until the following year, but the move was primarily tactical in nature, as he and his colleagues sought to buy time in order to make preparations for war.

## Lean to One Side

When Vietminh forces launched their surprise attack on French installations in North Vietnam on December 19, 1946, the first Indochinese war got under way. Ho Chi Minh did not despair of an eventual negotiated settlement, and in the early months of 1947 he sent out diplomatic feelers to Paris suggesting a resumption of peace talks. When they were rejected, the DRV sent covert signals to Washington stressing the moderation of its domestic and foreign policy objectives. But the Truman administration was increasingly suspicious of the communist leanings of the Vietminh, and it too ignored the overtures.[7]

For the time being, then, the Vietminh were forced to fight alone. In Moscow, Joseph Stalin was suspicious of Ho Chi Minh's ideological orthodoxy and virtually ignored the spreading conflict in far-off Southeast Asia. The DRV's most promising potential source of support was the Communist Party in China, many of whose leaders had become acquainted with Ho during the 1920s and watched the Vietnamese revolution with sympathetic eyes. But the CCP headquarters was now based in North China, where it was mired in its own civil war with Chiang Kai-shek's Nationalist government. A few communist military units—popularly known as the People's Liberation Army (PLA)—were based in the southern provinces and gave some secret assistance to Vietminh forces operating in the vicinity of the frontier.

With its peace feelers rejected, Vietminh war planners lacked an alternative and turned to a policy of self-reliance, based on the Maoist strategy of protracted war. Their hope was to build up the political and military strength of the movement in preparation for an eventual general offensive to drive the enemy into the sea. A description of Vietminh strategy written at the time by ICP General Secretary Truong Chinh made only a brief reference to the possibility of a diplomatic solution, noting that "false negotiations" might be used to distract the enemy and undermine French morale.[8]

By the end of the 1940s, however, the situation changed dramatically, as the communist victory in the Chinese civil war brought a potentially powerful ally to the very northern border of Indochina and provided the Vietminh, for the first time, with a clear prospect of outside assistance. But there was a price to pay for the new relationship. Whereas in the past Vietminh leaders had deliberately downplayed their ties with socialist countries in a bid to win the support of moderates at home and abroad, the new government in Beijing now demanded that they publicly avow their allegiance to the principles of Marxism-Leninism in return for diplomatic recognition and military assistance. Recognition from the Soviet Union followed shortly after, but Moscow established a clear division of labor in carrying out socialist bloc assistance to the DRV, as Stalin assigned primary responsibility for the task to China. Vietnamese leaders were quick to return the favor. In succeeding months, Vietminh news sources publicized the new relationship with China and declared that they would formulate their war strategy and their approach to nation-building on the Chinese model.[9]

The new posture was a gamble, for in drawing closer to the nations of the socialist camp, the DRV ran the risk of drawing the United States into the war on the side of the French. As the prospects for victory in Indochina seemed steadily to recede, Paris began to seek U.S. military assistance, and in March 1949 it had created an autonomous government in Vietnam under the titular rule of former emperor Bao Dai in a bid to win support from Washington. The Truman administration, which remained distrustful of French intentions in Indochina, placed stringent political and military conditions on any prospective aid agreement. But the communist victory in China later that year inflamed anticommunist sentiment in the United States, and with the DRV now moving steadily into the socialist camp, pressure increased on the White House to enter the lists on the side of the French. Within days of the Moscow's recognition of the DRV, Washington announced formal ties with the new Bao Dai government. Economic and military assistance, to be channeled through the French, soon followed.

With its decision to identify more closely with the Sino-Soviet bloc, the DRV was for the first time positioned directly on the global ideological divide. Vietnam's new prominence as a major factor in the Cold War had been signaled in a speech by Chinese Premier Liu Shaoqi in December 1949, when he declared that the new China would give its firm support to struggles for national liberation elsewhere in Asia and specifically referred to the one in Indochina. In all likelihood, Liu's comments were greeted with some discomfort by Ho Chi Minh, who for years had not only tried to avoid identifying his movement directly with the socialist bloc not only in the hope of maximizing its internal appeal, but also in the hope of preventing U.S. intervention. However, the hardening of ideological position of the Cold War and the obvious lure of Chinese aid had been impossible to resist.

It did not take long for the new strategy to bear fruit. In a dramatic battle in the fall of 1950, Vietminh forces defeated French units along the Sino-Vietnamese border and thus opened up the entire border area to Chinese assistance. With the help of Chinese advisors, Vietminh units gradually improved their performance on the battlefield, and in 1951 the high command ordered a major offensive on French-held territories on the fringes of the Red River delta. But for once Ho Chi Minh had overreached, and the Vietminh attacks were driven back with high casualties.

The results of the 1951 campaign sobered Ho's war planners, who were now forced to realize that massive frontal attacks had only minimal success in the face of the enemy's superior firepower. In succeeding years they adopted a more cautious strategy in the hope of dividing the enemy's forces and undermining morale in France, where discontent with the course of the war in Indochina was on the rise. In neighboring Laos and Cambodia, where autonomous royal governments had just been established by the French, ICP leaders sponsored the formation of new revolutionary movements (popularly known as the Pathet Lao and the Khmer Rouge respectively) to operate under Vietminh tutelage. Vietnamese strategists now became increasingly aware of the benefits of waging a protracted war to wear down a more powerful enemy.

In later years, Vietminh commanders would learn how to combine battlefield successes with diplomatic overtures designed to win friends and influence adversaries. Now, however, isolated in their mountain fastness and perhaps temporarily giddy over the prospects for a total victory, they made little use of the weapon of diplomacy as a means of influencing public opinion. When asked by the occasional visiting journalist about the possibility of a negotiated settlement, Vietminh sources consistently downplayed the prospects for peace talks and insisted that the war could come to an end only with a complete victory on the battlefield. Even Ho Chi Minh appeared to believe in the prospects for a total military victory, declaring to one visiting French communist that the DRV was willing to enter peace talks but would make no major concessions.[10]

## Devil's Bargain

But the Vietminh were about to be presented with the bill for the Faustian arrangement they had entered into three years earlier. With Indochina now squarely placed within the socialist camp, the DRV was now increasingly vulnerable to the blandishments of its major allies. At first, China had provided active support and encouragement to the Vietminh in the belief that a direct confrontation with the United States in East Asia was sooner or later inevitable. But by the fall of 1953, Beijing had learned the high costs of its own military intervention in Korea and sought a negotiated settlement in Indochina in order to reduce military expenditures and channel scarce resources into domestic projects. In Moscow, a new post-Stalin leadership under Georgyi Malenkov was determined to follow a similar path. With the Indochina conflict at a virtual stalemate on the battlefield, Moscow and Beijing saw few advantages in extending the war and began to pressure the DRV to accept a compromise settlement that could bring an end to the hostilities before they escalated into a global conflagration among the major powers.

DRV leaders were initially skeptical. In a speech to intellectuals about the cease-fire reached on the Korean peninsula in July, Ho Chi Minh warned his audience that they should harbor no illusions about the immediate prospects for a satisfactory peace settlement in Indochina. The French must be thoroughly defeated, he declared, so that they would meet Vietnamese conditions and withdraw. Yet Ho always was careful to avoid alienating potential benefactors, and in a lengthy interview with a Swedish reporter in October, he expressed a cautious willingness to listen to French proposals for the restoration of peace in Indochina, although he warned his colleagues in a speech shortly after that conditions were not yet entirely favorable for a settlement.[11]

Moscow and Beijing quickly followed up on Ho Chi Minh's remarks, and in January 1954 plans were launched to hold multilateral talks on the Indochina question at a peace conference to convene in Geneva in May. When Ho visited Moscow and Beijing in April to formulate a common negotiating strategy, he was advised by his hosts to be realistic and flexible in his demands. To sweeten the pot for their Vietnamese allies, Chinese leaders promised to increase the level of their military assistance to Vietminh forces to help bring about a major victory on the battlefield and thus strengthen the DRV's position at the conference table. The focus of that effort was to take place at the border post at Dien Bien Phu, recently occupied by French forces to hinder the movement of Vietminh units into neighboring Laos.

At Geneva, Chinese and Soviet delegates publicly supported Vietminh demands for the complete withdrawal of French forces and the total independence of all three Indochinese states. But privately they urged their allies to compromise on key issues. At a short meeting with Chinese Foreign Minister Zhou Enlai at Liuzhou in early July, Ho Chi Minh reluctantly agreed on a peace settlement that would call for the temporary division of Vietnam into two separate regroupment zones and a recognition of the royal governments in Laos and Cambodia as the legitimate authorities of two neutral and independent states. In return, Zhou promised that Chinese aid to the DRV would be increased, and he assured Ho that unification surely would come about within a few years. Some of Ho's colleagues were angry at his decision to bow to Chinese advice (Pham Van Dong, the chief DRV negotiator at Geneva, had to be ordered to accept the agreement by the party politburo), but eventually Ho had his way.[12]

What did DRV leaders learn from their experience at Geneva? There was certainly some bitterness in Vietminh circles, particularly among those fighting in the South, that Vietnamese national interests had been betrayed by their allies. But Ho Chi Minh, despite his own evident reluctance to accept a compromise peace, recognized the logic of Zhou Enlai's advice, and at a meeting of the Vietnam Workers Party (VWP) Central Committee in July, he warned that "some comrades" did not see the United States behind the French. Still, it took all of Ho's persuasive efforts to convince his colleagues that they needed strong and powerful allies and that without a peace settlement in Indochina, the United States would inevitably intervene. In the end, Ho had his way, but the legacy of the Geneva agreement hovered like a shadow over the later history of the Vietnamese revolution and undoubtedly heightened the reluctance of many party leaders to make compromises as they pursued their goal of national reunification.[13]

## Disillusionment

A political declaration drawn up at the Geneva Conference had called for national elections to unite the two regroupment zones two years after the close of the conference. The document had not taken the form of a binding commitment on the administrative authorities in each zone, however, but was merely a statement of intent, approved by a verbal agreement among delegations at the conference. Even then representatives of the United States and the Bao Dai government—now to serve as the governing authority in the South—had refused to give their assent. Washington's refusal to commit itself to the provisions of the Geneva agreement undoubtedly worried many of Ho's supporters (Pham Van Dong was quoted as remarking "You know as well as I do that the elections will never take place"). But Ho Chi Minh, placing his confidence in Zhou Enlai's pledge of support in July, expressed optimism that a political solution ultimately would be found. In preparation for such a contingency, the DRV leadership, which had returned to Hanoi in October, left a small infrastructure of supporters in the South to promote national elections. In case elections were not held, these followers would provide the nucleus for a return to armed struggle.

By the summer of 1955, any optimism in Hanoi that pressure from Moscow and Beijing would help to bring about national reunification had dissipated. That spring the prime minister of Bao Dai's' government in Saigon—the veteran Catholic politician Ngo Dinh Diem—had announced that he had no intention of holding consultations with representatives from the North on possible future elections. The Eisenhower administration was uneasily aware that Diem's adamant refusal to hold elections contravened the spirit of the Geneva agreement, but, fearing that Ho's popularity would tilt the results of such elections in Hanoi's favor, it was no less anxious to avoid them, and eventually the White House decided to back Saigon in its decision. Diem now proceeded with plans to form an independent state, known as the Republic of Vietnam (RVN), in the South.

Diem's rebuff of Hanoi's offer of consultations, combined with his government's vigorous efforts to suppress all opposition to his rule in South Vietnam, aroused considerable anger in the North, especially among those southerners (variously estimated at 70,000 to 80,000 in number) who had been sent north after the cease-fire as part of the exchange of refugees called for by the accords. For many party leaders, still bitter at the compromises imposed on them at Geneva, Diem's action was no surprise, and preparations were intensified to expose many of these "regroupees" (as the refugees from the South were named) to training in agitprop activity and guerrilla war, in the event that renewed hostilities broke out in the near future. But Ho Chi Minh did not yet despair of a political solution and urged his colleagues to use diplomatic means to turn the new situation to their advantage. To split Paris from Washington, the DRV offered cultural and economic concessions in the North to the French. Then Ho embarked on a trip to Moscow and Beijing to seek bloc support for a demand to reconvene the Geneva conference. But Chinese and Soviet leaders continued to seek a reduction in Cold War tensions and gave only lukewarm support to the Vietnamese appeal. In a public speech on his return to Hanoi, Ho thanked Moscow and Beijing for their support but warned his audience that reunification would come about only through a policy of self-reliance.[14]

Indeed, the new situation presented Hanoi with a knotty dilemma. Discontent within the ranks over the situation in the South needed to be dealt with, but several factors militated against the adoption of a more aggressive policy designed to bring about reunification by forceful means. In the first place, living conditions in the North were depressed, and the national economy badly needed an infusion of foreign capital and technology to lay the foundation for a modern industrial society. At the same time, the North Vietnamese armed forces needed to be modernized to prepare for a possible future confrontation with the Diem regime in South Vietnam. Under the circumstances, a policy of caution appeared in order. In a public letter to the Vietnamese people, Ho Chi Minh promised eventual victory, but only after the DRV had built a strong foundation.

In the meantime, party leaders began to intensify their lobbying efforts to win the support of Hanoi's allies for a future advance toward national reunification. At international conferences held in the Soviet Union and Eastern Europe during the late 1950s, Vietnamese delegates publicly praised the new Soviet policy of "peaceful coexistence" but privately argued that a policy of revolutionary violence might be required in societies where the imperialists refused to concede power in a peaceful manner. But to the anger and frustration of militant elements in Hanoi, Moscow continued to turn a deaf ear to their appeal. Vietnamese pleas for support encountered a more receptive hearing in Beijing, which in 1958 had begun to enter a more radical phase in its foreign as well as in its domestic policy. Still, Chinese leaders were equally reluctant to sanction a strategy that could lead to a Cold War crisis in Indochina, and urged Vietnamese comrades to be patient in pursuing their goal of national reunification.[15]

## Call to Action

By the end of the 1950s, pressure was building among Vietminh sympathizers in the South for a more aggressive posture in defending the revolution. The Diem government in Saigon had intensified its efforts to suppress all opposition, and thousands of southerners who were suspected of allegiance to Hanoi were convicted at drumhead tribunals throughout the country and imprisoned or executed. Although Hanoi had authorized its local operatives in South Vietnam to build up their self-defense forces, in some areas the movement was at skeleton strength or had been virtually wiped out. In January 1959 the issue was raised for discussion by the party Central Committee (in 1951 the ICP was renamed the Vietnam Workers' Party [VWP]). Some VWP leaders were opposed to action, not only because it would irritate Hanoi's chief allies, but also on the grounds that the North had just begun its march to socialism with a three-year program to launch the collectivization of agriculture throughout the countryside. Ho Chi Minh advised caution in order to avoid provoking the United States. But Le Duan, a figure of increasing prominence in Hanoi and soon to be named VWP first secretary, had just completed a secret inspection visit to the South and argued strongly for action. In the end party leaders reached a compromise, approving a resumption of revolutionary war in the South, but with the degree of political and military struggle to be applied left unresolved.[16]

After the conference adjourned, Ho Chi Minh left Hanoi on a mission to Beijing and Moscow to explain the decision and plead for bloc support. But despite his formidable diplomatic skills, the reaction of Soviet and Chinese leaders was disappointing. Moscow was noncommittal, and Chinese leaders, although sympathetic, were cautious. Conditions in Indochina and around the world, Mao Zedong warned his guest, were not yet ripe. Indeed, it might take up to 100 years to bring about Vietnamese national reunification. It was hardly a message that Ho's more zealous colleagues in Hanoi wished to hear.[17]

One powerful motive for a policy of caution, of course, was the need to determine the attitude of the United States. After the Geneva Conference of 1954, the Eisenhower administration had given its firm support to the government of Ngo Dinh Diem, and Diem was invited to Washington, D.C., on a formal state visit in 1957. At that time, conditions in the RVN appeared stable, inspiring some enthusiastic U.S. commentators to remark that Diem was America's answer to Ho Chi Minh. By the end of the decade, however, such pronouncements rang hollow, as the increasing effectiveness of anti-Diem forces (popularly known in the West as the Viet Cong, or Vietnamese Communists), combined with a bitter conflict between the rightists within the royal Lao government and the Pathet Lao, aroused rising concern in Washington and provoked the White House to consider U.S. military intervention in Laos to prevent a communist victory. Concerned at the prospects of a direct U.S. military presence in Indochina, Hanoi warned Pathet Lao leaders not to exacerbate the situation to the point of threatening the survival of the shaky royal government in Vientiane.

In the meantime, DRV leaders had an additional problem elsewhere, as an ideological dispute was beginning to flare up between Moscow and Beijing over the threat or use of force to protect and extend the socialist community throughout the world. Ho Chi Minh, who feared that the growing tensions between his country's two major allies would hinder Hanoi's effort to achieve unified bloc support for the Vietnamese revolutionary cause, tried to maintain an even-handed stance between the two powers. In a visit to China in August 1960, he suggested bilateral talks to resolve Sino-Soviet differences. Both sides, he chided Mao, were at fault. But Ho's remarks were not appreciated in Beijing, where Foreign Minister Chen Yi remarked that Ho was unable to stand up to the Soviets. Ho had no better luck in Moscow, where Soviet party chief Nikita Khrushchev rebuffed his plea to adopt a conciliatory posture, on the grounds that China was now a big power whose pride had to be taken into account.[18]

Still, Ho Chi Minh was temporarily successful in helping to keep the dispute from coming into the open. At a conference of Communist parties held in Moscow in November 1960, he persuaded an angry Liu Shaoqi to return to the meeting, thus avoiding a public rupture between China and the Soviet Union. But Ho's attempt to maintain good relations with both countries aroused irritation in Hanoi, where some of his more militant colleagues began to remark privately that Ho was too inclined to defer to Moscow. Their concerns may have had some justification, for Ho was increasingly suspicious of Mao Zedong's imperial pretensions and tended to support the Soviet view on most international issues.

The continuing desire of most DRV leaders to maintain friendly relations with both of their country's chief benefactors undoubtedly complicated Hanoi's attempt to formulate a coherent policy to bring about reunification with the South. In September 1960 the VWP had held its Third National Congress. The conference focused its primary attention on the domestic scene, when it approved a five-year plan to enter the stage of transition to a fully socialist economy during the early 1960s. No changes were announced in the party's strategy toward the South, as the conference declaration simply affirmed the current uneasy balance between political and military struggle and stated that reunification would have equal billing with domestic concerns in future years. Representatives from both China and the Soviet Union attended the congress and (undoubtedly to Ho Chi Minh's relief) did not engage in mutual polemics during the meeting.

Still, changes in the regime's approach to national reunification were in the wind. Responding to the rapid growth of local revolutionary forces in the South, Hanoi ordered the creation of a new united front—to be known as the National Liberation Front for South Vietnam—to lead the movement there. Henceforth the NLF, as it was popularly known, would play a role similar to the old Vietminh Front as a broad-based alliance of all forces opposed to the Diem regime. Its stated objective was to bring about the departure of U.S. advisors and the formation of a coalition government dedicated to maintaining peace and neutrality. To reassure foreign observers and moderate elements in the South, there was no mention of communism or of direct future ties with the DRV.

If one of the purposes of the creation of the NLF was to allay U.S. suspicions of the links between the insurgent movement in the RVN and the North, it had little success, for the growing effectiveness of the Viet Cong aroused concern in Washington. Shortly after his accession to the White House in January 1961, President John F. Kennedy ordered the creation of a task force to assess the situation in South Vietnam and recommend measures to prevent a communist takeover in Saigon. Later that year he ordered a dramatic increase in U.S. military assistance to the GVN. But of more immediate concern to Washington was the situation in Laos, where Pathet Lao operations against the rightist government in Vientiane threatened to bring that country under communist rule. Unwilling to commit U.S. military forces to landlocked Laos, Kennedy opted for new peace talks in Geneva to bring about a cease-fire and the formation of a new neutralist government there.

## Tiger Trap

Washington's decision to take the crisis in Laos to the conference table was a welcome sign to Hanoi that the United States was looking for a way out of the morass in Indochina. In party meetings, Ho Chi Minh had argued that the United States, which lacked vital security interests in the area, was simply trying to save face in Indochina. Although Duan, along with other militant elements, was increasingly critical of Ho's penchant for seeking diplomatic solutions, in this case he agreed. In a letter to a leading party operative in South Vietnam, Duan predicted that Washington eventually would back down in Indochina, as it had done previously in Korea and in China. In that belief, Hanoi sought to find a means of easing the United States out of South Vietnam through negotiations to create a coalition government that ostensibly would be neutralist but surreptitiously would be dominated by the communists.[19]

Hanoi's optimism about the mood in Washington was misplaced, however, for distrust of communism and a fear of falling dominoes in Southeast

Asia continued to dominate the political scene in the United States. Although tentative feelers between U.S. and DRV officials took place in the summer of 1962, the White House lost interest once it became clear that the North Vietnamese had no intention of honoring Soviet assurances at Geneva that the DRV would not take advantage of the Laos agreement to increase the infiltration of personnel and supplies through Laos into the RVN. According to historian Robert Brigham, author of an impressive new study on the diplomatic activities of the NLF, Hanoi also may have decided to withdraw its peace feelers as a result of protests from senior party representatives in the South, ever wary of compromises that might delay once again the final goal of national reunification. The moment of opportunity thus died stillborn.[20]

Hanoi's failure to lure the United States into a face-saving peaceful solution to the conflict in South Vietnam did not deter party leaders from their belief that Washington could be lured into withdrawing from South Vietnam short of an all-out war. During the spring and summer of 1963, Ngo Dinh Diem's police suppressed demonstrations by Buddhists who were protesting what they alleged to be Diem's pro-Catholic bias. This Buddhist Crisis climaxed in the self-immolation of monks in South Vietnam. DRV leaders, perhaps expecting that the White House would decide to withdraw its support from the RVN as a result of the crisis, reacted cautiously to the rising tensions between Washington and Saigon over the issue. When Diem was deposed by a military coup in early November, Hanoi quietly issued peace feelers to the new leadership in Saigon to explore the possibility of a negotiated settlement. But when those overtures were rejected, party leaders concluded that President Lyndon B. Johnson, who had just replaced Kennedy in the White House, was not yet ready to accept Hanoi's terms for a settlement.

## Between Moscow and Beijing

With prospects for a U.S. withdrawal from South Vietnam temporarily foreclosed, Hanoi returned to the military option. In December 1963 the party Central Committee gave urgent consideration to a proposal by militants to escalate the military pressure on the South in the hopes of achieving a quick victory before Washington could decide whether to intervene. Any such decision, however, raised the distinct possibility of a wider war. An intensification of the conflict would not cause major problems with Beijing, which was now willing to take risks in order to win Hanoi's support in the Sino-Soviet dispute, but it could anger the Soviet Union, anxious now more than ever, since the 1962 Cuban Missile Crisis, to improve relations with the United States.

The debate was heated, since many senior party leaders, including Ho Chi Minh himself, were still reluctant to offend Moscow or provoke Washington, but Duan and his allies were now in the ascendant in Hanoi, and eventually the proposal was approved. To appease doubters, it was decided that no North Vietnamese regular force troops would be dispatched to take part in the fighting in the South. Although some of the more militant elements in the party leadership appeared willing to risk a total break with the Soviet Union, Duan had no desire to cut all ties to Moscow, and the VWP sent a circular letter to bloc parties that promised that the war could be contained within the boundaries of South Vietnam. At Duan's urging, a critical reference to Soviet "revisionism" (a direct slap at Soviet leader Nikita Khrushchev) was deleted from the letter. Still, the message was clear. North Vietnamese officials suspected of pro-Soviet views were purged from the ranks of the party and the government, and articles critical of alleged "revisionism" appeared in the official press. For the first time, the regime had broken from its careful policy of neutrality in the Sino-Soviet dispute.[21]

In its hope that the United States might react to the heightened conflict in South Vietnam by reducing its role there, however, Hanoi had miscalculated the mood in Washington. As the political and military situation in the South deteriorated in the months following the coup, the Johnson administration showed no signs of weakening resolve and approved measures that threatened to increase the U.S. role in the conflict. When, in early August of 1964, North Vietnamese naval units responded to clandestine operations by South Vietnamese guerrillas in the southern provinces of the DRV by attacking U.S. warships operating in the nearby coastal waters of the Tonkin Gulf, the White House quickly ordered retaliatory air strikes on DRV territory. To party leaders, the U.S. response demonstrated conclusively that Washington had no intention of seeking a face-saving exit from South Vietnam. A few weeks later, the VWP Politburo approved plans to dispatch the first North Vietnamese combat units to the South. The decision further soured relations with Moscow, but it received approval in Beijing, which promised to step up its military assistance and even offered to send Chinese troops if they should become necessary. Chinese leaders, however, did not want to get lured by Hanoi (at the possible instigation of Moscow) into a confrontation with Washington, and Mao warned Duan not to overreact to U.S. provocations.[22]

In October 1964 Nikita Khrushchev was overthrown by a cabal of his rivals in the party Presidium and a new leadership led by Leonid Brezhnev and Alexei Kosygin took power in the Kremlin. Although the coup had little effect in easing the polemics between China and the Soviet Union, it had a significant impact in Hanoi, since the new leaders in Moscow, hoping to isolate China within the socialist camp, seemed more receptive to DRV appeals for increased military assistance. For the remainder of the war, the Soviet Union became an irreplaceable source of advanced military equipment, such as MiG fighters and surface-to-air missiles, that enabled the regime to defend DRV airspace against U.S. air attacks. In return, Hanoi assured Soviet leaders that it would not permit the conflict in Indochina to get out of hand.[23]

It was one thing to restore a measure of balance in the DRV's relations with its two major benefactors; it was another to maintain it. The Chinese were irritated at Hanoi's decision to accept increased military aid from the Soviet Union and did not hesitate to say so. From Beijing's point of view, close relations between Hanoi and Moscow represented a blatant gesture of ingratitude by the former for the considerable amount of assistance that China had provided to the Vietnamese revolution over four decades. When Deng Xiaoping visited Hanoi in December, he demanded that the DRV refuse any future offers of military assistance from Moscow and to rely entirely on Beijing. His hosts flatly refused, and Chinese leaders, fearful that the Vietnamese would shift further toward Moscow, backed down. Hanoi was finally learning how to use the split to its own advantage. But the seeds of later difficulties with Beijing had been sown.

## Four Points for Peace

Backed with reasonably firm support from its chief allies, so long as the war could be kept from spreading beyond the borders of South Vietnam, Hanoi had earned some precious breathing room to deal with the rapidly evolving situation in South Vietnam. In the winter of 1964–1965, the political situation in Saigon descended to the point of chaos, as one regime followed another with bewildering rapidity. In the countryside, Viet Cong forces took advantage of the disarray and adopted more aggressive tactics against the demoralized South Vietnamese armed forces. According to U.S. intelligence estimates, the NLF now controlled over 80 percent of the total land area of the RVN. Such signs of progress in the South led to a brief moment of euphoria in Hanoi that victory was at hand. Even the ever-cautious Ho Chi Minh predicted that negotiations with the United States might not be necessary, since victory in the South was imminent. At a meeting of the VWP Central Committee in February 1965, party leaders decided not to send additional North Vietnamese troops down the Ho Chi Minh Trail in the hope that local Viet Cong forces could bring about a collapse of the Saigon regime by midsummer. Even when the White House reacted to a Viet Cong attack on a U.S. Special Forces base in the Central Highlands by ordering bombing raids over the North, Hanoi initially concluded that Washington was simply escalating in order to improve its situation on the battlefield and lay the groundwork for a negotiated withdrawal.

With that in mind, Hanoi returned to the diplomatic offensive in April, when Prime Minister Pham Van Dong issued his famous "Four Points," calling for a settlement based on a withdrawal of U.S. forces, a return to the provisions of the Geneva agreement, a peace settlement based on the program of the NLF, and the peaceful reunification of the two zones without foreign interference. But the proposal was soon embroiled in controversy, as a "five-point" program issued almost simultaneously by the NLF appeared to demand a U.S. withdrawal before negotiations could even get under way. U.S. officials also were concerned that point 3 of Hanoi's Four Points might require the total surrender of the current government in Saigon. Washington sought to clarify the situation through diplomatic contacts with DRV officials, but Hanoi was evasive, and after several meetings in midsummer, Hanoi suddenly broke off the contacts.[24]

According to historian Robert Brigham, North Vietnamese officials had drawn back from negotiations primarily out of deference to the views of their followers in the South, who (rightly or wrongly) feared the possibility of another sellout by Hanoi and its allies. But another factor was undoubtedly Duan's conclusion that Washington—which had now begun to introduce U.S. combat troops into South Vietnam—was not yet prepared to make major concessions at the conference table. As Duan remarked in a letter to southern commanders in May, Hanoi did not wish to enter peace talks until the situation on the battlefield was clearly favorable to the revolutionary forces. "Only when the insurrection [in South Vietnam] is successful," he remarked, "will the problem of establishing a 'neutral central administration' be posed again. In the meantime, the lure of negotiations could be used to win sympathy within the international community and seduce the Johnson administration into further concessions."[25]

By late summer, however, it had become clear that the current Viet Cong offensive would not succeed in toppling the South Vietnamese government, while the steady increase in the number of U.S. combat troops in the South forced Hanoi planners to realize that only a drastic increase in the number of their own troops could avoid a stabilization of the Saigon regime. The leading exponent of this view was General Nguyen Chi Thanh, the newly appointed commander of North Vietnamese forces in the South, who had devised an aggressive strategy to pressure U.S. and South Vietnamese forces throughout the RVN to force them to surrender. Hanoi did not close off the negotiating track entirely—during the fall and winter DRV sources continued to refer to the possibility of a negotiated solution to the conflict—but Duan and his allies within the party leadership had decided that the times were not favorable for negotiations. At a meeting of the Central Committee in November, Duan declared that Hanoi's offer of peace talks was primarily intended as a lure to "tantalize the United States." As a test of U.S. intentions, and to reassure hard-liners who opposed any consideration of the diplomatic option, DRV sources posed two conditions for the opening of talks: a total bombing halt of the North and U.S. acceptance of point 3 of the Four Points.[26]

## Stab in the Back

The escalation of the war, a process that was now under way on both sides, made it ever more vital for Hanoi to achieve crucial support from its allies. Moscow could be kept in line so long as Hanoi prevented the war from spreading beyond the borders of South Vietnam and indicated an interest in a possible future diplomatic settlement. Soviet officials did express frustration, however, that Vietnamese leaders refused to consult with them about DRV war plans. The Soviet military attaché in Hanoi was consistently informed by North Vietnamese officials that DRV strategists had "their own views" on the formulation of strategy in the South.[27]

As always, relations with Beijing were more complicated. Party leaders in Hanoi wanted China to serve not only as a key source of military assistance but also as a powerful deterrent to dissuade the United States from expanding the war beyond the borders of South Vietnam. During the early months of 1965, Beijing had promised Vietnamese leaders that China would serve as the "great rear" of the Vietnamese revolution, providing military equipment, technical assistance, and, if necessary, even combat troops to help their Vietnamese comrades to achieve their objectives. In April the two countries signed an aid agreement providing for the dispatch of Chinese support troops to North Vietnam. Two months later bilateral discussions in Beijing reached agreement that China would respond in kind to any further U.S. escalation of the war.

In fact, however, some Chinese leaders were becoming increasingly concerned that they might get dragged into a direct confrontation with the United States, and Beijing began to signal Washington that, while it was quite willing, if necessary, to intervene directly in the Vietnam conflict to protect its national interests, it had no intention of provoking a conflict with the United States. If Washington did not directly threaten China, the messages hinted, the latter would not involve itself directly in the war. After a bitter midsummer debate among party leaders in Beijing, China rejected Hanoi's request for Chinese combat pilots and rebuffed a Soviet proposal for united action to provide assistance to the DRV. An article allegedly written by Chinese Minister of Defense Lin Biao that was published in September implicitly advised party leaders in Hanoi to adopt a policy of self-reliance and protracted war in the South.[28]

To North Vietnamese war planners, China's decision to limit its commitment in Vietnam represented a "stab in the back," which seriously hindered their ability to dissuade the United States from using its technological superiority to seek a total victory in the war.[29] Early the following year, Duan responded to China's unsolicited advice as conveyed in Lin Biao's article, retorting that "it is not fortuitous that in the history of our country, each time we arose to oppose foreign aggression, we took the offensive and not the defensive."[30]

Duan's testy response was a blunt message to Beijing that Hanoi intended to follow its own dictates in drafting war strategy. Still, although Vietnamese party leaders were reluctant to admit it, China had become one of their most potent weapons in facing down the United States. Although Chinese leaders had been careful to qualify the degree of their commitment to the DRV, the implicit threat of Chinese intervention was undoubtedly a major factor in constraining the Johnson administration from undertaking a more aggressive approach to the war. Moreover, during the next few years, Chinese military assistance to North Vietnam increased dramatically, while the number of Chinese civilian and military personnel serving in Vietnam reached to over 100,000.[31]

But even the steady flow of Chinese personnel and equipment into the DRV did not resolve differences between Beijing and Hanoi, in part because the expanding Chinese presence was a growing irritant among the people of North Vietnam. The situation was exacerbated during the late 1960s, when visiting Red Guards began to spout the slogans of the Great Proletarian Cultural Revolution to their Vietnamese hosts. Party leaders in Hanoi had their own way of signaling their displeasure, as articles about the tradition of Chinese "feudal aggression" began to appear in the official press. The none-too-subtle hint was soon picked up in Beijing. If our presence is irritating to you, Deng Xiaoping remarked to Duan in April 1966, "we will withdraw at once."[32]

## Fight and Then See

Meanwhile, on the battlefield, the cost in both human and material terms of Nguyen Chi Thanh's aggressive strategy was enormous, with potential benefits that were as yet unclear. By early 1967 dissent against existing policy was being expressed in both civilian and military circles in Hanoi. Some apparently even expressed a renewed desire to pursue the negotiating track. With the peace movement in the United States and around the world growing rapidly, there was some optimism in Hanoi that the Johnson administration might be prepared to offer major concessions to bring an end to the war. In January 1967 DRV foreign minister Nguyen Duy Trinh signaled Washington that if the U.S. bombing campaign over North Vietnamese territory were to be halted unconditionally, prospects for the opening of peace talks would improve. Hanoi's previous condition—that the United States must accept its Four Points as a precondition for opening negotiations—had thus been tacitly abandoned. To White House officials, however, the ambiguity of Hanoi's message (did "there could be talks" mean the same thing as "there will be talks"?) aroused suspicions that were not clarified in succeeding contacts, and eventually Washington rejected the proposal as inadequate.

The Johnson administration had not lost interest in opening peace talks, however, and by June further contacts were under way, as the White House pushed a new proposal—known variously as the Pennsylvania or the San Antonio formula. The plan called for a halt in U.S. bombing of the North, provided that peace talks began and that DRV officials gave assurances that they would not take advantage of the cessation to escalate their military operations in the South. In Hanoi there was some interest in the proposal, but since plans were already under way for a major military offensive in South Vietnam sometime early in the following year, DRV sources eventually rejected the offer. War planners hoped that a major assault could further destabilize the situation in the RVN and lay the groundwork for major U.S. concessions. If necessary, the U.S. proposal could be revived later.[33]

The Tet Offensive broke out throughout South Vietnam at the end of January 1968. There has been considerable debate among historians over the objectives of the campaign, but Vietnamese sources make it clear that policymakers themselves were not certain of the likely outcome, thus reflecting Duan's view (citing Lenin) that "we must fight and then see." Hanoi's maximum goal was to use a combination of armed attacks and popular uprisings to bring about the collapse of the Saigon regime, leading to immediate negotiations and an early withdrawal of U.S. military forces. But its minimum objective was to destabilize the situation in the South sufficiently to force the United States to seek negotiations under unfavorable conditions. As it turned out, the results of the Tet Offensive were mixed. Viet Cong forces sustained heavy losses and did not succeed in toppling the Saigon regime. But the campaign did have a significant effect on public support for the war in the United States, and in persuading many American officials that the war could not be won at an acceptable cost. The White House reluctantly decided to launch heightened efforts to bring about peace talks.[34]

## Fight and Talk

The first breakthrough came in early April, when Hanoi agreed to open discussions with U.S. representatives to seek agreement on an unconditional U.S. bombing halt as a means of bringing about the beginning of negotiations. Hanoi's decision created immediate problems with China, which for the past three years had been warning Hanoi not to abandon the Four Points as a precondition for engaging in peace talks. In a discussion with Pham Van

Dong that same month, Zhou Enlai criticized the Vietnamese for considering a partial bombing halt, charging that it would cause the revolutionary forces in South Vietnam to lose the initiative. Dong retorted that the DRV was simply trying to use adroit diplomatic tactics in order to mobilize world opinion against the United States and force Washington into concessions. When Zhou noted that the Chinese had more experience in dealing with the United States than had Vietnamese negotiators, Dong thanked him for his opinion while noting that "we are the ones who are fighting against the U.S. and defeating them." So, he concluded, it is we who should be responsible for undertaking both military and diplomatic activities.[35]

Chinese leaders reiterated their criticisms in the autumn, when the DRV agreed to open peace negotiations with representatives of the United States, the RVN, and the NLF in Paris. Beijing charged that Hanoi thus had given the Saigon regime a degree of international legitimacy that it had never possessed in reality. By now, however, the atmosphere in Sino-Vietnamese discussions had become increasingly strained. North Vietnamese officials bluntly rejected Beijing's suggestions, pointing out that the DRV had made a mistake by listening to Chinese advice at Geneva in 1954. Eventually Mao Zedong gave his imprimatur to Hanoi's fight-and-talk strategy, while warning Vietnamese visitors to be wary of U.S. tricks.[36]

For the moment, then, strains between Beijing and Hanoi had been papered over, with both sides skeptical of an early diplomatic solution. North Vietnamese leaders continued to use the peace talks in Paris primarily as a forum for swaying public opinion while simultaneously attempting to build up their armed forces in the South for another assault on the Saigon regime. When the neutralist government of Prince Norodom Sihanouk in Cambodia was overthrown by a military coup led by General Lon Nol in 1970, the two countries were able to cooperate in setting up a fragile alliance between Sihanouk's supporters and the Khmer Rouge.

But although Mao had given his blessing to Hanoi's fight-and-talk strategy, Chinese leaders were still free with their advice, counseling their Vietnamese counterparts to adopt a protracted war strategy on the battlefield and warning against putting too much confidence on the negotiations in Paris. In September 1970 Pham Van Dong assured Zhou Enlai that DRV war planners had no illusions about a diplomatic settlement at that point (the talks in Paris, he remarked, are just "a play of words"), since Washington was still seeking a victory in the war. Hanoi's current conditions for a settlement (establishing a timetable for the full withdrawal of U.S. troops and the removal of South Vietnamese President Nguyen Van Thieu prior to the formation of a coalition government) were not intended for serious consideration, but only to "corner" the Americans and build up popular sympathy for the revolutionary movement inside South Vietnam and around the

world. The diplomatic struggle, he insisted, thus playe
with the military effort on the ground.[37]

## The Nixon Shock

But in the early 1970s, policymakers in Hanoi suddenly were
uncomfortable new reality when China decided to seek a ra
with the United States. For much of Asia, the prospects for imp
U.S. relations were a welcome indication that the Cold War in
was finally beginning to thaw. But for party leaders in Hanoi, the st
stunning setback to their war strategy, since the latter had been based
premise that China's hostility to the United States was a stable fac
world affairs. Now the DRV was faced with the disagreeable possibility
Chinese leaders (who had once urged toughness in the struggle against
imperialist forces) would now collude with Washington to deprive the Vie
namese of the fruits of their revolutionary struggle.

As Chinese leaders undoubtedly argued, the possibility did exist that improved relations between Beijing and Washington could prove advantageous to the cause of Vietnamese reunification, since it would serve to reduce U.S. concerns about communist expansion in Southeast Asia and enable the White House to focus attention on other parts of the world. But that view was not shared in Hanoi, where North Vietnamese leaders feared that the projected visit of President Richard M. Nixon to China—first announced on July 15, 1971—would undercut their own efforts to undermine public support for the war in the United States and that China now would actively promote a compromise peace settlement in Indochina in order to satisfy its own changing security interests.[38]

Hanoi's fears that Beijing would begin to pressure the North Vietnamese to accept a compromise peace settlement soon took on substance, for Chinese leaders had become convinced that Washington was planning to seek an honorable withdrawal from Indochina. North Vietnamese war planners now focused their own hopes for success on plans for a new general offensive in South Vietnam that could further erode the authority of the Saigon regime and bring about further U.S. concessions in peace talks. The Easter Offensive, launched in late March 1972, vividly displayed the superiority of North Vietnamese forces against South Vietnamese units—now operating without U.S. ground support. Still, U.S. air strikes blunted the offensive, and the RVN, although severely shaken, remained in place.

For the next several months, North Vietnamese leaders assessed the situation in light of the new realities. In July Zhou Enlai advised Le Duc Tho to be more flexible in the peace talks and, if necessary, to recognize Nguyen Van Thieu as a potential member of the future tripartite coalition. Tho was ptical, because Nixon's major opponent in the 1972 presidential cam- ign, Democratic Senator George McGovern, was campaigning on a plat- rm of immediate U.S. withdrawal from South Vietnam. But by early fall had become clear that Senator McGovern was going to be soundly de- eated in the presidential elections, while Nixon was threatening to escalate U.S. military pressure in Vietnam after the election if a peace settlement did not appear a likely possibility.

On October 8 Tho abandoned Hanoi's demand for the resignation of Nguyen Van Thieu and the formation of a coalition government as a condition for a peace agreement. Instead, he accepted a plan calling for a "ceasefire in place" and the recognition of two administrative entities in South Vietnam—the Saigon regime under President Nguyen Van Thieu and the Provisional Revolutionary Government, or PRG (a shadow government created by Hanoi to serve as its representative in the South in 1969). U.S. military forces were to be withdrawn, while a tripartite subdiplomatic organization called the National Council of Reconciliation and Concord (NCRC) and composed of representatives of the PRG, the RVN, and neutralist forces in the South was to be created to smooth the way for a future coalition government and national elections. The final treaty embodying these terms was finally signed in Paris in January 1973.

To many members of the NLF, the Paris agreement was ominously reminiscent of the betrayal that had taken place at Geneva two decades previously, and VWP leaders went to considerable lengths to assure them that the cause of reunification had not been forgotten. In fact, however, Hanoi appeared to feel no sense of urgency to complete national reunification. Now that U.S. military forces had been withdrawn from the RVN, North Vietnamese leaders were confident that victory in the South was only a matter of time. In talks with held in Beijing in June, Zhou Enlai suggested that "during the next 5 to 10 years, South Vietnam, Laos, and Cambodia should build peace, independence, and neutrality." Duan appeared to agree, remarking to Zhou that the DRV was in no hurry to transform the current government in Saigon into a socialist one (he mentioned the possibility of ten to fifteen years), so long as it had been transformed into "a democratic and a nationalist one."[39]

As it turned out, it did not take nearly that long to complete the reunification of North and South Vietnam. When the Thieu regime balked at carrying out the provisions of the Paris agreement and aggressively attacked enemy-held areas in South Vietnam, DRV leaders revised their plans and launched a major offensive in the South beginning in early 1975. The decision aroused some anxiety in Moscow and Beijing, but when Washington did not react (Nixon had been replaced by President Gerald Ford in August 1974, and the latter had no stomach for resuming the war), South Vietnamese resistance rapidly crumbled, and Saigon fell to a North Vietnamese assault on April 30, 1975. Reunification took place a year later, and the regime drafted plans to complete socialist transformation throughout the country by the end of the decade.

## Conclusion

In the months and years that followed the fall of Saigon, official sources in Hanoi ascribed victory to a variety of factors: the firm and astute leadership provided by the party, the unyielding patriotism and heroism of the Vietnamese people, and the personality and strategical genius of its great leader, Ho Chi Minh. Relatively little credit was assigned to the role of diplomacy or to the assistance provided by Hanoi's chief allies. To the contrary, Vietnamese leaders, now locked in an increasingly bitter dispute with China, consistently downplayed the support that they had received over the decades from outside sources, and especially from Beijing, whose assistance to the DRV was now portrayed as having been motivated by self-seeking purposes.[40]

In fact, however, diplomacy had been a weapon of crucial importance to the party in its struggle to bring about national reunification on its own terms. Like the ancient Chinese military strategist Sun Tzu, Vietnamese war planners had recognized at an early stage of their struggle that a pragmatic understanding of their own strengths and weaknesses, as well as those of their adversaries would be a key prerequisite for final victory. And they had realized that the international environment would have to be artfully managed to isolate their enemy and maximize support for the revolutionary cause.

In formulating their diplomatic approach, the weapon of choice was the Leninist concept of the united front, which the Bolshevik leader had devised as a means of rallying support for the revolutionary forces against a more powerful adversary. Like Lenin, Vietnamese leaders applied the concept both internally, against their nationalist rivals, and in foreign affairs, where they sought to drive a wedge between their chief adversaries of the moment (first the French and later the United States) from other interested governments on the world scene. Neutral forces were carefully cultivated, even though their long-term sympathy for the party's ultimate objectives was decidedly limited.

Such tactics were not uniformly successful. Ho Chi Minh's persistent efforts to win U.S. support for the cause of Vietnamese national independence after World War II were fruitless. His later confidence that Washington could be persuaded not to intervene directly in South Vietnam was equally not borne out by events. Such miscalculations were obviously a major factor in his declining influence at the height of the Vietnam War. Similarly, DRV leaders had only limited success in coordinating assistance from their chief allies to their best advantage. Despite Ho's best efforts to mediate the Sino-Soviet dispute, relations between Moscow and Beijing deteriorated rapidly during the 1960s and hindered Hanoi's ability to present Washington with a united front.

Once the scope of the challenge had been made clear, however, Vietnamese strategists were adept in finding solutions. The united front approach originally devised by Ho Chi Minh in the 1920s proved highly effective in winning worldwide sympathy for the cause of Vietnamese national liberation. Vietnamese leaders learned to effectively manipulate the Sino-Soviet dispute to gain crucial military and diplomatic support from both Moscow and Beijing. Finally, Vietnamese policy planners effectively orchestrated the issue of opening peace talks in a manner that presented a public impression of flexibility while actually refusing meaningful negotiations until a time of Hanoi's choosing.

In the end, of course, Hanoi made a number of significant compromises to bring about the peace agreement that was signed in January 1973. For Vietnamese strategists, however, the concessions made at Paris were more apparent than real, since they realized, better than their counterparts in Washington, that once the U.S. shield had been removed from the South, the Saigon regime would be no match for its adversary to the North. DRV leaders apparently expected a lengthy period of time to elapse before the final victory and were prepared to accept a compromise settlement in the form of a coalition government dominated by the NLF. But the resignation of President Nixon in August 1974 brought an unexpected dividend when his successor proved reluctant to intervene to counter the 1975 spring offensive. In the end, Hanoi's strategy had succeeded even more than party leaders had anticipated.

Much of the credit for the party's diplomatic success must go to Ho Chi Minh, whose astute grasp of international affairs compensated for the lack of experience of many of his colleagues. A clear measure of his importance is that after his death in 1969 Hanoi's relations with China rapidly deteriorated, leading to the Sino-Vietnamese War a decade later and a series of foreign policy reverses that were not fully rectified until the 1990s. Although Ho had made a number of errors in his assessment of the international environment during the era of the Cold War, his sage advice was a major factor in enabling the party to vanquish its adversaries in the thirty-year struggle for total power in Vietnam.

## Notes

1. For a brief discussion of the traditional Sino-Vietnamese relationship, see King C. Chen's classic study, *Vietnam and China, 1938–1954* (Princeton NJ: Princeton University Press, 1969).

2. For an overview of this period, see Huynh Kim Khanh, *Vietnamese Communism, 1925–1945* (Ithaca, NY: Cornell University Press, 1982).
3. Details of the establishment of this arrangement between the Vietminh Front and U.S. military intelligence units in South China are provided in Archimedes L. A. Patti, *Why Viet Nam? Prelude to America's Albatross* (Berkeley: University of California Press, 1980).
4. Ho Chi Minh's efforts at the close of World War II to deny his past experience as an agent of the Comintern are well known. Only in the late 1950s, when the DRV had become a loyal member of the socialist camp, did he disclose his real identity. See my *Ho Chi Minh: A Life* (New York: Hyperion Press, 2000), especially chapters 9, 10, and 14.
5. Ho's speech, which was presented to the ICP Central Committee in mid-August, was eventually included in a resolution entitled "Nghi quyet cua Toan quoc Hoi nghi Dang Cong san Dong duong" (Resolution of the national conference of the Indochinese Communist Party) and printed in *Van kien Dang* (1930–1945) (Party Documents [1930–1945]), vol. 3 (Hanoi: Ban Nghien cuu lich su Dang Truong uong, 1977), 412–417.
6. The letter was written in August 1945. See Charles Fenn, *Ho Chi Minh: A Biographical Introduction* (New York: Scribners, 1973), 8.
7. The DRV's abortive overtures to the United States are discussed in Mark Bradley's "An Improbable Opportunity: America and the Democratic Republic of Vietnam's 1947 Initiative," in Jayne S. Werner and Luu Doan Huynh eds., *The Vietnam War: Vietnamese and American Perceptions* (Armonk, NY: M.E. Sharpe, 1993), 3–23.
8. For his analysis, see Truong Chinh, *The Resistance Will Win,* translated in *Truong Chinh: Selected Writings* (Hanoi: Foreign Languages Press, 1977).
9. Moscow also agreed for the first time to grant diplomatic recognition to the DRV, but Stalin made it clear that China would be assigned primary responsibility for carrying out socialist bloc assistance to the DRV. For a discussion and references, see my *Ho Chi Minh,* 422.
10. Cited in ibid., 450.
11. The interview, which appeared in the journal *Expressen,* was summarized in U.S. Embassy (Stockholm) to Department of State, November 29, 1953, in Record Group (RG) 59, U.S. National Archives. For a Vietnamese-language version, see *Ho Chi Minh Toan Tap* (The complete writings of Ho Chi Minh), 1st ed., (Hanoi: Su that, 1980–1989), vol. 6, 494–496. (Hereafter cited as *Toan Tap.)*
12. For a discussion, see Qiang Zhai, *China and the Vietnam Wars, 1950–1975* (Chapel Hill: University of North Carolina Press, 2000), 60–62.
13. Report to the Sixth Plenum, in *Ho Chi Minh: Selected Writings* (Hanoi: Foreign Languages Press, 1977), 181–183.
14. Ho's speech is printed in *Toan Tap,* vol. 1, vol. 7, 286–289.
15. Cited in *Cuoc khang chien chong My cuu nuoc 1954–1975* (The Anti-U.S. War of National Salvation, 1954–1975) (Hanoi: Quan doi Nhan dan, 1980), 35.

16. Ibid., 49–50.
17. Ang Cheng Guan, *Vietnamese Communists' Relations with China and the Second Indochina Conflict, 1956–1962* (Jefferson, NC: McFarland, 1997), 86–87.
18. Zhai, *China and the Vietnam Wars,* 88, 90–91.
19. Le Duan, *Thu Vao Nam* (Letters to the South) (Hanoi: Su That, 1986), 63–66.
20. Robert Brigham, *Guerrilla Diplomacy: The NLF/s Foreign Relations and the Viet Nam War* (Ithaca, NY: Cornell University Press, 1999), 47–48.
21. For a discussion of the decision and its domestic and foreign policy consequences, with citations, see my *Ho Chi Minh: A Life,* 534–539.
22. Zhai, *China and the Vietnam Wars,* 132–133; Ilya Gaiduk, *The Soviet Union and the Vietnam War* (Chicago: Ivan R. Dee, 1996), 13–14.
23. During his visit to Hanoi in February 1965, Kosygin did warn his hosts not to provoke the United States. Although the warning had little immediate effect—the Viet Cong attack on Pleiku took place shortly afterward—Soviet leaders were generally confident that pragmatists within the DRV would contain the war to the South. Gaiduk, *Soviet Union,* 67.
24. For a discussion of this issue between Vietnamese and American representatives thirty years later, see Robert S. McNamara, James G. Blight, and Robert K. Brigham, *Argument Without End: In Search of Answers to the Vietnam Tragedy* (New York: Public Affairs, 1999), 224–232.
25. Duan, *Thu Vao Nam,* letter to Xuan, May 1965. Brigham, *Guerrilla Diplomacy,* 44–48.
26. Zhai, *China and the Vietnam Wars,* 168.
27. Gaiduk, *Soviet Union,* 17.
28. See the illuminating discussion in Qiang Zhai, *China and the Vietnam Wars, 1950–1975,* 134–139.
29. The "stab in the back" remark was by Vo Nguyen Giap. See Douglas Pike, *Vietnam and the Soviet Union: Anatomy of an Alliance* (Boulder, CO: Westview, 1987), 87.
30. Donald Zagoria, *Vietnam Triangle* (New York: Pegasus, 1967), 84.
31. Zhai, *China and the Vietnam Wars, 1950–1975,*138–139.
32. As for the Red Guards, Mao Zedong told Pham Van Dong, "just hand them over to us." Odd Arne Westad et al., *77 Conversations Between Chinese and Foreign Leaders on theWars in Indochina, 1964–1977* (Washington, DC: Woodrow Wilson Center, 1998), 96, 104.
33. For a discussion, see McNamara et al., *Argument Without End,* 292–301.
34. Duan's comment, which initially had been made on an earlier occasion, is from *Thu Vao Nam,* letter to Xuan [Nguyen Chi Thanh], February 1965.
35. Westad et al., *77 Conversations,* 125–129.
36. Ibid., 140, 143.
37. Ibid., 159.
38. Zhai, *China and the Vietnam Wars,* 194–197.
39. Westad et al., *77 Conversations,* 189–191. The meaning of this conversation is admittedly somewhat ambiguous, since both Zhou and his Vietnamese

visitors insisted on the importance of party leadership over the government in the South, something that had certainly not been achieved in the Paris agreement. According to Duan, the current government in Saigon could exist for ten to fifteen years before being transformed into a socialist entity.

40. The most lengthy account of Hanoi's complaints against its northern neighbor appeared in Hanoi's White Paper entitled *The Truth About Vietnam-Chinese Relations over the Last Thirty Years* (Hanoi: Ministry of Foreign Affairs, 1979).

## CHAPTER TWO

# FIGHTING WITHOUT ALLIES

## The International Dimensions of America's Failure in Vietnam

GEORGE C. HERRING

No question has more perplexed Americans since 1975 than that of why, despite its vast power, the United States could not impose its will on what Lyndon Baines Johnson once contemptuously dismissed as that "raggedy-ass little fourth-rate country." Some Americans, scholarly voices in the wilderness for the most part, have had the temerity to suggest that the North Vietnamese and National Liberation Front of South Vietnam had a great deal to do with it. But the answers that most Americans seem to prefer have focused on the misuse of the nation's admittedly vast military power. The United States did not employ its military power wisely or decisively, it is argued. Military leaders such as General William C. Westmoreland, some say, did not understand the type of war they were in and used the wrong strategy. Others claim that civilians such as Johnson and Secretary of Defense Robert S. McNamara imposed restrictions on the use of America's military power that made it impossible for the military to win.[1]

This chapter argues that America's failure in Vietnam was as much diplomatic as military. For the United States, the lack of international support for its policies in Vietnam and indeed in some quarters virulent international opposition limited its military options and undermined its commitment to the war. On the other hand, widespread international support and voluminous and vital material aid from the Soviet Union and China contributed mightily to North Vietnam's ability to resist the United States and its determination to prevail. America went to war ostensibly to sustain its international position. Ironically, by early 1968 the war had drastically undermined that position, politically and especially economically, playing a key role in Johnson's dramatic March 31 decisions to stop escalation, seek a negotiated settlement, and withdraw from the presidential race. Richard Nixon was much more sensitive to the diplomatic aspects of the war than was his predecessor and indeed he attempted to use diplomacy as a key instrument in his quest for peace with honor. But his strategy also was fundamentally flawed and failed to achieve the goals he had set. The international dimension is rarely discussed in either the popular or the scholarly literature as a major reason for America's failure in Vietnam. But it is crucial to understanding why the war took the course it did and why it ended as it did.

Lyndon Johnson undertook the American War in Vietnam in an international system increasingly less favorable to U.S. hegemony. The bipolar world of the early Cold War had given way by the mid-1960s to a much more fluid and dynamic world in which both major alliance systems were in disarray and polycentrism was running amuck. The post - World War II process of decolonization was in its final stages, and new nations throughout the southern hemisphere were asserting their independence from former colonial masters and from both sides in the Cold War as well. China and the Soviet Union were engaged in open ideological warfare that in 1969 would lead to a brief shooting war along their long common border. France's Charles de Gaulle had directly challenged a Western alliance that was already coming apart, most notably on Southeast Asia, where he had called for neutralization and U.S. withdrawal. Even in its own bailiwick, the western hemisphere, there were challenges from Cuba and longtime protectorate Panama. The rampant instability that came with the new world of the 1960s was one reason Johnson decided to escalate the war in Vietnam. At the same time and in a variety of ways, it made realization of U.S. aims there much more difficult.

Winston Churchill is supposed to have observed that there is only one thing worse than fighting with allies, and that is fighting without them. The task of diplomacy in war is to maximize international support for one's position and minimize support for the enemy. For Churchill, the great challenge was to hold together a fragile alliance composed of great nations with conflicting interests. Lyndon Johnson failed in both diplomatic tasks in Vietnam, and he found himself without allies.

It is interesting to speculate what might have happened if LBJ had taken the approach to going to war in Vietnam in 1964–1965 that Dwight D. Eisenhower had taken ten years earlier. Had he made U.S. escalation contingent on what Secretary of State John Foster Dulles had called United Action, the active support of key allies, there seems no doubt of the result.[2]

He did not, of course, and his decision not to do so in some ways reflected his personality, priorities, and leadership style. Like most public figures of his generation, LBJ was nominally internationalist, but domestic issues were what really engaged his attention and where he hoped to realize his huge ambitions. He found diplomacy frustrating. He was not comfortable meeting with leaders of other nations. "Foreigners are not like the folks I am used to," he once admitted, only partly in jest. Uneasy with diplomacy and diplomats, he was not inclined to consult with allied governments. He often took personally the differences of interest and opinion that are basic to diplomacy. An acknowledged master of the art of persuasion, he was not a good listener. Rather, in the best tradition of the renowned "Johnson treatment," he sought to bend foreign leaders to his will, and he could be very heavy-handed in doing so.[3]

But the major reason that he did not make his 1965 escalation of the war contingent on allied support was that he and his advisors understood very well that America's European allies would respond at best tepidly to such a move. Through much of 1964, the administration had energetically pursued a "More Flags" campaign to get troop commitments from its allies. Such contributions, it was reasoned, would make it easier to justify increasing U.S. forces in Vietnam. The very word "allied" conveys a good cause and broad support, and backing from America's friends would give the war at least a measure of legitimacy and a veneer of international respectability. American diplomats also relentlessly pushed the line that by fighting the communists in Asia, the United States was defending Europe.[4]

At various points, the president himself got directly involved. In July 1964, in best Johnsonian fashion, he literally commanded his ambassadors in key capitals: "I am charging you *personally* [emphasis added] with the responsibility of seeing to it that the Government to which you are accredited understands how seriously we view the challenge to freedom in Viet Nam and how heavily the burden of responsibility for defending that freedom falls on those Governments who possess freedom in their own right." When British Prime Minister Harold Wilson in February 1965 proposed to help resolve the Vietnam problem by sponsoring a peace conference, an angry LBJ retorted: "If you want to help us some in Vietnam send us some men." Later in the year, he harangued West German Chancellor Ludwig Erhard in language that alarmed his own advisors, emphatically reminding his listener of all the United States had done for Germany and making clear that it was time to pay back.[5]

The results were disappointing. All European and some Asian allies saw in a way that Americans never seemed to the dubiousness of the U.S. cause in Vietnam. They questioned whether the stakes were really as high as the United States claimed, whether its credibility was in fact on the line. Some, like West Germany's Willy Brandt, dismissed the Europe/Asia defense analogy as "oversimplified and unfounded." Many Europeans feared—correctly, as it turned out—that American credibility might suffer more from a failed intervention than from a face-saving withdrawal. In any event, they doubted, given the weakness of South Vietnam—so obvious in these days when, as Johnson aide Jack Valenti sarcastically put it, the coat of arms of the rickety South Vietnamese regime was a turnstile—that even a massive injection of U.S. power could do more than delay an inevitable defeat. Despite veiled threats, blandishments, and some monetary inducements from Washington, only Australia—for reasons of its own—came through with major commitments of troops. In 1965 a frustrated LBJ asked, "Are we the sole defenders of freedom in the world?" Thus the president determined that, if necessary, America would fight with minimal international support and that is precisely what happened, with important consequences.[6]

Britain's failure to provide troops was particularly disappointing. The British did assist the United States in Vietnam with intelligence, arms sales (sometimes clandestine), and counterinsurgency expertise, but Wilson's Labour government refused to send even the symbolic "platoon of bagpipers" requested by the United States. Americans on occasion pondered a "Hessian option," the possibility of threatening to withhold support for the pound sterling if Britain did not come through with troops. But they did not want to buy the troops. And in the interdependent world of the 1960s, leverage worked both ways. A threat against the pound might force Britain to devalue its currency or pull its troops out of Asia, thus, for reasons to be noted later, putting additional economic strains on the United States. The Johnson administration was frustrated with its dilemma. "When the Russians invade Sussex," an angry Secretary of State Dean Rusk once snarled to a British journalist, "don't expect us to come and help you."[7]

In one sense, outside of France, the allied response in 1965 was not all bad. If the European allies did not provide troops or money, neither did they, despite strong reservations about U.S. policy, object openly or loudly to what the United States was doing. They could not help but recognize LBJ's special sensitivity on the subject. They were aware, in some cases painfully so, of their continued reliance on the United States, and they were sufficiently concerned about good relations with their ally to mute their reservations about U.S. policy. Thus, as historian Fredrik Logevall has concluded, from the American perspective, the outcome of the campaign was "mixed. The Johnson administration may have failed spectacularly in its bid to generate enthusiasm among key allies for the Asian war, but it had considerable success in the more limited objective of damage control, of keeping allied grumbling largely private."[8]

In this sense, interestingly, Johnson's deliberately low key approach to escalation in July 1965 served the administration's diplomatic as well as its domestic needs. A smaller, quiet escalation as opposed to a noisy, drastic expansion of the war would give America's allies no obvious cause for concern and therefore avert the sort of loud, open criticism the administration so desperately wished to avoid. Just as Johnson gambled that he could achieve his goals in Vietnam before domestic criticism built up, so also he gambled that he could succeed before international opposition assumed threatening proportions.

Here, as at home, of course, the administration miscalculated. Despite subsequent repeated U.S. efforts to get international support, only the Pacific allies contributed troops. They shared with the United States to a much greater degree than the Europeans a concern about communist, and especially Chinese, expansion in Southeast Asia. Some were even dependent on U.S. security guarantees and aid for their very survival. At least several saw an opportunity to extort additional aid and other concessions from the United States in return for modest contributions of troops. Among the Pacific allies, only Australia provided significant numbers of troops (over 7,000 at its peak number) and paid for them itself. Thailand furnished 11,000 troops in return for significant U.S. concessions. New Zealand, "the most dovish of the hawks," neatly balanced its concerns not to offend the United States and not to inflame domestic critics by sending an artillery battery of 552 men. South Korea provided the most troops, about 50,000 at its peak, but drove a very hard bargain in terms of additional military aid, subsidization of the troops, and U.S. security commitments. The Philippines' Ferdinand Marcos secured maximum gain from a small investment. Sensing Johnson's desperation, Marcos provided a small engineering battalion. He then offered to mobilize ten battalions of troops at U.S. expense, but kept them at home and used them for his own political benefit. Recognizing that he had been had, Johnson warned an aide: "If you ever bring that man near me again, I'll have your head."[9]

By late 1967, however, the Asian allies had grown weary and wary. When presidential advisors Clark Clifford and Maxwell Taylor toured Southeast Asia in search of additional troops, they met a considerably less than lukewarm response, even among the more hawkish allies. By this time, Australian opinion had begun to turn against the war, a sizable antiwar protest had developed, and the official response was "polite but unhelpful." South Korean President Chung Hee Park made the visiting Americans "sit through a dissertation on *his* political difficulties." Marcos was "adamantly uncooperative," and a planned Clifford-Taylor visit to Manila was canceled. The response from such key allies helped persuade soon-to-be secretary of defense Clifford of the futility of further escalation and the need for extrication.[10]

In other ways, the absence of allied support undermined the U.S. war effort. Most European leaders continued to soft-pedal their opposition to U.S. policy in Vietnam. The longer the war went on, however, the more it became an object of bitter political discord in all European countries and a source of political embarrassment for leaders who valued ties with the United States. Throughout Western Europe, the war set off protest movements even among America's staunchest allies, such as West Germany, provoking rising anti-Americanism and calling into question the alliance itself. Thus allied leaders found themselves caught between their ties to the United States on one hand and mounting domestic protest on the other. Most continued to refuse to break openly with the United States, even at political cost to themselves. Some attempted to deal with Vietnam by refusing to talk about it. Canada's Lester Pearson and Britain's Wilson on occasion sought to save the United States from itself and themselves from political turmoil and perhaps political defeat by promoting a negotiated settlement of the war. Such efforts were unavailing. They were not appreciated in Washington, it goes without saying, and earned for Pearson and Wilson the wrath of an increasingly embattled commander in chief. A war undertaken ostensibly to save the western alliance strained it to the breaking point. "Europe does not understand America any longer, America is not understanding Europe," Italian Socialist leader Pietro Nenni told Vice President Hubert H. Humphrey in 1967. "The root of the discord is the Viet Nam war."[11] The United States by late 1967 thus found itself isolated on Vietnam. The absence of open criticism from allied leaders was increasingly drowned out by the rising volume of popular protest against the war in Europe. On occasion, U.S. officials had to be sneaked out of places where they had made public appearances to avoid angry crowds.

Sweden posed special problems. Traditionally neutral in world affairs, Sweden also had a long history of close ties with the United States, but the Vietnam War drove the two nations apart. Over strong U.S. objections, the Swedish government permitted philosopher and pacifist Bertrand Russell to hold war crimes trials in Stockholm, with America the absent—and undefended—defendant. Even more galling to Washington, Sweden became a haven for U.S. war deserters, and the Swedish government assisted them by giving them work permits, temporary housing, and a small pension. In 1968 Sweden reduced its representation in South Vietnam to consular status, and in 1969 it recognized North Vietnam.[12]

The administration could do little to reverse the unfavorable trend. Periodically, LBJ would mount a noisy diplomatic offensive sending scores of top advisors around the world to explain his policies and seek international support. These initiatives produced few results, however, and the administration was reduced to professing not to be affected and stubbornly insisting that it would stay the course—alone, if necessary.

In fact, U.S. isolation and its status as international whipping boy took a considerable toll. U.S. policymakers of the World War II generation generally had acted on the assumption that their nation was always right, and to hear otherwise, even from close allies, troubled many a great deal and gave some sober second thoughts. If Ronald Reagan was the Teflon president, to whom nothing stuck, LBJ, to a considerable degree by his own choice, was the fly-paper president, to whom everything clung, and he took each item of criticism personally and to heart. As domestic antiwar critics never tired of pointing out, moreover, one of the most compelling arguments for negotiations or even withdrawal from Vietnam was the enormous damage the war was doing to America's "world position" and to its relationship with its major allies.

International pressures had other effects. They limited the Johnson administration's ability and willingness to escalate the war. They pushed the president to undertake peace moves, such as bombing pauses that he would have preferred not to make and that North Vietnam was able to exploit, and to respond to peace initiatives from elsewhere that he recognized, correctly in most cases, were not likely to produce results he could live with, thus undermining the U.S. strategy of coercion. In all, they contributed significantly to the inability of the United States to achieve more than a stalemate in Vietnam by the end of 1967.[13]

In terms of dealing with America's major adversaries, the Soviet Union and China, Johnson and his advisors may have fared even worse. They achieved their major goal-keeping a limited war limited. But they fundamentally miscalculated in counting on Soviet help to bring North Vietnam to the conference table. More important, they appear not to have anticipated the extent to which Soviet and Chinese supply of North Vietnam would limit their ability to force North Vietnam to give in. Once aware of it, they were powerless to stop it.

The United States escalated the war in Vietnam in 1964 and 1965 to contain and deter the People's Republic of China, discourage any Soviet tendencies toward "adventurism," and uphold the credibility of U.S. commitments. While doing this, Americans hoped also to exploit the steadily widening Sino-Soviet split to improve relations with the Soviet Union and thereby reduce the danger of nuclear war. Thus, while expanding the war, they also kept the door open to the presumably more conciliatory Soviets to broker a settlement in Vietnam, explored the possibility of negotiations on arms control, and sought to build bridges to the Soviet Union and Eastern Europe through trade and cultural exchanges.

The Johnson administration focused mainly on keeping the war limited. Vividly recalling Chinese intervention in the Korean War in 1950 and the terror of the more recent Cuban Missile Crisis, LBJ and his advisors sought to avoid steps that might widen the war. They escalated the U.S. commitment gradually and quietly to minimize the danger of confrontation with the major communist powers. They repeatedly assured Moscow and even Beijing that their goals were limited. They scrupulously avoided the sort of rash military moves that might provoke a Soviet or Chinese response. Johnson tightly restricted the bombing near the Chinese border and around Haiphong Harbor. He lived in mortal terror, by some accounts, that an American pilot (from Johnson City, Texas, in his most vivid nightmare) would drop a bomb down the smokestack of a Soviet freighter, thus starting World War III.

Johnson's caution appears to have been warranted—and to have paid off. There is ample evidence that a serious threat to destroy North Vietnam would at least have posed a very hard choice for the Soviet Union and China, at most have brought them into the war. There is no evidence, on the other hand, to indicate that at any time between 1965 and 1968 the war came close to a flashpoint. In this one important respect, the Johnson strategy worked, and for this the administration deserves some credit.

Gradual escalation had an obvious downside, of course. It gave Hanoi time to adapt to the bombing, shield its most precious resources, and develop one of the most deadly air defense systems ever employed in warfare, all of which increased its capacity to resist U.S. military pressures.

Johnson and his advisors also badly miscalculated in other areas, and these miscalculations were costly in terms of their ability to achieve their goals. They overestimated, first, the influence of the Soviet Union over its North Vietnamese ally. Until it left office in 1969, the administration clung stubbornly to the notion that the Soviet Union could and would broker a peace settlement acceptable to the United States. Major U.S. peace initiatives in 1965 and again in 1967 sought to find a way to Hanoi through Moscow. Johnson pressed the matter hard with Soviet Premier Alexei Kosygin at their 1967 summit in Glassboro, New Jersey. After negotiations opened in Paris in 1968, the United States continued to seek, finally with some limited success, to use the Soviet Union as an intermediary. Even in its last days, it persisted in believing that the Soviets could pull off a diplomatic miracle by brokering a negotiated settlement of the war.[14]

Such hopes were at best misplaced. The war offered both opportunities and dangers for the Soviet Union. It distracted and weakened Moscow's two major enemies, enhanced its moral authority in the world, and permitted the test of new weapons under combat conditions. On the other hand, it posed a major obstacle to Moscow's efforts to improve superpower relations and reduce the risk of nuclear war. Soviet officials shared America's fears of escalation and indeed had their own quagmire theory, perhaps a product of their memories of the Cuban Missile Crisis, of being dragged into war by reckless allies and stubborn enemies.[15]

In terms of brokering a settlement, the Soviets were notably cautious and ultimately unhelpful. Soviet leaders went to considerable lengths to minimize conflict with the United States and at times worked cautiously to bring the belligerents together. They encouraged their Eastern European allies to undertake peace initiatives, and in early 1967 Kosygin collaborated with Britain's Wilson on a joint approach to Hanoi and Washington. But there were limits beyond which they could not go. They found (much as the United States had found with Saigon) that their massive aid to North Vietnam did not give them commensurate influence. Having been burned by the Soviet Union and China at the Geneva Conference in 1954, Hanoi tightly guarded its freedom of action. In any event, the Soviet Union could not push North Vietnam too far for fear of playing into the hands of its rival, China. Soviet leaders limited themselves to the role of a "postman," who would deliver messages to and from Hanoi, or a "night watchman," who would encourage negotiations. They played an important role in brokering the bombing halt of October 1968 and the momentary breakthrough in negotiations that followed. For a variety of reasons, however, that breakthrough did not produce a settlement, and that was about the extent of Soviet influence.[16]

Ironically, significantly, and in ways the United States appears not to have anticipated, its own escalation of the war forced the Soviet Union and China to sharply increase their assistance to North Vietnam, thus undercutting U.S. military pressures. Up to 1964, both Moscow and Beijing had been consummate pragmatists, neither hindering nor in any major way assisting North Vietnam's efforts to "liberate" the South. U.S. escalation, however, forced ideology back to the forefront. Competing with each other for leadership of world communism, the Soviet Union and China had little choice but to expand dramatically their assistance to North Vietnam. The North Vietnamese brilliantly played one off against the other—what have you done for me lately?—all the time keeping control of their destiny in their own hands. The Soviets provided crucial modern weapons such as fighter planes, surface-to-air missiles (SAMS), and tanks, and 3,000 Soviet technicians took direct part in the war by manning antiaircraft batteries and SAM sites. The Chinese provided huge quantities of small arms, vehicles, and food, and more than 300,000 Chinese troops helped to maintain the vital supply route from China to Vietnam. The total of Soviet and Chinese aid has been estimated at more than $2 billion. This assistance helped neutralize U.S. air attacks, replace equipment lost in the bombing, and free North Vietnam to send more troops South. It played a crucial role in Hanoi's ability and will to resist U.S. military pressures. The United States apparently did not anticipate this development, and Johnson could do nothing about it short of the kind of provocative measures that he so feared would dangerously escalate the war.[17]

One of the principal reasons Johnson escalated the war in 1965 was to uphold his nation's position as a world power. America's Cold War empire was built on an intricate and "inextricable intertwining" of alliances, armed forces, and economic connections. The empire was already shaky when Johnson launched the war in Vietnam in 1965. Ironically, the war undertaken to maintain the empire shook it to its foundations, causing the worst economic crisis since 1933 and leading some influential Americans by early 1968 to push for liquidating the war on the periphery to save the empire's center.

The American empire was built mainly on force of arms and the strength of the dollar, and the rapidly expanding Vietnam War put enormous strains on both. Robert McNamara's Defense Department had prepared itself in the 1960s to fight two and a half wars: one against Soviet forces in Europe; another against China in Asia; and a half war in a smaller theater with a second or third level adversary. By 1967, the "half" war in Vietnam was consuming the lion's share of America's available defense forces. Johnson's steadfast refusal to mobilize the reserves meant that almost all combat-ready units had been committed to Vietnam to meet its pressing need in Vietnam. Forces in Europe were stripped of experienced men, and those remaining in the United States consisted of little more than a training establishment.[18]

A crisis in the Western alliance, itself in part triggered by U.S. commitments in Vietnam, further strained allied military capabilities and economic resources. As defense costs skyrocketed and the Soviet threat to Western Europe appeared to ease, America's allies in the North American Treaty Organization (NATO) increasingly went their own way. De Gaulle withdrew 70,000 French troops from the alliance and cut off French funds for its operations. In early 1967 an economically beleaguered Britain announced plans to reduce its overseas forces by one-third and threatened to remove all its troops from Europe unless West Germany assumed the entire foreign exchange cost of supporting them. West Germany, in turn, threatened to curtail the purchases of U.S. and British military equipment that had helped offset those nations' military expenditures and thereby ease their balance-of-payments problems. The European moves provoked angry demands from a Congress already restive over Vietnam to withdraw U.S. forces from Europe.[19]

A crisis was averted—temporarily—when the Germans agreed to procure U.S. and British goods on a reduced scale, and the United States and Britain agreed to "redeploy" troops from Germany to home territories, keeping them under NATO command and ready to redeploy again if needed. But Britain went ahead with further cutbacks in July, and West Germany indicated that it would reduce its forces to 400,000 instead of building them up to 508,000 as originally planned. By late 1967 the "NATO shield appeared to be disintegrating under the combined influence of nationalism, political complacency, and mounting financial pressures."[20]

Defense matters were closely linked with economic issues, and growing economic problems in the Western nations, both cause and effect of the

NATO crisis, intensified the sense of urgency. To save his Great Society programs, Johnson had carefully concealed the costs of the war and refused to seek an increase in taxes until late 1967. Mounting expenditures for Vietnam thus imposed a burden of as much as $3.6 billion a year on an already overheated U.S. economy, stoking inflation and increasing America's balance-of-payments deficit. These combined to weaken the dollar in international money markets. Since the dollar propped up the world economy, its weakness placed the entire world monetary structure in jeopardy. The United States had bailed out a faltering pound sterling three times between 1964 and 1966. But a financial crisis in Britain in late 1967, leading to devaluation of the pound, brought further cutbacks in British overseas forces and threatened the dollar. The dollar was pegged to gold and all other Western currencies to the dollar, and rising fears about the world and the U.S. economy also set off a run on gold, causing enormous American losses. The administration had to defend an embattled dollar, Johnson warned in late 1967, or "we will wreck the Republic."[21]

All of these military, economic, and political chickens came home to roost in March 1968 when Washington was already reeling from the North Vietnamese/NLF Tet Offensive. Pressure on the dollar began to mount again, and by the end of the first week gold purchases reached a new high. In early March Britain announced plans to withdraw all troops east of Suez by the end of 1971, placing added defense burdens on the United States and more pressure on the dollar. The next day came word of General William C. Westmoreland's request for 206,000 additional troops to hold the line in Vietnam. These events combined to cause a growing lack of confidence in the U.S. economy and wild speculation in gold. On March 14 alone, the United States lost $372 million in gold trading, "the largest gold rush in history," *Time* magazine called it, "a frenetic speculative stampede that threatened the Western world."[22]

The troop request plus the gold crisis provoked a full-fledged political crisis in Washington. Johnson's budget director warned that increased spending for Vietnam might take the defense budget above $100 billion and add $500 million to the balance-of-payments deficit. Such expenditures would require cuts in domestic programs up to $3 billion and another tax increase at a time when the president's belated request for a 10 percent surtax was already stalled in Congress. In this context, leading organs of business opinion began to question the nation's ability to finance the war at existing or higher levels. Vietnam made clear, *Business Week* insisted, that "even the mighty U.S. lacks the means to fight anywhere, anytime and prevail," and it called for a policy of deescalation in Vietnam and fiscal restraint at home.[23]

Simultaneously, leading establishment figures, including, most important, some of the major architects of the nation's Cold War containment policy, concluded that the war was destroying the nation's overall national security position and pressed for fundamental changes in policy. W. Averell Harriman, Paul Nitze, Dean Acheson, and Clark Clifford, all key advisors from the administration of Harry S. Truman, formed the core of a cabal that mobilized in March 1968 to push Johnson to change course in Vietnam. Acheson was the leader. The sophisticated easterner could not stand the earthy and often crude Texan—a real Centaur, Acheson labeled him, "half man, half horse's ass." But he put aside his personal dislike to save the larger defense structure he and the other Truman people had brought forth at what Acheson would later call, in near-biblical terms, "the creation." "Our leader ought to be concerned with areas that count," the imperious former secretary of state insisted. Acheson assumed the lead in the famous meeting of the Wise Men's group on March 26–27, the "high water mark of U.S. hegemony," journalists Walter Isaacson and Evan Thomas have called it, helping to persuade the distinguished group of informal presidential advisors to recommend that LBJ deescalate the war in Vietnam.[24]

It was in this atmosphere of gloom and doom about the Western alliance, the international and domestic economic crises, and Vietnam that LBJ made his March 31 decisions. Justifying himself to his generals—and, as was his wont, seeking to get others to feel his pain, he moaned and groaned about an "abominable fiscal situation, panic and demoralization" in the country, near universal opposition in the press, and his own "overwhelming disapproval" in the polls. "I will go down the drain," he gloomily concluded.[25] Thus, on March 31, 1968, he announced to a stunned nation his momentous decisions to stop escalation of the war, seek negotiations, and withdraw from the presidential race. A war originally undertaken to sustain American hegemony by March 1968 had to be scaled back to maintain a larger economic and military system on the verge of collapse. Those same international factors that had led the United States to undertake the war in the first place became a major reason for it to change course.

Where Johnson's diplomatic strategy was essentially defensive, his successor, Richard Nixon, sought to seize the initiative. As vice president under Eisenhower and as a presidential aspirant, Nixon was much more internationally minded than his predecessor was. He was keenly interested in world politics and diplomacy, had thought deeply and written extensively about such subjects, and fancied himself a skilled diplomatist. Diplomacy in fact was the centerpiece of his strategy to end the war in a way that would salvage for the United States "peace with honor."

Unlike Johnson, Nixon wasted little time fretting over allied support or lack thereof. He later admitted that concern about a possible international "uproar" limited his military options, at least at the start of his presidency. For the most part, however, up to December 1972, European leaders gave

Nixon the benefit of the doubt. They respected the U.S. dilemma. They wanted the war to be over, if for no other reason than to end the turmoil in their own countries, but they were willing to keep quiet as long as they believed Nixon was seriously committed to getting out of Vietnam. De Gaulle's successor, Georges Pompidou, made clear that as long as the United States was seeking to get out of Vietnam, he would not second-guess the president. In any event, the Europeans generally recognized their inability to influence U.S. decisions and remained reluctant to alienate their most important ally.[26] Even neutral Sweden, largely because of its own increasingly serious economic difficulties, soft-pedaled its criticism of the United States without changing its views on the war.[27] When Nixon drastically escalated the war in response to the North Vietnamese Easter Offensive of 1972, the NATO allies privately expressed support for the administration and no one publicly opposed it. Nixon appreciated the relative freedom of action the Europeans accorded him.[28]

Relations with the major Pacific allies during this phase of the war were much more complicated, and the strains evident during the 1967 Clifford-Taylor mission deepened significantly. All the Asian allies, especially the most vulnerable nations, such as Thailand and South Korea, were alarmed by signs early in Nixon's administration that the United States was shifting military responsibility to the South Vietnamese and scaling back its own commitments in South Vietnam and Southeast Asia. Their concerns for their own security grew and their faith in U.S. defense guarantees wavered. The Nixon Doctrine, which was announced in June 1969 and unilaterally imposed on the allies greater responsibility for their own defense, increased their concerns. Indications in late 1971 that the United States was seeking a rapprochement with China sent some Asian allies scurrying to make their own diplomatic adjustments.

The modus operandi favored by Nixon and his top foreign policy aide, Henry Kissinger, strained relations even more. Operating in secrecy, the administration did not consult with its allies regarding its withdrawals of troops from Vietnam, and it ignored allied requests for timetables. While withdrawing large increments of its own troops from South Vietnam, the administration pressured its allies to maintain their own troops there at full strength. Australia and New Zealand, who mostly paid their own way, were further infuriated by congressional exposés and stories in the press indiscriminately labeling the Pacific allies "mercenaries" and belittling their contributions to the war effort.[29]

The administration made some effort to repair the damage, with no more than mixed results. Thailand was especially important as the "hub" of the U.S. war in Vietnam, and its air bases were crucial to the defense of South Vietnam and the region. The administration thus treated Thailand with special care, working out an agreement for a phased withdrawal of Thai troops from South Vietnam and U.S. troops from Thailand. The Thais were nevertheless "stunned" when they learned about Nixon's 1972 visit to China and began a diplomatic reassessment of their own looking toward improving ties with China.[30] The United States also worked out an arrangement with the South Koreans by which some forces would be withdrawn, but two divisions remained in South Vietnam until the cease-fire of March 1973. Ironically, some of the worst problems were with the oldest and most faithful Pacific ally, Australia. Already annoyed at Nixon's refusal to consult regarding troop withdrawals, Canberra was shocked by the size of the April 1970 withdrawal and shortly after announced the reduction of its own forces from three to two battalions. When the Australians learned of Nixon's visit to China, they assumed that meant an end to the war and pulled out the rest of their forces.[31]

Nixon and Kissinger's major diplomatic ploy was to exploit the dramatic changes in world politics to end the Vietnam War and improve America's global position even as its power declined. Presidential candidate Nixon had sharply criticized Lyndon Johnson in 1968 not only for using American military power badly but also for squandering America's diplomatic assets. The Soviet Union wanted expanded trade and improved relations with the United States, Nixon reasoned, and that could provide the leverage to secure Soviet aid in ending the war in Vietnam.

Shortly after taking office, Nixon set out to employ this strategy. Certain that his reputation as a hard-line anticommunist would work to his advantage, he passed word through Soviet officials that if North Vietnam did not negotiate a satisfactory peace agreement by November 1, 1969, it could expect a forceful response from the United States.[32]

This effort to bludgeon the Soviet Union and North Vietnam into productive peace talks worked no better than Johnson's quiet diplomacy. However much it may have wished better relations with the United States, Moscow was not willing to push Hanoi to the point of a break, and nothing short of that could have budged North Vietnam from its position. In some ways, for Nixon, the timing could not have been worse. The death of North Vietnamese leader Ho Chi Minh in September 1969 made any major concessions on North Vietnam's part unlikely. In any event, the North Vietnamese believed their military position was weak at this point, and they were extremely reluctant to negotiate. They also believed that time was on their side and that it was to their advantage to delay. The deadline passed, and Nixon did nothing.

Nixon and Kissinger continued, however, to rely on great power diplomacy to end the war. Intent on improving relations with both the Soviet Union and China as a way of exploiting the dispute between the two communist powers and improving America's position, they also hoped thereby to isolate North Vietnam from its major allies and suppliers, leaving it no choice but to accept a settlement that would permit the United States to claim peace with honor.

The Nixon-Kissinger strategy worked—to a point. Nixon was able to arrange dramatic summit meetings in Beijing and Moscow in 1972, making Hanoi very nervous and, diplomatically at least, leaving it isolated. China rejected North Vietnamese Premier Pham Van Dong's late 1971 request not to receive Nixon and indeed urged Hanoi to settle with the United States. "As our broom is too short to sweep the Americans out of Taiwan," Chinese leader Mao Zedong cooed, "so yours is too short to do the same in South Vietnam."[33] China and the Soviet Union went ahead with summits with the United States in 1972, despite Nixon's drastic escalation of the war during the Easter Offensive, provoking the North Vietnamese newspaper *Nhan Dan* to denounce its allies for "throwing a lifeline to a drowning pirate." Under these circumstances and reeling from the destructive force of U.S. air power in the summer of 1972, the North Vietnamese made major concessions.[34]

But it worked only to a point. To secure substantive negotiations, the United States, too, had to make major concessions that would cripple its ability to achieve the sort of peace Nixon wanted. Having learned hard lessons about the unreliability of its allies at the Geneva Conference in 1954, the North Vietnamese, in approaching the final negotiations, preciously guarded their freedom of action. They made sure not to place themselves at the mercy of Moscow and Beijing. While making concessions that permitted South Vietnam's Nguyen Van Thieu government to stay in power temporarily, they held out for terms that would enable them to achieve their long-term aim of unifying Vietnam under their own control.

In addition, although both the Soviet Union and China at this point in the war gave higher priority to their relations with the United States than to the conflict in Vietnam, their continuing rivalry prohibited either from leaving Hanoi at the mercy of the United States. Thus before, during, and after the Easter Offensive, each dramatically stepped up its aid to North Vietnam as a means of demonstrating its continued support and preventing the other from making inroads at its expense. Thus, ironically, while pushing Hanoi to agree to terms, they gave it the means to fight on to final victory. Chinese aid reached record levels in 1971 and 1972 and was particularly important in countering the U.S. mining of Haiphong Harbor. Soviet aid was even greater, helping to replace the enormous matériel losses suffered in the Easter Offensive and facilitating the conventional offensive that would bring the fall of Saigon in 1975.[35]

When Nixon and Kissinger launched the so-called Christmas bombing in December 1972 after the peace negotiations again reached a deadlock, the Nixon administration found itself even more isolated internationally than in the worst days of the Johnson administration. Across the world, outrage spewed forth from enemies, allies, and neutrals against the intensive U.S. bombing of Hanoi and Haiphong. The Soviet Union and China loudly denounced the United States while quietly pressing North Vietnam to end the war. "Not one NATO ally supported us or even hinted at understanding our position," Kissinger later complained. The bombing "made the world recoil in revulsion," the *London Daily Mirror* exclaimed, and Hamburg's *Die Zeit* protested that "Even allies must call this a crime against humanity." Pope Paul VI spoke of the bombing as an "object of daily grief," and in a statement that infuriated Nixon, Swedish Prime Minister Olof Palme compared U.S. actions against North Vietnam to those of the Nazis against the Jews. Even a relatively mild private criticism by Australian Prime Minister Edward Whitlam provoked fury in the Nixon White House.[36]

The Christmas bombing undoubtedly pushed North Vietnam back to the conference table. On the other hand, the international reaction, along with obvious signs that Congress would soon attempt to take control of the war from the White House, pushed Nixon and Kissinger toward a settlement in January 1973. Although Nixon insisted at the time and later that he had attained peace with honor, the Paris agreements attained neither. The war continued, and within a little more than two years North Vietnam and the National Liberation Front scored a total victory over America's client, South Vietnam, and the United States could do nothing more than carry off a hasty and humiliating withdrawal.

International factors thus played an important role in the outcome of the war. International opposition to U.S. policy, including that from some of America's key allies, limited the nation's freedom of action militarily and undermined its will to persist. On the other hand, Soviet and Chinese aid encouraged North Vietnam's will to resist and facilitated its ability to counter U.S. moves. A war fought to maintain the American empire exposed and exacerbated its fundamental economic, diplomatic, and military weaknesses, leading to calls from its creators to scale back the war to save it. The United States learned the hard way the truth of what Winston Churchill had spoken in an earlier war.

## Notes

1. For an introduction to the debate, see George C. Herring, "American Strategy in Vietnam: The Postwar Debate," *Military Affairs* 46 (April 1982): 57–63, and Gary R. Hess, "The Military Perspective on Strategy in Vietnam: Harry G. Summers's *On Strategy* and Bruce Palmer's *The 25-Year War*," *Diplomatic History* 10 (Winter 1986): 91–106.

2. George C. Herring and Richard H. Immerman, "Eisenhower, Dulles, and Dienbienphu: 'The Day We Didn't Go to War' Revisited," *Journal of American History* 71 (September 1984): 343–363.
3. Fredrik Logevall, *Choosing War: The Lost Chance for Peace and the Escalation of War in Vietnam* (Berkeley: University of California Press, 1999), 78–79.
4. Ibid., 149–150; Fredrik Logevall, "America Isolated: The Western Powers and the War," paper delivered at the German Historical Institute, Washington, D.C., November 19–22, 1998, 11–14.
5. Logevall, "America Isolated," 15–16; Logevall, *Choosing War,* 339. The conversation with Erhard is recounted in George McGhee, *At the Creation of a New Germany: From Adenauer to Brandt* (New Haven, CT: Yale University Press, 1989), 184–185.
6. Suzanne Brown, "United States Ambassador George Crews McGhee and the Vietnam Crisis: American Involvement in South Vietnam and United States-West German Relations," *The Maryland Historian* 24 (Fall/Winter 1993): 38–39.
7. Quoted in Logevall, *Choosing War,* 133. See also John Dumbrell, "The Johnson Administration and the British Labour Government: Vietnam, the Pound and East of Suez," *Journal of American Studies* 30 (1996): 220–224, 231.
8. Logevall, "America Isolated," p. 5.
9. Quoted in Stanley Karnow, *In Our Image: America's Empire in the Philippines* (New York: Random House, 1989), 377. For Australia, see Peter Edwards, *A Nation at War: Australian Politics, Society and Diplomacy During the Vietnam War 1965–1975* (Sydney: Allen & Unwin, 1997); for New Zealand, see Roberto Rabel, "'The Most Dovish of the Hawks': New Zealand Alliance Politics and the Vietnam War," in Jeffrey Grey and Jeff Doyle, *Vietnam: War, Myth and Memory* (Sydney: Allen & Unwin, 1992), 14–30; for South Korea, see Nicholas Evan Sarantakes, "In the Service of Pharaoh? The United States and the Deployment of Korean Troops in Vietnam, 1965–1968," *Pacific Historical Review* 68 (August 1999): 425–449; for Thailand, see Robert J. Flynn, "Preserving the Hub: U.S.-Thai Relations During the Vietnam War, 1961–1975," Ph.D. dissertation, University of Kentucky, 2001.
10. Peter Edwards, "The Strategic Concerns of a Regional Power: Australia's Involvement in the Vietnam War," paper presented at the German Historical Institute, Washington, D.C., November 19–22, 1998; Edwards, *Nation at War,* 150–152; Sarantakes; "Service of Pharoah," 442–443; and Marshall Wright memo for William Jorden, August 22, 1967, Lyndon Baines Johnson Papers, Lyndon Baines Johnson Library, National Security File, Country File, Box 279, Philippine Memos, Vol. IV.
11. Quoted in Leopoldo Nuti, "The Center-Left Government in Italy and the Escalation of the Vietnam War," paper presented at the German Historical Institute, Washington, D.C., November 19–22, 1998.
12. Fredrik Logevall, "The Swedish-American Conflict over Vietnam," *Diplomatic History,* 17(Summer 1993): 429–434, and Logevall, "Sweden and the

ASPEN Channel," paper presented at the Lyndon Baines Johnson Library, Austin, TX, April 2001.

13. For the difficulties posed by the peace initiatives, see George C. Herring, *LBJ and Vietnam: A Different Kind of War* (Austin: University of Texas Press, 1994), 88–120.
14. See, for example, Tom Johnson, Notes on Meeting, November 26, 1968, Lyndon Baines Johnson Papers, Lyndon Baines Johnson Library, Tom Johnson Notes on Meetings, Box 4.
15. Ilya V. Gaiduk, "The Vietnam War and Soviet-American Relations, 1964–1973: New Russian Evidence," *Cold War International History Project Bulletin* (Winter 1995–1996): 253; Anatoly Dobrynin, *In Confidence: Moscow's Ambassador to America's Six Cold War Presidents (*New York: Times Books, 1995), 135–136, 140.
16. Ilya V. Gaiduk and Oganez V. Marinin, "The Vietnam War and Soviet-American Relations," unpublished paper in possession of author.
17. Soviet aid is documented in ibid. The scope and importance of Chinese aid is covered in Chen Jian, "China's Involvement in the Vietnam War, 1964–1969," *China Quarterly* 142 (June 1995): pp. 371–380, Xiaoming Zhang, "The Vietnam War, 1964–1969: A Chinese Perspective," *Journal of Military History* 6 (October 1996): 731–762, and Qiang Zhai, *China & the Vietnam Wars, 1950–1975* (Chapel Hill: University of North Carolina Press, 2000), especially 35–139.
18. Hanson Baldwin, "U.S. Forces Spread Thin," *New York Times,* February 21, 1966.
19. George C. Herring, "Tet and the Crisis of Hegemony," in Carole Fink et al., eds., *1968: The World Transformed* (New York: Cambridge University Press, 1998), 34.
20. Richard B. Stebbins, *The United States in World Affairs, 1967* (New York: New York University Press, 1968), 197–206.
21. Quoted in Dumbrell, "The Johnson Administration and the British Labour Government," 226.
22. Quoted in Robert M. Collins, "The Economic Crisis of 1968 and the Waning of the 'American Century,'" *American Historical Review* 101 (April 1996): 396.
23. Quoted in Herring, "Tet and the Crisis of Hegemony," 41.
24. Ibid., 41–44.
25. Tom Johnson, Notes on Meeting, March 26, 1968, Lyndon Baines Johnson Papers, Lyndon Baines Johnson Library, Tom Johnson Notes on Meetings, Box 2.
26. Henry A. Kissinger, *White House Years* (Boston: Little, Brown, 1979), 424–425. Kissinger even claims that European leaders shared the administration's concern about U.S. credibility in Vietnam.
27. Logevall, "Swedish-American Conflict Over Vietnam," 437–438.
28. Kissinger, *White House Years,* 1195.

29. Edwards, *Nation at War,* 237–243; Laking to Carner, June 23, 1969, and Carner to Laking, July 15, 1969, and Washington to Wellington, September 4, 1970, New Zealand External Affairs Archives, 478/4/6, Wellington, NZ.
30. Flynn, "Protecting the Hub," 188–195.
31. Edwards, *Nation at War,* 237, 239–241.
32. George C. Herring, *America's Longest War* (New York: 1996), 246–247.
33. Quoted in Zhai, *China & the Vietnam Wars,* 204–205.
34. Ibid., 201–204.
35. Ibid., 203–204.
36. International reaction to the Christmas bombing is covered in James R. Powell, "Going for Broke: Richard Nixon's Search for 'Peace With Honor,' October 1972-January 1973," Ph.D. dissertation, University of Kentucky, 1998, 227–228; Jeffrey Kimball *Nixon's Vietnam War* (Lawrence, KS: University Press of Kansas,1998), 366, Kissinger, *White House Years,* 1453–1454, William Bundy, *A Tangled Web: The Making of Foreign Policy in the Nixon Presidency* (New York: Hill and Wang, 998), 362; Walter Isaacson, *Kissinger: A Biography* (New York: Simon and Schuster, 1992), 470–471; and Edwards, *Nation at War,* 322–332.

Chapter Three

# Why the South Won the American War in Vietnam

Robert K. Brigham

The question before us—Why did the North Win the Vietnam War?—represents a long tradition in the thinking of U.S. policymakers and American and Vietnamese historians alike. It is, however, as the contributors to this volume make clear, essentially the wrong question because it gives primacy to northerners within Vietnam's modern revolution and it inaccurately divides the struggle in Vietnam along geopolitical lines that have no cultural or historical precedent. The question as posed without any caveat accepts the official U.S. explanation and justification for the war. During the 1960s, Washington used this "North-South" paradigm to defend U.S. national security interests in Vietnam and to validate American intervention. In December 1961 the White House released an important White Paper entitled "A Threat to Peace: North Vietnam's Efforts to Conquer South Vietnam."[1] In this document, Kennedy's advisors claimed that the National Liberation Front (NLF) was nothing more than a puppet on a string, a false facade constructed to allow communist North Vietnam to take independent South Vietnam by force. To combat this aggression, the report concluded, the United States had to supply its South Vietnamese ally with technical, economic, and military support. After twenty-five grueling years, according to the official U.S. account, North Vietnam finally prevailed because it was willing to sacrifice 3 million of its own people to win a protracted war.

Ironically, postwar histories from Hanoi support this view. Several suggest that the People's Army of Vietnam (PAVN), Hanoi's military arm, marched South with Prussian-like precision to liberate Vietnam.[2] Because of the glorious sacrifices of the North, these histories tell us, all of Vietnam was saved.[3] In the postwar period, southerners were routinely excluded from historical conferences on the war, thus guaranteeing the official northern stamp on all that was published.[4] Historian George Kahin has correctly suggested that the rewriting of the war's history was necessary because northerners within the party wanted to wrestle control from southerners. For nearly two decades, southerners had dominated several key positions within the Political Bureau. By overstating the significance of the northern contribution to the southern liberation war, northerners could justify their exclusion of the NLF in the postwar government.[5] As the new government formed, many southerners found themselves isolated from the corridors of power, even though the revolution had moved forward on their backs. In one recent survey, for example, Hanoi calculated that its wartime losses were near 3.2 million.[6] Of these, nearly 65 percent were southerners. Clearly, the writing of history in postwar Vietnam was a political act.

Surprisingly, most U.S. historians have largely accepted Washington's official construction and Hanoi's postwar perspective. In the war between the United States and Vietnam, only northerners count. In several recent books, including Michael Lind's *The Necessary War* and Lewis Sorley's *A Better War,* northerners make all significant military decisions.[7] Furthermore, "North Vietnam's" decision to march South provides an axiomatic starting point from which the rest of the war naturally follows. The problem, of course, is that most northerners had opposed such measures in the mid-1950s. It was only after a "southern wind" had swept over Hanoi that southern party members convinced a majority on the Political Bureau that the war was necessary. The decision to create the NLF was not a carefully calculated scheme by "North Vietnam" to take "South Vietnam" by force. Instead, it was the result of intense, bitter, and often acrimonious debates within the Communist Party. In the end, a handful of southerners in Hanoi convinced the Political Bureau to change its policy. Their strategic political victory was an unlikely one: They faced overwhelming opposition from a majority within the Political Bureau, Military Commission, National Assembly, and Central Committee. Furthermore, the desire to use arms in the South went directly against the wishes of two of the most powerful policymakers in Hanoi during the 1950s, Truong Chinh, the party's secretary general, and Vo Nguyen Giap, the head of the military. What follows, then, is the story of how a radical, southern worldview came to dominate Vietnam's modern revolution against all odds.

Every effort to understand the Vietnam War must begin with some knowledge of Vietnam's Communist Party. The party, founded in 1929, was a unified, nationwide organization, drawing its members and leaders from all corners of Vietnam. Since its birth, the party always had incorporated the dual goals of national independence and social reform. However, party leaders continually stressed that national liberation was the most crucial problem facing the Vietnamese people. This emphasis on patriotism taught cadres to think of Vietnam as "one nation, one people, with four thousand years of history."[8] The party, of course, was trying to combat regional tensions created by French colonialism. The French had separated Vietnam into three administrative regions: Tonkin, Annam, and Cochinchina, hoping to keep the country divided and weak. As part of its "civilizing" mission in Vietnam, France had claimed that it was in Indochina to bring peace and stability to a region that had known nothing but tribal warfare for years. This fallacy included French efforts to force Vietnam to accept Vietnamese psychocultural distinctions based on regionalism. It now seems clear that one of the party's earliest successes was in revitalizing a sense of national identity. The party accomplished this task through its massive education programs that emphasized national unity through a shared geographic past. This populist appeal resonated loudly in the countryside where most of Vietnam's citizens lived.

By the time of the French defeat in 1954, the party had a sophisticated network throughout all of Vietnam. According to Carlyle A. Thayer, an expert on the party in the 1950s, nearly one-third of all Vietnamese living south of the seventeenth parallel lived in areas controlled by the party.[9] Still, for the next two decades, the party struggled to liberate the South and reunify the country. During this period, Hanoi remained the geographic center of the national party. Many southerners traveled North to take significant positions of power within the party's infrastructure. The Political Bureau and the Central Committee, the party's two most important policymaking bodies, had southerners and northerners in its ranks. The labels so commonly used in the West—"North Vietnam" and "South Vietnam"—are problematical therefore for several reasons. For one, many party leaders usually labeled in the West as "North Vietnamese" were actually from the South. For another, labeling someone as a "South Vietnamese" simply because they lived South of the seventeenth parallel does not speak accurately to political affiliation. Many southerners were communists who had spent most of their lives in service to the revolution. As our story begins, then, in 1954 with the signing of the Geneva Accords, northerners and southerners within the Communist Party were having an intense debate over the future of the liberation war.

In 1954, the warring parties in Indochina were invited to Geneva to participate in an ongoing conference about conflict between East and West, especially in Asia. At Geneva, Soviet and Chinese leaders convinced Hanoi to allow France a face-saving defeat by dividing Vietnam at the seventeenth parallel. This would grant Paris a grace period for a phased withdrawal after 100 years of colonial rule. After a two-year period, the protocols called for nationwide elections to reunify the country. The Vietnamese Communist Party accepted this compromise peace to placate it allies and its enemies. At Geneva, the Chinese Communists had made clear their opposition to a harsh armistice. Beijing believed that a provocative settlement might entice the United States to intervene in Indochina, and this was unacceptable. As one China expert in Hanoi recently reported, "The Chinese feared another land war in Asia so close to the Korean peace of 1953. The last thing Mao wanted was an open invitation for the Americans to return to the region."[10] More important, the Soviet Union wanted to keep the United States at bay. It was beginning a period of détente with the United States, and by 1956 the Soviet leadership made a concerted effort to reach out to the West. Premier Nikita Khrushchev denounced Joseph Stalin and outlined a policy of peaceful coexistence with the United States and its allies. In this climate, it would have been difficult for Vietnam's Communist Party to extract an austere peace from its former colonial overlords. Accordingly, Hanoi adopted Moscow's emphasis on the political struggle as the way to reunite Vietnam following the Geneva meetings. By political struggle, party leaders meant the willingness to persuade legal and semi-legal organizations to agitate for implementation of the political provisions of the Geneva Accords.

Most strategists in Hanoi clearly understood that the United States and its allies in Saigon were not likely to go along with the accords. No representative from either government had signed the compact, and the Southeast Asia Treaty Organization conventions made the Geneva agreement obsolete in the minds of most policymakers in Washington and Saigon. Within months of the end of the French war, the United States had backed the return to Vietnam of Ngo Dinh Diem, a former official in Emperor Bao Dai's government. Diem was a staunch anticommunist and a devout Catholic. He shunned a political accord with Hanoi and sought support in the U.S. Senate for the creation of counterrevolutionary alternative south of the seventeenth parallel. At the height of the McCarthy hysteria at home, the Eisenhower administration was more than willing to support anticommunist nation-building abroad. Diem used this support to create the Republic of Vietnam (RVN), or "South Vietnam," and its national army, the Army of the Republic of Vietnam (ARVN). He also enlisted the help of his brother, Ngo Dinh Nhu, who took control of organizing a national security police. Diem used these state organs to move swiftly against communist cadres in the South. Beginning in 1955, he authorized massive sweeps against suspected communists. By early 1956, according to journalist Stanley Karnow, Diem had reduced the former communist cells by nearly 90 percent.[11] Diem filled his jails with his political opponents; stories of torture at Poulo Condore and other prisons were common. He even helped pass a law that gave the security police the right to hold anyone suspected of being a communist indefinitely without bringing formal charges.

Diem's repressive policies were so effective that many party leaders called these the "darkest days" of the revolution.[12] Cadre ranks shrank, and it was difficult to recruit new members. From the first anticommunist sweeps, several southern party leaders urged Hanoi to respond in kind. "We needed to fight fire with fire," one former party spokesperson recently reported. "We in the South wanted to take up arms immediately."[13] In Hanoi, however, party officials adhered to Moscow's line. "We were committed to unification through political means," one former member of the Foreign Ministry explained. "We thought that an all-Vietnamese solution through elections held out the best hope for Vietnam."[14] In late April 1956, as Diem was beginning his fiercest attacks on southern Vietnam's mass organizations, the Political Bureau in Hanoi again confirmed its commitment to the political struggle alone. At the Party's Ninth Plenum, Truong Chinh, the party's secretary general, dismissed calls for a military offensive. He believed that the political struggle promised new "reasons to be confident in the correctness of the policy in the struggle for national reunification."[15] Furthermore, he severely criticized those who wanted to take up arms against Diem. "There are some people who do not yet believe in the correctness of this political program and in the policy of peaceful reunification of the country."[16] With the secretary's overwhelming opposition to a military response, the party endorsed the political struggle as the only path toward reunification.

During these troubled times, a powerful voice emerged from the party's ranks supporting a more militant response in the South. Le Duan, a southerner and longtime party member, quickly became the leading advocate for sending men and arms to the South to combat Diem's oppressive government and to liberate southern Vietnam. Duan was born in Quang Tri, near Hue, in 1908. He had spent nearly ten years in French prisons during the 1920s and1930s, emerging as a committed Leninist. After his release from prison, Duan was assigned to the civilian defense forces in his region. He was outraged at this treatment, thinking that he deserved a military position with high rank and responsibility. From his early writings, it is clear that he supported revolutionary war as the answer to Vietnam's anti-imperial cause. By 1954 he believed that military success in the South was inevitable and that the enemy "could be defeated in a relatively short period of time."[17] After the French war, when others headed north to regroup, Duan remained in the south and quickly became one of the region's most important political figures.

Few in the party recognized Duan as a potential national leader, however. For one thing, he was dogmatic. For another, there were constant rumors in Hanoi about his overall intelligence. In a postwar memoir, Bui Tin, the former editor of the party's daily newspaper, claimed that Duan had always been the subject of much ridicule within the party.[18] His arrogance was also legendary.

Following President Ho Chi Minh's death in September 1969, Duan reported: "As for me, well, I am better than Uncle Ho. He opened his mouth and talked along the lines of the Confucian code of morality, like human dignity, loyalty, good manners, wisdom and trustworthiness. What is that? It is outmoded feudalism. As for me, I am for the collective mastery of the workers."[19]

Many of Vietnam's modern revolutionaries spoke the language of Marxism, but few believed it as passionately or followed it as blindly as Duan. The party leadership was, by and large, far more pragmatic.

Duan, then, was an unlikely leader of Vietnam's modern revolution, and his views certainly were in the minority in 1954. Slowly, however, Duan developed supporters within the party's top leadership, including the influential Political Bureau member Le Duc Tho, a northerner who was close to Ho Chi Minh. Some party officials feared that if they did not allow southern cadres to fight back, Hanoi would lose control of the anti-Diem movement. Desperately searching for a way to link southern opposition to Diem with the party's own liberation goals, party leaders invited Duan, the head of the Nam Bo Regional Committee (the party's southernmost region), to make a formal report on conditions in the South. He delivered the report, entitled "The Revolutionary Path in the South," at the Party Plenum in December 1956. In an uncharacteristic fashion, the usually doctrinaire southerner claimed that the Vietnamese Communist Party desired peace. He wrote:

> First of all, we must determine what it means for a revolutionary movement to adhere to a peaceful line. The movement must use the political forces of the people as its base, instead of using the people's armed forces to achieve the revolutionary objective. A revolutionary movement struggling according to a peaceful line is considerably different from a reformist movement. For example, a reformist movement relies on established laws to achieve change, while a revolutionary movement relies on the revolutionary political forces of the masses as its base. Another difference is that a revolutionary movement struggles for revolutionary objectives, while a reformist movement struggles for reformist goals.
>
> With an imperialist, feudalist, dictatorial, fascist government like the U.S.-Diem government, is it possible for a peaceful political movement to achieve its objectives?

He further emphasized that the natural political leanings of the party were not aimed at class warfare and that armed violence came only in response to the Diem regime. For example, he explained the party's peaceful aspirations in this way:

> We must recognize that all accomplishments in every country stem from the people. This is a definite law and cannot be otherwise. Therefore, the line of

> the revolutionary movement must be in accord with the inclinations and aspirations of the people. Only in this way can a revolutionary movement be mobilized, and only in this way can it achieve eventual success. The highest priorities of the Southern people are lasting peace and national unification. We must clearly recognize this longing for peace: the revolutionary movement in the South can mobilize and achieve success only by grasping the flag of peace in harmony with popular sentiments. On the contrary, the U.S.-Diem regime is using fascist violence to provoke war, contrary to the will of the people. Therefore, it must certainly be defeated.[20]

After all of the talk of peace, however, Duan eventually concluded, "the only way for the people to oppose the U.S.-Diem regime is by the path of revolution."[21]

As the party considered Duan's recommendations, it also listened to many northerners who insisted that the time was not right for a fight in the South. The leading voice of opposition to war belonged to Truong Chinh, former party secretary general and president of the National Assembly. Truong Chinh, a pseudonym used by Dang Xuan Khu meaning "long march," was a northerner who had joined Ho Chi Minh's Thanh Nien (Youth League) in 1929, and was one of the founding members of the Indochinese Communist Party. From the start, Truong Chinh was one of the party's leading theorists. He was also a committed Maoist, but he questioned the efficacy of the general counter offensive, the last stage of the three stages of Mao's guerrilla war strategy.[22] The problem, according to historian Greg Lockhart, was that Truong Chinh opposed the use of troops in "human waves" as Mao had done in Korea.[23] Instead, he believed that the revolutionary movement required "balanced institutional development so that the power of the People's Army would come from the people's willingness to support it."[24] Truong Chinh believed that Vietnam's modern revolution needed a people's war strategy that never developed faster than local conditions would allow. The military had to be supported locally through the proper development of revolutionary social forces before it could act. He also believed that the construction of socialism in the North was the revolution's primary goal. He contended that the moral superiority of the North's socialist experiment would bring the Saigon government to its knees without firing a single shot. Truong Chinh was aware that many in the party would see his theory as caution, and so he purposefully adopted the name *Anh Thanh* (Brother Cautious).[25]

In his debate with Duan, Brother Cautious argued persuasively that the social and political factors for successful revolution had not yet been met in the South and that the party risked inviting a wider war if it moved too quickly. He had the support of many northerners who also concluded that the party should move against Diem only when it had overwhelming "objective force."[26] In other words, it was safe to strike against the Saigon government only when socialism had been properly developed because the social factors of the revolution were more important than the military. Without the proper economic and social support, some northerners argued, the war in the South would be a waste. "We would be sending good men to die for nothing," one former PAVN officer commented secretly.[27] Furthermore, many in the party, especially northerners, believed that the South would never be fully liberated under arms and that the social development there would be handicapped by the lack of military control. "We could not mount the kind of military offensives that Duan and others were calling for in the late 1950s," reported one former party military leader, "because we did not have the local resources to see the fight through."[28] In people's war, northerners reminded their impatient southern comrades, men under arms were self-sufficient. Any outside requirements meant that the objective conditions for armed struggle had yet to be met.

To make his point even more forcefully, Truong Chinh republished an influential essay written in 1951 shortly after the party's heavy losses against the French at Vinh Yen and Mao Khe. The article had received tremendous praise in the days when Truong Chinh was the party's most influential theorist. In this important treatise, he had argued:

> Naturally, we must build a force completely capable of meeting its strategic and tactical responsibilities on the battlefield. But if you do not take into account the people's capacity to shoulder the burden and the financial potential of the government, it is adventurous and dangerous to mobilize and concentrate forces that have no rice to eat and clothes to wear and no weapons to fight with. The number of people emancipated from production is far too high, the development of the economy is not sufficient to guarantee re-supply, the people do not have the strength to nourish the army.[29]

A dangerous adventure is exactly how Truong Chinh viewed Duan's calls for war in the South. No doubt most northerners shared the National Assembly leader's view. After the long struggle against the French, the People's Army needed a respite from heavy fighting. Why would southerners purposefully intensify the conflict and risk provoking the United States? As it stood now, the United States was not heavily involved in the ground war, and the entire North was spared. That was precisely the point, according to Duan. Southerners were carrying the burden of the next phase of the revolution, and it was time to allow them to fight back.

After careful consideration, party leaders concurred with Duan's findings, concluding that "self-defense and armed propaganda forces are needed to support the political struggle, and eventually armed forces must be used to carry out a revolution to overthrow Diem. The revolution in the South is to use a violent general uprising to win political power."[30] It now seems clear that Duan's position gained favor in Hanoi against all odds because the situation in the South had deteriorated so rapidly and the party feared that a radical peasant movement against Diem might be launched without its control or guidance. The French historian Philippe Devillers, a longtime student of Vietnam, supports this conclusion. In an influential essay in the early 1960s, he declared that southerners "were literally driven by Diem to take up arms in self-defence." He also argued that the insurrection existed before the communists decided to take part and that "they were simply forced to join in" or they would lose control of events in the South.[31] One of the leading antiwar scholars shares Devillers's views. According to George Kahin, "the Central Committee [of Vietnam's Communist Party] faced disagreement with its southern branch; it was already losing influence over some southerners, and further delay would cause greater loss among those who were still active."[32] Clearly, by early 1957, events in the South were forcing the party to side with Duan.

The party, however, did not release violence unchecked. The armed struggle was to develop along the lines of the political struggle and move to violence only "when conditions were ripe."[33] Southerners, relieved to be able to organize against Diem in any fashion, were quick to recognize Duan as their national spokesman. This development carried considerable political weight in Hanoi. As a result, in early 1957 the party invited Duan to become a member of the Political Bureau, the party's most important policy planning body.[34] Once safely seated in power, he advocated that the party adopt a war footing in the South. Because of his efforts, cadre ranks increased dramatically and new military bases appeared in all regions. "Le Duan was a rising star," one former party official recently explained. "No one much liked him, or thought he was very smart, but he had shown that he had a keen sense of the workings of the party, had harnessed enough political support for his cause, and many, many southerners truly believed that he was their voice in Hanoi. Isn't that the markings of a good politician? I don't think political leaders are always smart or well liked just effective."[35]

By the time the Nam Bo Regional Committee met in August 1958, most party leaders hailed Le Duan's leadership of the southern movement as one of the "revolution's great successes."[36] As for Truong Chinh, he carried a bitter taste in his mouth the rest of his life over his political defeat at the hands of Duan. Much like John Adams's fear of how history books would record the American revolution—Adams correctly predicted that Thomas Jefferson would get most of the credit—Truong Chinh reported, "Le Duan's ideas on revolutionary armed struggle were not the only ones, nor were they the first."[37] Of course, Truong Chinh could not have it both ways. He had opposed a rapid mobilization in the South, and now the party had moved forcefully in that direction. As he lost power, he blamed Duan for taking it. This personal conflict between two of the party's most influential policymakers outlines the nature of the political debate in Hanoi. During much of this ideological contest, Ho Chi Minh sat on the sidelines waiting for a consensus to emerge. According to William Duiker in his impressive biography of Ho, "he appeared to lead by persuasion and consensus rather than by imposing his will through force of personality."[38] Ho did, however, offer his tacit support to Duan's southern strategy.

Still, many senior party officials feared that the southern rebellion was moving too quickly. Party leaders were concerned over reports that Diem had launched new anticommunist sweeps because of the increased activity and that several radical peasant groups had retaliated. One internal party document suggested that cadres in the highlands had openly rebelled, killing several Saigon troops.[39] The results had been disastrous as the secret police targeted urban areas in the South for the first time. "We understood that we had to fight back in the South," one former party leader recently commented, "but we did not want to move so quickly as to draw the United States into the war or to give Diem further cover to unleash his national security forces. The revolution in the South at that point was a delicate balancing act, and Le Duan was constantly pushing us toward a more aggressive stance."[40] Even after Duan had replaced Truong Chinh as the Party's most influential policymaker, the path to war in the South was not readily apparent. Duan needed to find a way to articulate his position without losing the support of those few northerners who had favored war all along.

In late 1958 Duan made an important trip South that seemed to cement his thinking on the war and provide him with its rationale. He was particularly influenced by reports from the Nam Bo Regional Committee that stressed the importance to southerners of fighting back. One young communist, Nguyen Thi Dinh, described the situation in her province: "Sister, we must arm ourselves to survive, otherwise we'll die. If you let us kill the security police to get weapons, we'll do it right away. . . . We've heard that people in Hong Ngu and Dong Thap province have taken up arms. How about our province? Have we been allowed to strike back?"[41] At the party's plenum in January 1959, Duan reported on his most recent southern trip. He argued that conditions had deteriorated and that the political struggle movement had stalled. It was time, he concluded, to create a broad based united front to harness opposition to Diem. The front would combine the diplomatic, political, and military struggle movements into a unified whole and eventually would remove Diem from power at the end of gun.

At that party plenum, it was clear that Duan's position would receive the Political Bureau's full support because events were getting out of control. Duan also had figured out how to explain his vision of what was needed to a broader audience. His report concluded that the party must embrace war and must organize a broad-based front in the South directly under the control of the Central Committee. Such control would satisfy northern fears that the party would have no control over the southern revolution. This important new development persuaded the party to accept Duan's recommendations. Accordingly, it passed what is now known as Resolution 15. In May 1959 the Political Bureau approved Resolution 15 and fully supported the creation of a united front in the South. By summer, cadres in the Central Highlands had received word that "the green light for switching from political struggle alone to political struggle combined with armed struggle" had been given.[42] In September 1960, at the party's Third National Congress, leaders in Hanoi selected Duan as the new secretary general, replacing Ho Chi Minh, who had been acting secretary since Truong Chinh's ouster in 1954 for the failed land reform campaigns. Duan's rise to the most powerful policymaking position within the party is proof enough that the southern view dominated the revolution at this point. From his new position, Duan again called for the immediate creation of a broad-based front to "rally all patriotic classes and sections of the people to oppose the U.S.-Diem regime."[43] Shortly after the congress, on December 19, 1960, in the mangrove swamps of Tay Ninh Province in southern Vietnam, sixty southern Vietnamese revolutionaries met to proclaim the formation of the National Front for the Liberation of South Vietnam (NLF), derogatorily called the Viet Cong[44] in the West.

The creation of the NLF represents the triumph of Duan over Truong Chinh. It also symbolizes the way that the political tides were turning in Hanoi during the late 1950s. By 1959 the more militant southerners had found a way to frame the argument in terms acceptable to the largest number of party members. This had been the consensus that Ho Chi Minh had desperately desired. The party could now unleash a people's war in the South that had the full support of the Political Bureau, but that also harnessed all anti-Diem forces. In other words, the party, now led by southerners, could mobilize all southerners who opposed Ngo Dinh Diem into a united front that Hanoi controlled. We must be careful, however, to recognize that "Hanoi" does not mean "North Vietnam." Instead, it is merely the geographic center of a nationwide Communist Party. By 1959 southerners, not northerners, were clearly dictating party policy in Hanoi.

Once in operation, the NLF and its military arm, the People's Liberation Armed Forces (PLAF) put into practice Duan's views about the way the war should be fought in the South. PLAF regular infantry units continually attacked Saigon forces and harassed American advisors in the field. In the early years of the land war in the South (1961–1965), the PLAF dominated the battlefield. Impressive military victories helped fill cadre ranks and threatened to topple the Saigon government. It now seems clear that only massive amounts of U.S. aid kept the South from falling completely to the communists. Even with increased American support, however, there was never a stable government in Saigon. In the critical years of the war's escalation, Saigon experienced one coup after another as the PLAF intensified its attacks. The NLF grew bigger and stronger as the Saigon government became more dependent on U.S. aid and military support to survive.

Control of the NLF has always been a subject of intense debate among scholars and policymakers in the West. Recently released Vietnamese-language sources have given us greater insight into the decision-making process in Hanoi, however, and we can begin to fill out the chain of command. For example, we now know that decisions made by the Political Bureau in Hanoi and adopted by various party congresses and plenums were carried out in the South through the party's southern office, known in the West as the Central Office for South Vietnam (COSVN). During the war's major escalation, from 1965 to1967, the Director of COSVN was a southerner named Nguyen Chi Thanh. Thanh was actually a PAVN senior general, and his ascendancy to power within the party is another illustration of how regionalism propelled some into the spotlight. Thanh and Duan quickly became allies, mostly because they agreed early on that the path to victory in the South rested with the military. In a now famous exchange of letters from 1958 to 1965, the two southerners spelled out the theory behind military operations in the South.[45] They decided that the full mobilization of all disenchanted southerners joined with aggressive military tactics held out the best promise for a quick victory. As the war against Diem and the Americans entered its sixth year, Duan and Nguyen Chi Thanh became the chief architects of Vietnam's national liberation struggle. They shared a vision of how the war should be fought and understood better than most the sacrifices southerners had made.

Like Duan, Nguyen Chi Thanh's deep southern roots had a profound impact on his thinking. Born on New Year's Day 1914, in Quang Tri, near Duan's home village, General Thanh was raised by his maternal relatives on a small farm. He was a latecomer to communist politics, and probably joined the party in 1937 only because it "was attractive to young people during the Popular Front period."[46] Made the local secretary of the party, he was arrested repeatedly by the French. By 1950 Thanh had emerged as one of the leading political figures within the People's Army. His rise to power no doubt can be attributed to his ability to adapt to the changing ideological stances of the leadership in Hanoi and his loyalty to the cause of unification. In late 1950 the party named him its political commissar for the People's

Army and appointed him to its Central Military Committee. He quickly rose to the rank of three-star general, or colonel general, again probably because of his adroit political skills. From 1960 to 1965 the party asked Thanh to oversee the social aspects of the revolution, and he became an expert on collectivization. When southerners began to press for a more militant line, Thanh saw his chance to have more influence on events. He quickly supported the creation of the NLF and began to write extensively about the need for a more aggressive stance in the South.

While most leaders in Hanoi embraced Mao and his people's war strategy, Thanh clearly was attracted to Clausewitz's views on true war. Writing in the nineteenth century, Carl von Clausewitz, a Prussian military officer, had suggested that true war was all about the dramatic act of decisive battles and the primacy of the leader. He envisioned warfare so bloody and total that states would enter into it only when their national interest was truly at stake. Once committed, however, war was to be fought by big units and all out.[47] In the twentieth century, General Thanh advocated a land-based offensive strategy by large units as the only way to defeat the Americans. While others grew cautious in the face of continued U.S. escalation, Thanh claimed that southern cadres would make up in spirit what they lacked in material goods.[48]

Throughout 1966, PAVN and the PLAF launched offensive operations at points of vulnerability and where Thanh predicted great success. Clearly, Thanh had hoped to persuade Hanoi's top leadership that his offensive-minded strategy held out the best hope for victory. He advocated the total mobilization of the country behind the military effort. No sacrifice was too great for the national cause, including the conversion of all industry to production for the war effort.[49] When others in the party leadership wondered if the war was reaching a stalemate, Thanh argued that ultimate victory was near. In several essays and pamphlets in official party publications, Thanh promoted his aggressive approach against all detractors, especially General Vo Nguyen Giap, the leader of PAVN. General Thanh's theme was constant: "To attack unremittingly is the most active and effective method to maintain and extend our control of the battlefield."[50]

General Giap, however, had grown increasingly cautious in his use of force and found Thanh's massive attacks problematic. After the bloody counteroffensives in the 1951 Red River campaigns against the French, Giap wrote, "At the present time a careful analysis of our forces shows that in both the main force and regional force units the advanced level of organization is not commensurate with its needs and equipment potential."[51] Borrowing a page from Truong Chinh's argument, Giap became increasingly conservative in his use and support of firepower in the South during the American War in Vietnam. He supported a people's war in the South but did not want it to develop quicker than the capacity of local resources to support it. In other words, Giap and Truong Chinh thought that the NLF had to be self-sufficient and operate only in areas where the population could maintain its total needs. Giap was a master at moving men and supplies, but the new requirements of a war against the Americans seemed to be beyond his cautious grasp. In the West, Giap often is reported to be the brains behind the communist military victory, but in reality he was a reluctant warrior in the South and was severely criticized by his southern colleagues for being too deliberate. Giap blamed Thanh for this turn of events, and openly criticized the COSVN director's battle plans.

Some scholars have argued that the Giap-Thanh rivalry was not ideological but political.[52] Several military experts have suggested that Giap's power was diminishing by 1966 and that southerners within the party had begun to question his leadership.[53] In a postwar interview with the editor of the party's daily newspaper, Duan recalled: "During the war against the Americans, the Minister of Defense [Giap] was like a frightened rabbit. Therefore, we could not leave him in command. We had to take over the situation and pursue the struggle. In fact, we had to find somebody else to take over as Minister of Defense."[54] Still, in 1966 Giap was a commanding figure, and it would be difficult to influence party military decisions without the senior general's support. Giap had long criticized Thanh's military thinking, and he openly questioned the efficacy of Thanh's offensive strategy. He compared Thanh's battlefield exploits to those dark days of 1951 when the party lost thousands of troops in its ill-timed Red River Offensive, forgetting of course that he had planned those counterattacks himself. In any event, Giap grew increasingly cautious and pragmatic during the American War. Some say that this eventually cost him his political power.

In an essay written in 1966, General Giap declared that the conflict in the South was a protracted war and suggested that the proper military strategy might take years to achieve ultimate victory. Echoing earlier debates between northerners and southerners in the Political Bureau, Giap suggested that the party approach the war in the South more cautiously. "The people's war strategy of our Party," Giap explained in late 1966, "is based on using local resources to fight a protracted war. We do not believe in big unit battles for this favors the strategy of our enemy."[55]

Thanh could easily see that Giap's comments were aimed at his own effort in the South. He responded to Giap's criticisms immediately. In an essay written for the party's theoretical journal, *Hoc Tap* (Studies), Thanh declared that the offensive strategy in the South was the correct path to victory and charged that his critics' arguments were "empty-headed and illogical."[56] Thanh's argument did have certain logic. First, PAVN and PLAF were unified under his command in the South like never before. Both armies were at full strength despite heavy losses in the Ia Drang Valley, and Hanoi finally had agreed to send PAVN main force infantry divisions South. Most experts on the war agree that the communists were building up their strength in the South at twice the rate of U.S. escalation.[57] The American public, growing more disenchanted with the war each month, was not likely to support a full-scale draft given the limited nature of the war. President Johnson himself had refused to allow the mobilization of the reserves and already had begun to take U.S. troops from the North Atlantic Treaty Organization (NATO) force structures to assure a restricted conscription policy at home.[58] Second, the Saigon government was near complete collapse. Successive military coups had left the regime fragile and divided, and further political intrigue among the military made it almost impossible to govern effectively. Finally, and most important, Thanh had correctly sensed that the ARVN was in its weakest and most vulnerable state since the war began. "The general smelled blood," replied one former PAVN field commander recently. "He wanted to destroy what remained of the Saigon army quickly."[59] By 1965 the ARVN was no match for the combined PAVN and PLAF forces under Thanh's command, and this was the key to the communists' victory.

Indeed, from the earliest stages of the war, the Kennedy and Johnson administrations had agreed with their allies in Saigon that the ARVN was going to win or lose the conflict.[60] There was little that the United States could do if Saigon could not field an effective army that could stand its own against the communists. By early 1965 it had become clear that the ARVN could never fulfill this prerequisite for victory. Desertions were unusually high, manpower requirements were never met, there were significant problems in housing and food distribution, and military equipment often was used as coup protection instead of offensive machinery. Of all of these debilitating problems, desertions and poor command and control were perhaps the most significant. There were several reasons for the ARVN's high desertion rates, but most can be attributed to a repressive conscription, rotation, and leave policy that did not recognize the rhythms of peasant life in Vietnam. Unlike the communists, the Saigon government never extended family and village obligations to the larger community and state. As a result, the ARVN was never more than a collection of individuals. As individuals, ARVN enlisted men could easily desert the national army for what they perceived as more important family obligations. Saigon's response to the high desertions was to pass an even more restrictive conscription policy that only added to the problem it was trying to solve.

Sensing the growing military problems in the South, the U.S. government unknowingly took all of the teeth out of the ARVN just as General Thanh was planning his dry-season campaigns. In July 1965 John McNaughton, the assistant secretary of defense, suggested that the ARVN be given responsibility for "control over areas now held" and for "pacification operations and area control where possible."[61] Offensive operations, however, would be handed over to "U.S. and Allied forces, in conjunction with the GVN [ARVN] national reserve."[62] This concept, according to Jeffrey Clarke, the chief historian at the U.S. Army Center of Military History, "gave the bulk of the South Vietnamese regular army area security missions and left only eleven reserve battalions to participate in mobile offensive operations with U.S. ground units."[63] This meant, of course, that the United States had recognized the ARVN's weaknesses and had signaled to others that the South Vietnamese army was no match for the communists. The message became a self-fulfilling prophecy as ARVN morale plummeted and desertions reached an all-time high. Once the Americans abandoned the ARVN as an effective fighting force, Thanh understood that the war had been won.

In several meetings with the Military Commission of the Political Bureau, Thanh forcefully suggested that PAVN and PLAF forces launch coordinated attacks deep into the South. He argued that the growing U.S. commitment to the battlefield only represented the failure of the ARVN and its masters in Saigon. He confided to one colleague, "Now is not the time to act like cowards simply because the Americans are arriving now is the time to attack. Can't you see, American soldiers on Vietnamese soil is a sign that we are winning?"[64] Thanh correctly predicted that the United States was growing weary of the war and its recalcitrant ally, and that it was unlikely that Washington would respond to communist offensives with a major escalation. Furthermore, Thanh argued that the ARVN could not withstand an all-out offensive. Accordingly, he applied heavy pressure in the South throughout 1966 and early 1967. He decided where and when to hit the United States and the ARVN, and did so with cunning and remarkable agility. Thanh incurred heavy losses but held the United States to a stalemate, and in his mind that was the same as a military victory.

By mid-Spring, Thanh echoed the growing number of voices calling for a general offensive in the South. He believed that the United States had reached a point where it could no longer match communist escalation, and that the war had reached a turning point. Like many other PAVN military leaders, Thanh believed that a coordinated attack against key cities and provincial capitals would usher in the last phase of the war. Thanh was therefore part of the original planning team for the Tet offensive.[65] Ironically, it was Thanh's enthusiasm for that Tet offensive that led to his downfall. In June 1967 he traveled to Hanoi to promote the general offensive. Apparently, after some lengthy deliberations, he drank too much, went to his room for a warm bath, and died of a heart attack in his tub at the age of fifty-three.[66]

General Thanh's view that the people's war could never defeat the United States without the aid of big-unit warfare continued to carry influence in Hanoi, however, long after his death. From late 1965 until the end of the war in April 1975, more and more PAVN regular infantry divisions headed South. In fact, much of the way the party conducted the war against the Americans can be attributed to the "southern wind" that blew over Hanoi in the late 1950s. Southerners, not northerners, shaped the contours of the war and decided how the party would spend its limited resources on the battlefield. Every action taken in the South during the long war had the imprint of Duan, Nguyen Chi Thanh, and other influential southern party leaders. Northerners contributed to the victory too, but their efforts have dominated the history books for decades. This more balanced view of the war suggests that sacrifice in the liberation war was a national undertaking. We also should remember that even as PAVN tanks rolled South in 1975 to the party's ultimate military victory, they carried with them the NLF flag, because northern officers knew all too well that the South had paid a high price for victory.

## Notes

1. "A Threat to Peace: North Vietnam's Effort to Conquer South Viet Nam," United States Department of State, December 1961, Document No. 000358, Douglas Pike Collection, NLF Documents, Texas Tech University, Lubbock, Texas.
2. *Cuoc khang chien chong My, cuu nuoc, 1954–1975: Nhung su kien quan su* [The anti-U.S resistance war for national salvation of the fatherland, 1954–1975: Military events] (Hanoi: Nha Xuat Ban Quan Doi Nhan Dan, 1988); *Ho Chi Minh ve cong tac Dang cong tac chinh tri trong luc luong vu tran nhan dan* [Ho Chi Minh on Party tasks and political tasks in the people's army] (Hanoi: Nha Xuat Ban Quan Doi Nhan Dan, 1990); and especially *May van de tong ket chien tranh va viet lich su quan su* [Selected issues related to the conclusions and the writing of military history of the war] (Hanoi: Vien Lich Su Quan Su Viet Nam, 1987).
3. Ibid.
4. Tran Bach Dang, "Mau than: Cuoc Tong Dien Tap Chien Luoc" [Tet Offensive: A Strategic Rehearsal], *Tap Chi Lich Su Quan Su* (February 1988), 64. See also Ngo Vinh Long's essay in Marc Gilbert and William Head, eds., *The Tet Offensive* (Westport, CT: Praeger, 1996).
5. George Kahin, *Intervention: How America Became Involved in Vietnam* (New York: Doubleday, 1986).
6. Charles Hirschman, Samuel Preston, and Vu Manh Loi, "Vietnamese Casualties During the American War: A New Estimate," *Population and Development Review* 21 (December 1995): 783–812.

7. Michael Lind, *The Necessary War* (New York: Free Press, 2000); Lewis Sorley, *A Better War: The Unexamined Victories and Final Tragedy of America's Last Years in Vietnam* (New York: Harvest Books, 2000).
8. A famous quote repeated often by Ho Chi Minh, president of Vietnam's Communist Party.
9. Carlyle A. Thayer, *War by Other Means: National Liberation and Revolution in Viet-Nam, 1954–1960* (Sydney: Allen and Unwin, 1989), xxviii.
10. Author interview with Tran Quang Co, former deputy foreign minister, Socialist Republic of Vietnam, Hanoi, June 1997.
11. Stanley Karnow, *Vietnam: A History* (New York: Penguin, 1983), 227.
12. Author interview with Nguyen Khac Huynh, former member of the Democratic Republic of Vietnam's Foreign Ministry and ambassador to Mozambique, Hanoi, November 1995.
13. Author interview with Nguyen Van Hieu, former NLF cadre, Da Nang, March 1996.
14. Author interview with Nguyen Co Thach, former foreign minister, Socialist Republic of Vietnam, Hanoi, June 1997.
15. *Nhan Dan,* April 28, 1956, 3.
16. Ibid.
17. Le Duan, *Thu vao Nam* [Letters to the South] (Hanoi: Nha Xuat Ban Su That, 1986), 123.
18. Bui Tin, *From Cadre to Exile: The Memoirs of a North Vietnamese Journalist* (Chiang Mai, Thailand: Silkworm Books, 1995), 66–67.
19. Ibid. 66.
20. Le Duan, *Duong loi cach mang mien Nam* [The revolutionary path in the South], party document, c. 1956, Trung Tam Luu Tru Quoc Gia–1 [National Archives Center–1], Hanoi.
21. Ibid.
22. The three stages of Mao's guerrilla war strategy are defense, holding, and general counteroffensives.
23. Greg Lockhart, *Nation in Arms: The Origins of the People's Army of Vietnam* (Sydney: Allen and Unwin, 1989), 232.
24. As reported in ibid., 242.
25. Bui Tin, *From Cadre to Exile,* 4.
26. Author interview with a former PAVN officer who requested anonymity, Hanoi, June 1999.
27. Ibid.
28. Author interview with a former PAVN officer who requested anonymity, Hanoi, November 1995.
29. *Cuoc khang chien than thanh cua nhan dan Viet Nam* [The sacred resistance war of the Vietnamese people], Vol. 3 (Hanoi: Nha Xuat Ban Su That, 1958–1960), 25.
30. *Cuoc khang chien chong My, cuu nuoc, 1954–1975,* 20.
31. Philippe Devillers, "The Struggle for Unification in Vietnam," *China Quarterly* 9 (January-March 1962): 19.

32. Kahin, *Intervention,* 110.
33. Author interview with Nguyen Van Vinh, former NLF cadre, Hanoi, March 1999.
34. Thayer, *War by Other Means,* 111.
35. Author interview former party member who requested anonymity, Hanoi, June 1999.
36. *Nhan Dan,* October 4, 1958, 1.
37. Bui Tin, *From Cadre to Exile,* 43.
38. William Duiker, *Ho Chi Minh: A Life* (New York: Hyperion, 2000), 5.
39. "Tinh hinh va nhiem vu 59" [The situation and tasks for 1959], party document, circa 1959, Trung Tam Luu Tru Quoc Gia–1 [National Archives Center–1], Hanoi.
40. Author interview with former party official who requested anonymity, Hanoi, May 1997.
41. Nguyen Thi Dinh, *Khong con duong nao khac* [No other road to take] (Hanoi: Nha Xuat Ban Phu Nu, 1968), 58.
42. Ta Xuan Linh, "Armed Uprisings," *Vietnam Courier,* October 1974, 20.
43. Le Duan, "Political Report of the Central Committee of the Lao Dong," in *Third National Congress of the Vietnam Worker's Party: Documents,* Vol. 1 (Hanoi: Foreign Languages Publishing House, 1961), 62–63.
44. Viet Cong is an abbreviation for Viet Cong-san, meaning Viet Communist. Not all in the NLF were communists.
45. Le Duan, *Thu vao Nam.*
46. Author interview with former party official who requested anonymity, Hanoi, June 1999.
47. John Keegan, *A History of Warfare* (New York: Vintage Books, 1994).
48. William Duiker, *Sacred War: Nationalism and Revolution in a Divided Vietnam* (New York: McGraw-Hill, 1995), 187.
49. For example, the party outlawed the production and consumption of alcohol so that the production and distribution centers could be used for war matériel.
50. Duiker, *Sacred War,* 188.
51. *Cuoc khang chien than thanh cua nhan dan Viet Nam,* Vol. 3, 67.
52. Douglas Pike, *PAVN: People's Army of Vietnam* (Novato, CA: Presidio Press, 1986), 339–343, 348–351.
53. Author interview with Colonel Herbert Schandler (U.S. Army, retired), Bellagio, Italy, June 1998.
54. As quoted in Bui Tin, *From Cadre to Exile,* 132.
55. Vo Nguyen Giap, *Big Victory, Great Task* (Hanoi: Nha Xuat Ban Quan Doi Nhan Dan, 1966), 17.
56. Nguyen Chi Thanh, "Cang thuoc tu tuong cong viec giua luc luong vu trang va nhan dan o mien Nam va 1965–66 kho mua thang loi" [Ideological tasks of the army and people in the South and the 1965–66 dry season victories]," *Hoc Tap,* 12 (July 1966), 4.
57. Karnow, *Vietnam: A History,* 480.

58. Robert S. McNamara, James G. Blight, and Robert K. Brigham, *Argument without End: In Search of Answers to the Vietnam Tragedy* (New York: Public Affairs, 1999), 155–156.
59. Author interview with former PAVN Lieutenant General Dang Vu Hiep, Hanoi, June 1997.
60. McNamara, Blight, and Brigham, *Argument without End,* 324.
61. *U.S.-Vietnamese Relations, 1945–1967,* Vol. 5 (Washington, DC: Government Printing Office, 1971), Sec. iv, ch.6, 5.
62. Ibid.
63. Jeffrey Clarke, *Advice and Support: The Final Years* (Washington, DC: Center for Military History, 1988), 101.
64. Author interview with former party official who requested anonymity, Hanoi, June 1999.
65. Author interview with former PAVN General Doan Chung, Hanoi, February 1998.
66. Author interview with former party official who requested anonymity, Hanoi, January 2000. Several western sources have reported that Thanh died during a B-52 raid. See, for example, Pike, *PAVN,* 350. The high-ranking party official I spoke with in Hanoi in January 2000 insists that Thanh died as I have described. Others in Hanoi have confirmed this version of Thanh's death.

CHAPTER FOUR

# HOW AMERICA'S OWN MILITARY PERFORMANCE IN VIETNAM AIDED AND ABETTED THE "NORTH'S" VICTORY

JEFFREY RECORD

Conventional wisdom blames the lost war in Vietnam on American civilian decision makers. Clearly, political authority made the critical decisions to commit the United States to war in Indochina. It also established controversial limits on the application of force. Primary responsibility for America's ill-fated intervention in Vietnam rests with President Lyndon Johnson, Secretary of Defense Robert McNamara, Secretary of State Dean Rusk, and National Security Adviser McGeorge Bundy. These men fatally misread both the strategic significance of events in Vietnam and the effectiveness of U.S. military power in Indochina's revolutionary setting. Nor did they ever provide their subordinates in uniform clear military objectives in Indochina. On the contrary, they initially approached the use of force in Indochina as a means of coercing the enemy rather than defeating him.

Yet to conclude that the war in Vietnam was lost from the start by feckless politicians and meddling civilian crisis managers back in Washington is to ignore the remarkable political and military performance of the enemy in Vietnam. War is, after all, a two-sided affair, and to argue that the Vietnam War was entirely America's to win or lose is tantamount to examining Custer's destruction along the Little Big Horn without taking the Sioux into account.

Conventional wisdom also ignores the defective professional U.S. military performance in Vietnam *within* the political limitations imposed on the use of force. If the politicians were indeed stabbing the military in the back during the war, fairness demands recognizing that the military also was shooting itself in the foot. "[M]uch of the criticism of the Vietnam War has to do with 'political interference' in military operations," notes the late Vietnam veteran and military analyst, Harry Summers, Jr. "But such criticism is off the mark. Our problem was not so much political interference as it was lack of a coherent military strategy—a lack for which our military leaders share a large burden of responsibility."[1]

The performance of the armed services in the Vietnam War can and has been indicted on a host of grounds, including:

1. Failure of the senior military leadership to provide timely and useful professional advice to civilian authority.
2. Unwillingness to subordinate inter-service rivalry to the demands of wartime military effectiveness.
3. Pursuit of a firepower-attrition strategy based on palpably false premises.
4. Misuse of available military manpower.
5. Failure to recognize the limits of air power in the Indochinese strategic and operational setting.

Additionally, the senior military leadership back in Washington has been indicted for lack of moral courage to resist, on pain of resignation if necessary, what it regarded as war-losing policies imposed by civilian authority.

These indictments have been leveled, during and since the war, by civilian and military commentators alike, with retired and serving U.S. Army officers in the vanguard of the most persuasive and detailed criticism. These officers and their critiques include Edward L. King and his *The Death of the Army, A Pre-Mortem* (1972); Dave Richard Palmer and his *Summons of the Trumpet: A History of the Vietnam War from a Military Man's Viewpoint* (1978); Harry Summers Jr. and his *On Strategy: A Critical Analysis of the Vietnam War* (1982); Bruce Palmer Jr. and his *The 25-Year War: America's Military Role in Vietnam* (1984); Andrew F. Krepinevich and his *The Army and Vietnam* (1986); and H. R. McMaster and his *Dereliction of Duty: Lyndon Johnson, Robert McNamara, the Joint Chiefs of Staff, and the Lies That Led to Vietnam* (1997). Additionally, in 1977 retired army general Douglas Kinnard published *The War Managers, American Generals Reflect on Vietnam,* a book that summarized the highly critical findings of a survey of professional military opinion on how effectively the war had been conducted. Retired Marine Corps officer William R. Corson's *The Betrayal* (1968) also deserves inclusion.

Additionally, some air force officers have condemned the premises and conduct of the U.S. air war against North Vietnam. The key works here are Mark Clodfelter's *The Limits of Air Power: The American Bombing of North Vietnam* (1989) and Earl H. Tilford Jr.'s *Setup: What the Air Force Did in Vietnam and Why* (1991).

The unanswerable question is whether a more effective American military performance in Vietnam would have made any essential difference in the war's outcome. Even had civilian authority not imposed the restrictions that it did on the air war against North Vietnam and on the employment of U.S. ground forces outside of South Vietnam, it is far from self-evident that victory would have followed. A more vigorous military prosecution of the war still might not have broken Hanoi's own extraordinary will to win. Hanoi always had a far greater stake in the war than did Washington and therefore was prepared to sacrifice much more blood to get what it wanted. Greater U.S. military effectiveness in any event would not have budged the fundamental political obstacle to an enduring American success in Vietnam: namely, a politically illegitimate, militarily feckless, and thoroughly corrupted South Vietnamese client regime.

What is not in dispute is a faulty professional U.S. military performance in Vietnam that, by virtue of its flaws, aided and abetted—though certainly not caused—Hanoi's victory in the Vietnam War. In any war, one side's military mistakes play to the advantage of the other side, and this was true in Vietnam even though the United States was not militarily beaten there.

Before examining the flawed professional U.S. military performance during the Vietnam War, it is essential to recognize that there was no common military opinion on either the nature of the war or the best way to go about winning it. On both issues the services—and senior leaders within each service—brought differing views to the table. Moreover, on many issues senior civilians were just as guilty of mistaken judgment as senior military men. For example, in 1965 there was a broad consensus within the Pentagon and among the Pentagon and the White House and State Department that the United States had to fight in Vietnam because vital interests were at stake. For another example, key civilian and military decision makers alike badly underestimated the tenacity, will, and discipline of both the North Vietnamese state and the communist forces in the field.

But the civilians could not be blamed for the professional military's institutional disarray on war policy or the operational choices senior field commanders—most notably, General William Westmoreland—made within the confines of established political limits on the use of force. In contrast to the heavy political supervision of the U.S. air war against North Vietnam, the U.S. ground force commander in South Vietnam was given a relatively free operational hand in that country.

## Worthless Advice

The Joint Chiefs of Staff (JCS) proved incapable of providing timely and useful advice to President Johnson and Secretary of Defense McNamara.

The chiefs themselves failed more often than not to agree on what advice to give, and the JCS as an institution in the 1960s lacked the authoritative chairman established by Congress in the Defense Reorganization Act of 1986. It did not help that Johnson and McNamara, though for different reasons, had a visceral distrust of the senior military leadership.

The interservice rivalries that the Kennedy and Johnson administrations inherited were so acute as to preclude all but minimal cooperation on behalf of a common objective. The Joint Chiefs of Staff were a committee of equals with a relatively weak chairman, and the individual service chiefs had no mandate other than to advance their own parochial agendas. Accordingly, they tended to serve up conflicting advice, lowest-common-denominator advice, or no advice at all. The JCS were unable to provide useful and timely unified military advice and to formulate military strategy.[2] In the crucial decision-making period of mid-1964 to mid-1965, they could never seem to offer more than what amounted to single-service solutions stapled together.

> [E]ach of the services, rather than attempt to determine the true nature of the war and the source of the insurgency in South Vietnam, assumed that it alone had the capacity to win the war. The Air Force believed that bombing North Vietnam and interdicting infiltration routes could solve the problem of the insurgency in the South. . . . The Army viewed increased American involvement in Vietnam in the context of a protracted commitment of ground forces and believed that bombing the North might intensify the war in the South. . . . [The marines] advocate[d] bombing as only the first step in a larger program that included the introduction of large numbers of Marines into South Vietnam to establish secure 'enclaves' along the coast.[3]

Such a cacophony of views made it impossible for the JCS to meet their legal obligation of providing the president the best military advice. It also permitted those disdainful of military opinion in the first place to ignore whatever advice was proffered. As a populist, Lyndon Johnson had an innate mistrust of the military. "It's hard to be a hero without a war," he once told the historian Doris Kearns. "That's why I'm so suspicious of the military."[4] McNamara also had little use for military opinion, which he regarded as hidebound and simpleminded. The former Ford Motor Company executive was supremely confident in his own judgment, which rested on new analytical techniques and budgeting processes that he and his young, "whiz-kid" civilian assistants brought to the Pentagon in 1961. McNamara and his team "thought that their intelligence and analytical tools could compensate for their lack of military experience and education. Indeed, military experience seemed to them a liability because military officers took too narrow a view and based their advice on antiquated notions of war."[5]

It is doubtful that Johnson and McNamara would have paid much attention even to timely, useful, and unified military advice. The point here, however, is that such advice was rarely provided. Defenders of the military would have a much stronger case against Johnson and McNamara if they could establish the sustained presence of convincing military opinion, especially during the critical decision-making period from August 1963 through February 1965.

One wonders how different the situation might have been had the Defense Reorganization Act of 1986 been in place during the 1960s. During the Persian Gulf crisis, President George Bush received timely, useful, and unified military advice through a JCS chairman whose authority and ability to provide such advice—and to ignore the parochial counsel of the individual service chiefs—was clearly established. Indeed, the experience of the Vietnam War was a major impetus behind the 1986 act.

## Disunity of Command

If the combination of powerful interservice rivalry and a structurally weak Joint Chiefs of Staff gutted the quality of military advice in Washington, it had even more deleterious affects on the conduct of the war in Vietnam. Unity of command is an established principle of war that the American side violated repeatedly in Vietnam. In contrast to the superb unity of command displayed by the communists, who fielded basically a one-service military, the United States waged essentially three distinct wars in Indochina: a ground war in South Vietnam, a coercive air campaign against North Vietnam and an aerial interdiction campaign against the Ho Chi Minh Trail. Each of these wars was run by one or more separate command entities divided by service affiliation and often irreconcilable differences of opinion of how to win the war.

On the ground in South Vietnam was the Saigon-headquartered U.S. Military Assistance Command Vietnam (MACV), commanded by Army General William Westmoreland from 1964 to 1968. Westmoreland controlled U.S. ground force operations throughout South Vietnam, although in deference to interservice sensitivities he exercised only nominal command authority over the Marine Corps' 3rd Amphibious Force deployed in the critical I Corps region. Westmoreland had only token authority over the two South Korean divisions in the country and no command authority over South Vietnam's armed forces, which relegated themselves largely to static defense tasks.

Balkanization of the ground war was exacerbated by the mutual contempt between Westmoreland and the marines in I Corps; until 1968 they pursued two diametrically opposed strategies against the enemy based on two diametrically opposed conceptions of the nature of the war they were fighting. The marines believed they were fighting primarily an insurgency and took advantage of their long experience in counterinsurgency operations to pursue a program of political-military pacification based on expanding population enclaves.[6] The marines were not alone in their view of the war. A number of army officers, including Army Chief of Staff Harold K. Johnson, also viewed the war as first and foremost a counterinsurgent challenge, which arguably it was in 1965. These officers essentially rejected Westmoreland's view of the Vietnamese communists as a conventional military challenge (pacification tasks could be left to the South Vietnamese) that could be defeated through a strategy of attrition. Thus, even within the army, Westmoreland's take on the war and his choice of strategy were a source of division.[7]

Fragmentation of command authority was as bad as it gets in the prosecution of air operations. There was no single air component commander for the prosecution of the war, but rather several competing commands. The air force's Nebraska-headquartered Strategic Air Command retained operational authority over all B-52 bombers allocated to Southeast Asia, including the timing and target selection of all B-52 missions in Indochina. This in turn created tension with the Saigon-based U.S. 7th Air Force, which along with the Philippine-based 13th Air Force was responsible for most of the air force's share of the air war over both North and South Vietnam. (The 7th and the 13th also had a joint subordinate command in Thailand.) In the case of Laos, the 7th Air Force was granted control over U.S. Navy air operations in the southern part of the country (and in South Vietnam), but all proposed U.S. air operations in Laos had to be cleared personally by the U.S. ambassador in Vientiane. The U.S. Navy's air campaign against North Vietnam was run out of the Honolulu-based U.S. Pacific Command, to which both the air force's Pacific Air Force and the Navy's 7th Fleet reported.

Compounding this bureaucratic maze was the division of targets in North Vietnam into seven different "route packages," three farmed out to the air force and four to the navy. The 7th Air Force was assigned targets in the Hanoi area, northwestern rail lines, and in the area just north of the Demilitarized Zone (DMZ). The 7th Fleet was allocated the Haiphong area and northeastern North Vietnam. Westmoreland and his successors had no authority to pick air targets in North Vietnam except in the area adjacent to the DMZ. Nor did the MACV have operational control of the numerous C-130 cargo planes that operated in South Vietnam but were owned by the Pacific Air Force.

After the war, former 7th Air Force Commander William Momyer conceded that the route package system "compartmentalized our air power and reduced its capabilities and inevitably prevented a unified concentrated air effort."[8] Henry Kissinger got right to the point: The "bizarre way the air campaign was organized throughout the war told more about the Pentagon's bureaucracy than about military realities; indeed, it showed that Washington's organizational requirements overrode strategy."[9]

## A Dead-End Ground Strategy

Over a quarter of a century after the fall of Saigon, debate continues over whether the MACV should have pursued a different ground strategy in Vietnam. Many critics of Westmoreland's attrition strategy believe that a counterinsurgent strategy focused on separating the rural population from communist military danger and political penetration was the better strategy to have followed in 1965. Others believe that an earlier and sharper application of air power against North Vietnam and an accelerated program to create an effective South Vietnamese army might have obviated the need for massive U.S. ground combat intervention altogether.

The issue is compounded by the dramatic change in the nature of the war from the early 1960s to the early 1970s. During that decade, a southern, self-sustaining insurgency based on legitimate grievances metamorphosed into a North Vietnamese conventional military threat. Thus, what might have worked in 1965 might not have worked by 1972, and vice versa. The Tet Offensive and subsequent pacification initiatives greatly reduced the southern insurgent content of the communist war effort and compelled greater reliance on conventional North Vietnamese forces. Predictably, those forces proved more vulnerable to American firepower than the relatively irregular Viet Cong. Unfortunately for the United States, however, the dramatic impact of the Tet Offensive on American domestic political opinion compelled a shift in the U.S. war aim from defeating the communist threat in South Vietnam to extracting the United States from that country. Thus, ironically, by the time the insurgent threat had waned, the United States had lost its will to stay the military course against what had become an increasingly conventional threat. The lessening of the insurgent threat came too late to affect the war's outcome.

Even had Westmoreland opted for a counterinsurgency strategy, it is doubtful that the United States Army was in 1965 institutionally capable of performing such a strategy.[10] As for an effective South Vietnamese army, no amount of U.S. money, arms, and advice seemed capable of transforming a highly politicized, corrupt officer corps and a poorly trained, unmotivated soldiery into an effective battlefield competitor to the North Vietnamese army and Viet Cong. "Vietnamization" failed twice: in 1965, prompting U.S. intervention, and in 1975, handing Hanoi final victory.

Any chance of preserving a noncommunist South Vietnam after the Tet Offensive would have required, as in Korea since 1953, a permanent large

U.S. military garrison, but the Nixon administration chose unilateral military withdrawal followed by a 1973 Paris agreement that prohibited a U.S. combat presence. After 1973, moreover, there was never any prospect that the United States would reenter the war to enforce the Paris agreement. Under the circumstances, Congress is hardly to be blamed for refusing, two years later, to provide additional military assistance to a Thieu regime whose military forces were disintegrating in panic. Indeed, Thieu understood the Paris agreement for what it was, as did Alexander M. Haig Jr., Kissinger's emissary who was sent to Saigon to force Thieu to accept the agreement's terms: "a peace treaty with the North Vietnamese that everyone suspected Hanoi would never honor—and that depended for its credibility not only on massive American aid to Saigon but also, ultimately, on the fantasy that the United States would, if necessary, go back into South Vietnam in force to uphold it." Continues Haig: "[The] self-evident truth [was] that Thieu's regime could not survive if we permitted a huge communist army to remain inside his country."[11]

None of these judgments excuses Westmoreland's selection of an attrition strategy or obscures the reasons why it failed. Attrition's aim is simply to destroy or disable enemy forces and war-making capacity faster than the enemy can replace them. As one of Westmoreland's deputies put it, "The solution in Vietnam is more bombs, more shells, more napalm till the other side cracks and gives up."[12] Westmoreland himself explained it in 1967: "We'll just go on bleeding them until Hanoi wakes up to the fact that they have bled their country to the point off national disaster for generations. They will have to reassess their position."[13]

This was much easier said than done. Attrition and its search-and-destroy tactics were in fact doomed from the start, as many senior army officers suspected or believed at the time, including Army Chief of Staff Johnson and Westmoreland's own successor in Vietnam, General Creighton Abrams.[14] Attrition rested on three false premises: that there was a communist manpower breaking point within reach of U.S. firepower; that the United States could acquire and maintain the initiative on the battlefield, thereby forcing the enemy to lose control of his own losses; and that attrition's progress could be measured by keeping a reliable count of Vietnamese communists, both dead and alive.

The first premise assumed that the United States could kill more communist soldiers than North Vietnam and the Viet Cong could replace and that once this "cross-over point" (Westmoreland's term) had been reached, Hanoi would be willing to cease its sponsorship of the war in the South. In fact, U.S. firepower, lavishly employed though it was, never came close to competing with either the communist birth rate or Hanoi's willingness to sacrifice young men on behalf of its war aims. At the height of the war in

1968, North Vietnam and communist-controlled areas in South Vietnam had an estimated total military manpower pool of 2.3 million (only half of whom were soldiers), with 250,000 males annually becoming available for military service in North Vietnam alone. Even assuming a communist loss rate as high as the first half of 1968—during the Tet Offensive and its aftermath—it would have taken MACV thirteen years to have exhausted this manpower pool.[15] As British expert Sir Robert Thompson bluntly observed, to neutralize Westmoreland's attrition strategy, "all the people of North Vietnam had to do between 1965 and 1968 was to exist and breed," and the "United States Air Force could interrupt neither of those activities."[16] Westmoreland nonetheless continued attrition warfare throughout his tenure at the MACV even though "there was no compelling evidence that North Vietnam was hurting for manpower to keep on fighting."[17]

Attrition's second premise—that U.S. forces would have the battlefield initiative—also proved false. In fact, it was the enemy that assumed the initiative early and maintained it during most of the war. MACV and other studies revealed that communist forces, not the searching-and-destroying Americans, initiated 80 to 90 percent of all firefights, most of which were brief hit-and-run affairs, with communist forces breaking contact to escape the full weight of certain if delayed U.S. artillery and air responses.[18] By retaining the initiative, the communist forces essentially determined when and where they would fight and under what circumstances combat would take place. This in turn allowed them to control their own casualties and therefore avoid facing any "cross-over point." For example, when confronted with unexpectedly high casualties incurred during the Tet Offensive of 1968, the communists essentially retired to the jungle for the next couple of years and substituted artillery and rocket attacks for close-quarters combat.

Attrition failed also because of a "body count" mentality that miscounted both the living and dead enemy. The MACV definition of the communist order of battle (OB) excluded Viet Cong irregular forces, which numbered an estimated 300,000 on the eve of the Tet Offensive and performed indispensable support functions for North Vietnamese army and main force Viet Cong units. Moreover, pressure from on high for ever larger body counts encouraged commanders in the field to include all unarmed civilian dead in the count.[19] "The Saigon brass in their plush villas didn't believe that a VC youth of twelve who mined jungle paths and scouted for main force troops, or a fifty-year-old woman who tended VC wounded, should be counted as support troops," wrote combat veteran and later *Newsweek* commentator David Hackworth. "They didn't understand they were as much a part of the VC army as any of the half-dozen aides who kept Westmoreland's villa operating efficiently. The paradox was that though the generals insisted those non-regulars be arbitrarily dropped from the OB, when killed, they were included in the body count."[20]

## Manpower Misuse

Westmoreland's constant demands for more troops were in no small measure a function of the poor use he made of the ones he was given. The MACV employed its manpower in a way that greatly compromised its potential productivity, and it did so in the face of an enemy that squeezed the maximum combat power out of its forces in South Vietnam. The MACV's chosen personnel rotation policies and logistical improvidence seriously compromised potential U.S. military effectiveness in Vietnam by severely constraining the number of troops actually available for combat operations and by imperiling the quality of the tactical performance of those in combat.

President Lyndon Johnson's unprecedented refusal to mobilize reserve forces had already propelled the military toward a manpower crisis once the American buildup in Vietnam began in earnest, but Westmoreland made the crunch much worse than it otherwise would have been. Indeed, as military analyst Andrew Krepinevich correctly observed, "the Army in Vietnam instituted a personnel policy about as detrimental [to the war effort] as if it had set out with the worst intentions in mind."[21] By establishing a one-year tour of duty for enlisted men and even shorter tours for officers (six months for battalion commanders, three months for company commanders), Westmoreland gravely compromised small-unit cohesion in combat. The constant rotation of officers and men in and out of Vietnam bred units of what were essentially strangers, men unfamiliar with and often distrustful of their comrades in arms. Abbreviated tours of duty also compromised the ability of officers and men alike to accumulate and sustain knowledge of and skill in fighting the peculiar war in which Americans found themselves in Vietnam. "In and out like clockwork . . . just long enough to figure out what they didn't know," Hackworth noted.[22]

Westmoreland claims he instituted the short tours of duty because he believed the war would be long and therefore potentially injurious to troop morale and health (the threat of disease).[23] But this claim does not jibe with the unprecedented haste with which the MACV rotated officers in and out of command slots, a practice that was in fact aimed at satisfying the imperatives of an army in which careerism had trumped professional effectiveness on the battlefield.[24] Vietnam veterans Harold Moore and Joseph Galloway properly condemned the six-month limit on battalion and brigade command as pure "ticket punching: A career officer had to have troop command for promotion. The six-month tour meant that twice as many officers got that important punch in. The soldiers paid the price."[25]

Westmoreland's concern for troop morale and his reliance on massive firepower to "attrit" the enemy also fostered extraordinarily high ratios of support to combat troops, which further undermined the potential military productivity of the half-million troops he was ultimately granted to fight the war. To sustain the kind of capital-intensive war Westmoreland waged in so remote and logistically primitive country as South Vietnam in 1965, the MACV had to make an enormous investment in infrastructure and in the maintenance and servicing of U.S. combat forces. The result was a bloated military enterprise in which, by 1968, no more than 80,000—or 15 percent—of the 536,000 U.S. military personnel in Vietnam were actually available for sustained ground combat operations[26]; indeed, less than 10 percent of the total of 2.8 million Americans who served in what was first and foremost an infantry war served in line infantry units.[27] Given the high fat content of U.S. forces and the relative low tail-to-teeth ratio of the communist side, the MACV probably was outnumbered in effective fighting soldiers.

To be sure, expeditionary conventional military enterprises display high ratios of support to combat troops. In Vietnam, the United States built from scratch seven jet-capable and seventy-five smaller airfields, six deep water ports, twenty-six hospitals, and twenty-four permanent base facilities, many of them essentially small cities.[28] But military expeditions do not mandate the dumping of "stacks of paper plates, hot meals, ice cream, and mountains of beer and soft drinks in the forward areas" and an "insistence upon large and luxurious base camps with snack shops and swimming pools," all of which "greatly eroded the soldier's willingness to forgo such comforts in extended field operations."[29] The huge base at Long Binh occupied twenty-five square miles and boasted movie theaters, slot machines, steam baths, restaurant complexes, lawns, and flower beds; it also employed 20,000 Vietnamese, some of whom were undoubtedly communist agents.[30] "Never in any war has any force been so munificently pampered."[31] To be sure, many support personnel away from the big camps lived in relatively rugged conditions out in the countryside. But most lived in the relative safety and comfort of the big camps.

The dissipation of U.S. manpower in Vietnam stood in stark contrast to the far leaner communist forces, which relied more on stealth and cunning than firepower and upon hundreds of thousands of peasant coolies to perform logistical tasks.[32] Communist forces lived in the field, as had U.S. forces in World War II and Korea. Bruce Palmer Jr. one of Westmoreland's deputies, believed the base-camp idea was even worse than the one-year tour for enlisted men: "The manpower it soaked up was appalling, not to mention the waste of material resources and the handicap of having to defend and take care of these albatrosses."[33]

## Mistaken Confidence in Air Power

The massive U.S. aerial bombardment of North Vietnam and the Ho Chi Minh Trail failed to coerce Hanoi into ceasing its support of communist forces in the South. Nor did it destroy North Vietnam's capacity to wage war or decisively interrupt the flow of communist manpower and matériel from North Vietnam via Laos into South Vietnam. Despite the instructive experience of World War II and the Korean War, to say nothing of war-game outcomes and intelligence assessment conclusions, believers in "victory through air power" persistently refused throughout the war to recognize the very limited utility of air power in Indochina's distinctive political and military setting. The result was an excessive investment in air operations at the expense of potentially more effective military operations. The bombing of North Vietnam also played into Hanoi's political hand by strengthening the communist regime at home and its cause in Vietnam abroad.

As a fiercely nationalistic totalitarian state prepared to sacrifice entire generations of its sons to achieve Vietnam's reunification, North Vietnam was a very poor candidate for coercion through bombing. This should have been no surprise. The *United States Strategic Bombing Survey (European War)* of 1945 remarked upon the German people's "surprising resistance to the terror and hardships of repeated air attack" and concluded that "The power of a police state over its people cannot be underestimated."[34] Additionally, two JCS war games, SIGMA I and SIGMA II, played in April and September of 1964, concluded not only that bombing was unlikely to coerce Hanoi into stopping its support for revolution in the South but also that it would stiffen Hanoi's resolve while at the same time steadily erode U.S. public support for the war.[35] Subsequent Central Intelligence Agency assessments reached similar conclusions, as did two 1967 studies conducted for the Office of the Secretary of Defense by the Institute for Defense Analyses.[36]

Totalitarian regimes have shown themselves to be remarkably resistant to overthrow or intimidation via external military action short of the outright physical destruction of their armed forces or occupation of their territory. If Hanoi did have a breaking point during the war, it probably was reachable only through an invasion of North Vietnam or perhaps a bombing campaign aimed at the destruction of that country's agriculture or people themselves. Neither of these options, however, was ever seriously considered; they could not pass the tests of political and moral acceptability in a war that for the United States, if not for North Vietnam, was limited in terms of both political objectives pursued and military means employed.

As a preindustrial state, moreover, North Vietnam had little in the way of economic or military infrastructure targets whose destruction might cripple its capacity to make war. North Vietnam did have a military-industrial base, but it was located in the Soviet Union, China, Czechoslovakia, and East Germany; and while the United States could—and ultimately did—close down North Vietnam's main port, effective blockage of the overland flow of supplies into North Vietnam through China was impossible. The theory of strategic bombing as an autonomous war-winner presupposed like industrial adversaries presenting a large array of detectable and attackable economic and conventional military targets essential to a capacity to sustain combat.

The U.S. air war against the Ho Chi Minh Trail proved equally indecisive. Communist movement down the trail's myriad and superbly concealed avenues was difficult to detect, and even when enemy units were detected they were not easy to target and destroy, especially in bad weather, of which there was plenty. Even an invasion and occupation of southern Laos would have done nothing "to prevent Hanoi from simply shifting its trail activity farther West, into Thailand, much as the original Ho Chi Minh Trail had bypassed the Demilitarized Zone of Vietnam."[37] Westmoreland could not stop the movement of communist forces and supplies inside South Vietnam itself, amid U.S. troop concentrations. Then, too, at least until the Tet Offensive of 1968, the war in Vietnam remained largely a self-sustaining insurgency conducted by inhabitants of South Vietnam relying mostly on local logistical support. Although logistical dependence on North Vietnam steadily increased in the face of rising U.S. firepower - inflicted losses in men and matériel, it never reached the point where it could be effectively stanched by U.S. air attack. Like Chinese infantry in Korea, Viet Cong and even People's Army of Vietnam (PAVN) units were materially very austere by American standards. Communist forces in the South, by one estimate, never exceeded a dependence on food, fuel, and ammunition, of more than 380 tons a day—in contrast to the 750 to 2,000 tons a day a single U.S. infantry division consumed.[38] The bombing of North Vietnam, concluded one air force analyst, failed for two reasons: "First, in their pride American civilian and military planners did not, probably could not, imagine that North Vietnam could endure aerial attacks. Second, military leaders failed to develop and propose a strategy appropriate to the war at hand. Bombing strategic targets in the North and the unconventional war going on in the South had little direct interconnection."[39]

The evidence suggests that if anything bombing's unintended consequences played a greater role in the war's outcome than did its intended consequences. World War II provided ample testimony that bombing someone else's homeland tends to anger both its inhabitants and its government, affording the latter an increased claim on the former's willingness to sacrifice. The inspirational force of Churchill's call for "blood, toil, tears, and sweat" in May 1940 was immeasurably enhanced by nightly German bombing attacks on London and other British cities. Similarly, the U.S. bombing of North Vietnam made it easier for Hanoi's communist leaders to place the entire country on a wartime footing. The legendary Edward Lansdale observed that the very "presence of U.S. aircraft over North Vietnam gave visible veracity to the Politburo's claims that it was leading the people of

Vietnam in a struggle against an invading foreign power."[40] *The Pentagon Papers* narrative concludes that the "bombing clearly strengthened popular support of the regime by engendering patriotic and nationalistic enthusiasm to resist the attacks" and also "strengthened . . . Hanoi's political relations with its allies."[41] The bombing of the North also served to justify Hanoi's dispatch of more and more troops to the South and provided a major source of propaganda-assisted, David-versus-Goliath sympathy for the regime both inside the United States and abroad. According to journalist Harrison Salisbury in 1967: "[T]aking all factors into consideration—the groundswell of world opinion against the United States, the intense antagonisms the bombing had produced within the United States, the remarkable welding together of the North Vietnamese people under the impact of the bombs, the air program had been counterproductive. It had cost us far more than we had originally estimated (or even now would admit). It had not produced military, political or psychological results to justify its continuance."[42] On the contrary, observed nuclear war theorist Herman Kahn in 1968, the bombing helped create "empathy and support for the heroic little man in black pajamas and antagonism toward the white man in the B-52.[43]

## The Wrong Style of Warfare

The failure of the air war against North Vietnam to break Hanoi's will or capacity to fight[44] reflected a larger—if unavoidable—American military failure in Indochina. Put simply, the American style of warfare, although extremely destructive, was ineffective in Indochina compared to the style of warfare practiced by the Vietnamese communists.[45] It was hardly to be expected that the United States would practice a style of warfare foreign to its culture and historical experience, but that culture and experience were themselves alien to the Indochinese political-military setting.

The conventional warfare practiced by the United States in the 1960s was common within the industrialized world and rooted in the European military tradition. It primary goals are to seize enemy territory, to destroy enemy forces and war-making capacity, or both; success, accordingly, is measured in terms of territory taken, enemy forces destroyed or disabled, and war production capacity demolished. Conventional warfare is conducted on behalf of political objectives but makes little attempt to sway popular political loyalties in enemy or contested territory; it is a purely military undertaking dominated by operational considerations. Conventional warfare's principal means of victory are a bold maneuver of some kind that attempts to surprise the enemy into defeat or ineffectiveness or, more often, the application of massive firepower against enemy forces in the field and (since the emergence of air power) against military industrial targets in the enemy's homeland.

Conventional warfare's firepower/attrition variant plays to American material and technological superiority and offers a means of substituting machines for American blood; yet it is vitally dependent on the presence of detectable and destroyable enemy targets whose elimination will render the enemy defenseless or otherwise eager to terminate hostilities. Nazi Germany and Imperial Japan (and their forces in the field), and massed Chinese infantry in Korea, and later, Iraq armor in the desert, all proved highly suitable enemies for firepower/attrition.

But the enemy in Indochina did not. Revolutionary warfare as practiced by the Vietnamese communists was a weapon for the seizure of political power from a militarily superior foe; it was designed for insurgent groups in preindustrial states seeking to overthrow foreign rule or neocolonial governments. Vietnamese revolutionary war, which drew heavily on Chinese communist theory and practice, combined mass political mobilization of the peasantry and a reliance on guerrilla tactics that deprived a firepower superior conventional enemy decisive targets to shoot at. Indeed, the Vietnamese communists sought with considerable success to turn the MACV's excessive use of firepower in the South to their advantage. The U.S. destruction of much of the South Vietnamese countryside via air attack, free fire zones, and defoliation strengthened the communists' appeal to nationalism in South Vietnam. It also created millions of refugees whose political allegiance to the Saigon regime on whose behalf this destruction was being visited was hardly enhanced by their ordeal.

The keys to revolutionary war were elusiveness and protraction. The presence of a firepower-superior enemy dictated refusal to present decisive targets, which in turn dictated avoidance of pitched battles, heavy reliance on camouflage and night operations, hit-and-run attacks, and the use of terrain and populations as means of concealment. The fact that the communist forces sometimes violated these tactics to their great loss simply underscores their effectiveness. Nor does the communists' turn to primary reliance on conventional military operations in the early 1970s invalidate the utility of revolutionary war as a weapon against the Americans. Communist doctrine anticipated such operations in the final stages of revolutionary war. Moreover, the purpose of preconventional military operations was to break the enemy's will through a protraction of hostilities, which is exactly what the communists succeeded in doing during the three years of war culminating in the Tet Offensive.

Protraction essentially pitted time against American matériel superiority. Protraction played, as it had against the French in the First Indochina War, to the inherent impatience of Western democracies with costly and seemingly interminable wars waged on behalf of interests ultimately regarded as less compelling than those at stake for Vietnamese communism. As former

President Nixon acknowledged in his own book on the Vietnam War, "When a President sends American troops to war, a hidden political timer starts to run. He has a finite period of time to win the war before the people grow weary of it."[46] For the communists, there was no alternative to protraction because a swift victory against American military power was impossible. Protraction was thus both politically and militarily imperative. And it worked.

## Moral Cowardice at the Top

It was clear during the Vietnam War and even more so since its conclusion that the Joint Chiefs of Staff and other senior military leaders disagreed with their civilian superiors on fundamental issues of war policy. The major sources of contention were the Johnson administration's refusal to mobilize the reserves, imposition of highly restrictive targeting denials and rules of engagement on the air war against North Vietnam, and denial of permission for U.S. troops to invade southern Laos. Most of the military leadership believed that these policies, individually or together, cost the United States victory in the Vietnam War.

Yet not a single member of the Joint Chiefs of Staff or senior field commander ever resigned in protest. "Not once during the war did the JCS advise the commander-in-chief or the secretary of defense that the strategy being pursued most probably would fail and that the United States would be unable to achieve its objectives," noted retired army general Bruce Palmer Jr.[47] That at least the Joint Chiefs of Staff should have resigned has been the postwar judgment of many influential officers. "Somewhere in 1967 or early 1968," argued Phillip B. Davidson, Westmoreland's chief intelligence officer, "one or more of the Chiefs should have stood up and told the president publicly that that what he was doing in Vietnam would not work, and then resigned."[48] Harry Summers Jr. believed it "was the duty and responsibility of his military advisors to warn [the president] of the likely consequences of his actions, to recommend alternatives, and, as Napoleon put it, to tender their resignations rather than be an instrument of their army's downfall."[49] Army Chief of Staff Harold K. Johnson later regretted his failure to resign: "I should have gone to see the president. I should have taken off my stars. I should have resigned. It was the worst, the most immoral decision I've ever made."[50] Chief of Naval Operations David McDonald also lamented (in retirement), "Maybe we military men were all weak. Maybe we should have stood up and pounded the table. I was part of it and I'm sort of ashamed of myself too, At times I wonder, 'why did I go along with this kind of stuff'?"[51]

Whether the Joint Chiefs should have resigned to protest war policies with which they were in fundamental disagreement is a matter of continuing debate. It is improbable that threatened or actual resignation would have moved President Johnson to mobilize the reserves, lift the ban on U.S. ground force operations in southern Laos, and permit the air force and navy to pick the targets they wanted to strike in North Vietnam. It is also improbable, even had Johnson been so moved, that an earlier and relatively unrestricted application of U.S. military power in Indochina would have produced a fundamentally different outcome of the Vietnam War, although it likely would have raised, perhaps considerably, the cost of victory for the North in both blood and time. Thus, ironically, the Joint Chiefs aided and abetted Hanoi by lacking the courage of their convictions.

## Conclusion

The primary cause of the North's victory in the Vietnam War was Hanoi's superior political will and commitment to total war against a United States whose interests in Indochina, and therefore political will, were, by contrast, limited. To achieve their objectives in Indochina, the Vietnamese communists were prepared to—and did—sacrifice 1.4 million of their own (1.1 million dead and 300,000 missing in action), or almost *twenty-five times* the toll of American dead.[52] Ho Chi Minh and Senior General Vo Nguyen Giap understood, if American civilian and military leaders did not, that a combination of patience and the ability simply to deny victory to the Americans (while killing them in sufficient numbers) over a long enough period of time was itself enough to produce victory. In the end, American political resolve to continue fighting crumbled, not because of critical military reverses (the Tet Offensive was military disaster for the communists) but rather because of American political intolerance of prolonged and bloody military stalemate. The U.S. military nonetheless could have fought in Vietnam more effectively than it did. While it could not have been expected to change its basic style of warfare, it could have fought with less internal disunity and greater professional productivity. In so doing, it probably would not have changed the Vietnam War's outcome, but it could have increased the price of victory for Hanoi.

## Notes

1. Harry G. Summers Jr., *On Strategy, A Critical Analysis of the Vietnam War* (Novato, CA: Presidio Press, 1982), 143.
2. For a detailed assessment of JCS institutional weaknesses that in part prompted passage of the 1986 Defense Reorganization Act, see *Defense Organization: The Need for Change.* Staff Report to the Committee on Armed Services, United States Senate. 99th Congress: 1st Session. S. Prt. 99–86

Washington, D.C.: U.S. Government Printing Office, October 16, 1985), 139–274. The staff report was directed by James R. Locher III, a former U.S. Army officer.

3. H. R. McMaster, *Dereliction of Duty, Lyndon Johnson, Robert McNamara, The Joint Chiefs of Staff, and the Lies That Led to Vietnam* (New York: HarperCollins, 1997), 143,144.
4. Doris Kearns, *Lyndon Johnson and the American Dream* (New York: Harper & Row, 1976), 262.
5. McMaster, *Dereliction of Duty,* 328.
6. An early, informed, and energetic account of the Marine Corps pacification effort in I Corps is found in William R. Corson, *The Betrayal* (New York: W. W. Norton and Company, 1968).
7. See Lewis Sorley, "To Change a War: General Harold K. Johnson and the PROVN Study," *Parameters* (Spring 1998): 93–109.
8. William W. Momyer, *Air Power in Three Wars* (Washington, DC: Office of History, U.S. Air Force, 1978), 95.
9. Henry Kissinger, *The White House Years* (Boston: Little, Brown and Company, 1979), 1112.
10. See Jeffrey Record, *The Wrong War, Why We Lost in Vietnam* (Annapolis, MD: U.S. Naval Institute Press, 1998), 92–96.
11. Alexander M. Haig Jr. with Charles McCarry, *Inner Circles: How America Changed the World, A Memoir* (New York: Warner Books, 1992), 126, 299.
12. General William DePuy, quoted in George C. Herring, *America's Longest War, The United States and Vietnam, 1950–1975* (New York: McGraw-Hill, 3rd ed. 1996), 168.
13. Quoted in Guenter Lewy, *America in Vietnam* (New York: Oxford University Press, 1978), 73.
14. See Lewis Sorley, *A Better War, The Unexamined Victories and Final Tragedy of America's Last Years in Vietnam* (New York: Harcourt Brace and Company, 1999), 1–16; and Douglas Kinnard, *The War Managers, American Generals Reflect on Vietnam* (New York: Da Capo Press, 1979), 34–46.
15. See Record, *The Wrong War,* 80.
16. Robert Thompson, *No Exit from Vietnam* (New York: David McKay, 1969), 60.
17. Bruce Palmer Jr., *The 25-Year War, America's Military Role in Vietnam* (Lexington: University Press of Kentucky, 1984), 43.
18. *The Pentagon Papers: The Department of Defense History of United States Decisionmaking on Vietnam,* Senator Gravel ed. (Boston: Beacon Press, 1971), Vol. 4, 458; and Shelby Stanton, *The Rise and Fall of an American Army: U.S. Ground Forces in Vietnam, 1965–1973* (Novato, CA: Presidio Press, 1985), 86.
19. See Record, *The Wrong War,* 82–85. For a detailed account of the dispute between the MACV and the intelligence community over counting the enemy in Vietnam, see Sam Adams, *War of Numbers: An Intelligence Memoir* (South Royalton, VT: Steerforth Press, 1994). Also see Kinnard, *The War Managers,* 68–75.

20. David Hackworth, introduction to Adams, *War of Numbers,* xvi.
21. Andrew F. Krepinevich, *The Army and Vietnam* (Baltimore, MD: The Johns Hopkins University Press, 1986), 205.
22. David Hackworth and Julie Sherman, *About Face, The Odyssey of an American Warrior* (New York: Simon and Schuster, 1989), 524.
23. William C. Westmoreland, *A Soldier Reports* (Garden City, NY: Doubleday, 1976), 358.
24. See Kinnard, *The War Managers,* 109–117.
25. Harold G. Moore and Joseph L. Galloway, *We Were Soldiers Once—and Young: Ia Drang, the Battle That Changed the War in Vietnam* (New York: Random House, 1992), 405.
26. Thomas C. Thayer, *War Without Fronts: The American Experience in Vietnam* (Boulder, CO: Westview Press, 1985), 94.
27. James R. Ebert, *A Life in a Year: The American Infantryman in Vietnam, 1965–1972* (Novato, CA; Presidio Press, 1993), 1.
28. Ronald H. Spector, *After Tet: The Bloodiest Year of the War* (New York: Free Press, 1993), 43.
29. Stanton, *The Rise and Fall of an American Army,* 23.
30. Ebert, *A Life in a Year,* 89.
31. Dave Richard Palmer, *Summons of the Trumpet, A History of the Vietnam War from a Military Man's Point of View* (New York: Ballantine Books, 1978), 197.
32. For discussions of the organization, training, and field operations of communist forces in Vietnam, see Douglas Pike, *Viet Cong, The Organization and Techniques of the National Liberation Front on South Vietnam* (Cambridge, MA: MIT Press, 1966); and Pike's *PAVN: People's Army of Vietnam* (New York: Da Capo Press 1986). Also see Michael Lee Lanning and Dan Cragg, *Inside the VC and the NVA, The Real Story of North Vietnam's Armed Forces* (New York: Ivy Books, 1992). For two excellent histories of the communist side of the Vietnam War, see William J. Duiker, *The Communist Road to Power in Vietnam* (Boulder, CO: Westview Press, 1981), and Duiker's *Sacred War, Nationalism and Revolution in a Divided Vietnam* (New York: McGraw-Hill, 1995).
33. Palmer, *The 25-Year War,* 69.
34. *The United States Strategic Bombing Surveys (European War) (Pacific War).* (Maxwell Air Force Base: Al Air University Press, reprinted October 1987), 39.
35. McMaster, *Dereliction of Duty,* 89–91, 155–158, and 162–164.
36. See *Pentagon Papers,* Vol. 4, 115–120 and 222–225.
37. John Prados, *The Blood Road, The Ho Chi Minh Trail and the Vietnam War* (New York: John Wiley and Sons, 1999), 376.
38. Mark Clodfelter, *The Limits of Air Power: The American Bombing of North Vietnam* (New York: Free Press, 1989), 318.
39. Earl H. Tilford Jr., *Setup: What the Air Force Did in Vietnam and Why* (Maxwell Air Force Base, AL: Air University Press, 1991), 154–155.
40. Quoted in W. Scott Thompson and Donald D. Frizell, eds., *The Lessons of Vietnam* (New York: Crane Russak and Company, 1977), 127.

41. *The Pentagon Papers,* Vol. 4, 118.
42. Harrison E. Salisbury, *Behind the Lines—Hanoi* (New York: Harper Row, 1967), 222.
43. Herman Kahn, "If Negotiations Fail," *Foreign Affairs* 46 (1968): 629.
44. Linebacker II, the massive U.S. bombing of targets in the Hanoi/Haiphong area in December 1972, has been cited by air power proponents as proof that strategic bombing, properly conducted, could have broken Hanoi's will years earlier. There is no question that Linebacker II ended North Vietnam's boycott of the Paris peace negotiations, which in turn led to Hanoi's accession to the Paris Peace Accord of January 1973. But the critical U.S. concession—namely, tacit acceptance of a continued North Vietnamese military presence in Vietnam—that made the accord simply a vehicle for a decent interval separating the U.S. withdrawal from South Vietnam and the North's eventual takeover of that country had already been made months before Linebacker II. It is difficult to argue that Hanoi had to be bombed into signing an agreement which guaranteed an ultimate if delayed communist victory in the South and which South Vietnamese President Nguyen Van Thieu himself rightly understood to be Saigon's ultimate death warrant. In fact, Thieu was Linebacker II's real target. Thieu was refusing to accept the terms of the impending Paris Accord, and Linebacker II was aimed at reassuring him that the United States would use its air power to keep the North Vietnamese from violating the accord's cease-fire provisions. See Stephen E. Ambrose, "The Christmas Bombing," in Calvin L. Christman, ed., *America at War: An Anthology of Articles from MHQ, the Quarterly Journal of Military History* (Annapolis, MD: U.S. Naval Institute Press, 1995); George C. Herring, *America's Longest War, The United States and Vietnam, 1950–1975.* 3rd ed. (New York: McGraw-Hill, 1996), 276–283; and Tilford, *Setup,* 248–265.
45. See Record, *The Wrong War,* 64–70.
46. Richard Nixon, *No More Vietnams* (New York: Avon Books, 1986), 88.
47. Palmer Jr., *The 25-Year War,* 46.
48. Phillip B. Davidson, *Vietnam at War: The History, 1946–1975* (Novato, CA: Presidio Press, 1988), 462–463.
49. Summers, *On Strategy,* 121.
50. Quoted in Mark Perry, *Four Stars: The Inside Story of the Forty-Year Battle between the Joint Chiefs of Staff and America's Civilian Leaders* (Boston: Houghton Mifflin, 1989), 152. Se also Lewis Sorley, *Honorable Warrior, General Harold K. Johnson and the Ethics of Command* (Lawrence: University Press of Kansas, 1998), 302–304.
51. Quoted in McMaster, *Dereliction of Duty,* 262.
52. Record, *The Wrong War,* 36–37.

CHAPTER FIVE

# IMPATIENCE, ILLUSION, AND ASYMMETRY

## Intelligence in Vietnam

JOHN PRADOS

With reams of government reports, position papers, policy reviews, and streams of daily reporting, not to mention public and private commentaries and studies by institutes and scholars, the Vietnam conflict at the time was held to be the most analyzed war in American history. An important fraction of the studies and statistics consisted of intelligence estimates and reports. In addition, the intelligence available by the time of the Vietnam War came as the product, on the American side, of a highly evolved and sophisticated system for developing knowledge of an adversary's secrets. U.S. intelligence played an important role in the course of the war. South Vietnamese intelligence, arrayed alongside that of the Americans, had a closer cultural perspective on the arena of conflict and could be expected to contribute mightily as well. Yet expectations about outcomes were to be dashed, and North Vietnamese and Viet Cong spies trumped the American effort much as Hanoi triumphed over Saigon on the field of battle. This chapter examines the contributions of intelligence to the war effort.

On the road to defeat in Indochina, the United States and its allies sought in every way to avoid that outcome. Intelligence figured prominently in many tactical and strategic plans and in every battle of the conflict. A chronological narrative of actions and activities could easily take up a full volume, much more than the space available here. As an alternative, I propose to make a series of general points about the intelligence war for

Indochina. The aim is to approach the subject both at a high level of generality and with revealing detail.

The intelligence struggle was complicated by the type of warfare being waged in Southeast Asia. At times the conflict was a purely guerrilla war; at times it became conventional warfare. Observers still debate the instants when the war ascended to each of the successive stages of conflict, and indeed a cogent case also can be made that the level of operations on the continuum from insurgency to conventional warfare varied at any given moment in different places in Indochina, and varied from moment to moment at a given place. It is also true that developments in the war were not all in one direction; that is, the progress of the Vietnam war was less a simple march to victory by Hanoi than an ebb and flow of successes and failures, with Viet Cong and North Vietnamese forces in some locales and times being driven from conventional warfare back to a guerrilla existence, in others steadily succeeding at varied rates, sometimes stagnating for intervals before spurts of progress, and in some places going almost unchallenged. The point is that the needs of intelligence vary with the type and scale of warfare, a fact that creates huge headaches if the scale of warfare is changing in time and by place.

In conventional warfare, with adversary attacks and troop movements of major concern, the problem is tracking units and their strengths and intentions. Contributing to this is knowledge of the adversary's war production and supply lines. Both sides did a fairly good job collecting this type of intelligence. For insurgency warfare, on the other hand, adversary political and psychological initiatives are of primary importance and raw military strength figures of much less value. Here there remained a marked disparity between the intelligence capabilities of the two sides. If the type of warfare is then mixed up and down the scale of intensity across a series of places, the intelligence problem becomes complex indeed.

The United States possessed sophisticated intelligence resources in South Vietnam, with coverage throughout Indochina, supplemented by bases in Thailand and Okinawa, on aircraft carriers off the Vietnamese coast, and from satellites and high-altitude reconnaissance aircraft. Photographic reconnaissance units were in place in the theater beginning in 1961. The National Security Agency (NSA), the premier U.S. communications intelligence organization, sent its first detachment to South Vietnam in the spring of that year. Within the Military Assistance Command, Vietnam (MACV) and its antecedent advisory group, intelligence staff sections existed to analyze the information gathered. In Washington, substantial analytical capacity also resided within the Central Intelligence Agency (CIA); the Defense Intelligence Agency (DIA); the service intelligence branches, particularly Army G-2; and among staff specialists at the White House. The

South Vietnamese military had an intelligence section, and Saigon's Joint General Staff had another. Beginning in 1967 with the formation of the Combined Intelligence Center Vietnam (CICV), there would be a multinational analytical unit including both Americans and South Vietnamese. In short, there would be a wealth of raw data and analytical capability.[1]

During the early years of the Vietnam War particularly, however, the conflict was a guerrilla insurgency. In guerrilla warfare the important intelligence is less about operations than about organization and political initiatives. The guerrillas' advantages derived from their mass movement and the parallel hierarchy they built in competition with that of the Saigon government. The highly technical collection capabilities of the Americans and South Vietnamese had little capacity to gain information about guerrilla activities in the villages. Throughout the war the Americans and South Vietnamese continued to have trouble developing sources such as agents within the National Liberation Front (NLF) infrastructure who could provide reliable information on the inner workings of the enemy. In contrast, the NLF had a multiplicity of sources within the Saigon government and armed forces and with Vietnamese civilians who furnished goods and services to the American military. As a rough measure, U.S.-South Vietnamese penetrations of the NLF numbered in the hundreds and few of the agents were senior officials, while NLF and Hanoi penetrations of the Saigon side numbered in the tens of thousands. The disparity in resulting intelligence is palpable.

In addition, with its high-technology intelligence-gathering means, the United States remained preoccupied with those things that could be measured and counted. But such observables as Hanoi's stocks of guns, tanks, and planes only began to increase as the guerrilla forces entered the stage of conventional warfare; in other words, as Hanoi became successful, its military could keep forces in the field with impunity, and then the Americans could see them. Put another way, American intelligence could operate within its most efficient parameters only as American power failed to defeat the insurgency.

Hanoi's intelligence capabilities proved both less and more formidable than those of the Saigon side. The Central Research Agency, formed in 1957 as part of the Ministry of Defense, had an internal intelligence office that operated against South Vietnam and a foreign one active in other countries. The agency's Combat Intelligence Office did standard military spy work. At its greatest extent this agency was about the size of the U.S.-South Vietnamese CICV, about 1,200 people. Intelligence sections were attached to lower-echelon headquarters and field units in the same fashion as G-2 in the U.S. Army. The Central Research Agency also had a specialized battalion, a sort of intelligence commando unit, descended from Battalion 426, the "*trinh sat,*" special forces of the French war. Because the Vietnam People's Army increasingly emphasized sappers as commando units in the American War in Vietnam, few knew of the *trinh sat.*

Where the Central Research Agency excelled was in its agent networks. A *phai vien*, or field intelligence officer, who had two or more years' professional training in the North, controlled a cluster of three to five agent networks. The *phai khien*, a principal agent, controlled the individual networks. Sources were called *co cans*. As of 1971, after more than a decade and a half of intense counterintelligence work by the Saigon apparatus and three years of the anti-infrastructure Phoenix program (of which, more presently), the MACV Command History could still conclude that Hanoi's service "was capable of continuing high-level penetration operations, collecting tactical intelligence as a secondary mission," providing training, and starting a fresh emphasis on stay-behind operations to spy in Saigon-held areas.[2]

NLF capabilities represented a huge additional increment to Hanoi's overall intelligence effort. These were run by three elements of the elusive Central Office for South Vietnam (COSVN): the B-22 section for strategic intelligence, the B-2 section for military intelligence, and a Technical Reconnaissance Office. Directly descended from Hanoi's Central Research Agency, COSVN's B-22 used identical methods and was created in the summer of 1968 from the merger of fifteen different espionage cells of both the Hanoi agency and the NLF's Military Intelligence Bureau. Its agents, known in 1971, included a member of the Chamber of Deputies in Saigon and an advisor to President Thieu. Covert agents within the Saigon government and armed forces in fact included many more senior officials, as was revealed by events during the last phase of the war in 1975. A CIA analysis in 1970 estimated that the total of Hanoi and NLF agents among Saigon's bureaucracy and army could be as high as 30,000.[3]

The COSVN Technical Reconnaissance Office did signals intelligence, a responsibility it shared with the Radio Intercept Research Section in Hanoi. The Cryptographic Bureau of the People's Army General Staff handled codes and code-breaking. These technological services were dwarfed by U.S. and South Vietnamese abilities in these areas, but given the type of warfare in Vietnam, the asymmetries favored Hanoi and the Liberation Front. Their agent networks furnished invaluable and massive amounts of intelligence across the spectrum of conflict. The U.S. advantages in technical capabilities became most productive only as Saigon began to slide down the slope toward defeat.

The North Vietnamese and Liberation Front had a concept of "Struggle," a slow, steady process of warfare that eventually would lead to progress. The United States, in contrast, would be hampered by the delusion that there was some key to winning the war, some panacea promising victory, a formula that guaranteed success. Again and again, some idea or technique would be attempted as a model program and show promise but, when applied on a national level, did not generate the anticipated results. One example is the strategic hamlet program in the early 1960s, which enjoyed some success but became corrupted when extended to the national level. On the intelligence side, the "census grievance" program that began in 1966–1967 garnered good information about the Liberation Front infrastructure in villages when it was tried at that level in a few provinces. Converted to a national-level "revolutionary development" program, the teams responsible were again subjects of corruption. Also, their numbers were diluted by diversion to security projects and not accorded the resources to follow up initial efforts. The intelligence generated went into files at higher headquarters, where it contributed to sterile "orders of battle" but was rarely followed up operationally.[4]

A prime example of these failings would be the Phoenix program carried out from 1968 to 1973. Phoenix began as early as 1967 as a CIA initiative aimed directly at the Viet Cong infrastructure (VCI). It was prefigured by another CIA initiative (so-called Counter-Terror Teams), which successfully reduced the VCI when first tried in one province (Quang Ngai in 1964–1965). This effort resulted in a national program for Provincial Reconnaissance Units (PRUs) that continued under CIA control until 1969 and were then under U.S. (and CIA at the regional level) advice. Under the Phoenix concept, the PRUs were to utilize detailed local intelligence to neutralize the VCI, by arresting National Liberation Front cadres and supporters, engaging them in firefights as necessary, kidnapping where possible, and otherwise doing whatever had to be done to knock out the VCI. Backing the PRUs would be Saigon's police and security services, regional and popular forces, and American strike teams of Navy SEALs and other elite commandos. But the Phoenix target folders were full of data that was old or otherwise inaccurate. The folders often mentioned only the aliases of NLF officials, included merely the enemies of Saigon officials, the names of ordinary citizens whose removal would benefit Saigon officials or the government, or were empty altogether.[5]

A controversy developed in 2001 concerning the South Vietnamese villagers killed during a SEAL raid on Thanh Phong hamlet in the Mekong Delta in February 1969. The issue reverberated in American politics because the team in the incident had been led by Robert Kerrey, a man who subsequently attained prominence as a U.S. senator and possible presidential candidate.[6] The importance of Thanh Phong in this discussion of intelligence, however, lies in the way it demonstrates the weaknesses of the information that underlaid so many Phoenix operations. The NLF officials who were the targets here met sooner than the SEALs anticipated, in a different hut, in some other place, or perhaps not at all. The margin between a successful raid and a military atrocity was exceedingly thin, and this is true regardless of one's view of whether Kerrey's SEALs thought they were shooting at enemy guerrillas or unarmed civilians.

There were real Viet Cong, of course, and intelligence regarding Liberation Front activities improved after 1970, when pacification managers accepted a "green book" (for the color of its cover) with data correlating names and aliases. But the situation did not improve much until the pacification program began a systematic effort to weed out faulty files and changed incentives so that they did not value the lowest grades of supposed neutralizations. Even then the instances of first-rate intelligence work, like that of Orin Deforest in the Saigon area (III Corps), were far outnumbered by those in which work continued to be haphazard. Phoenix data show that in 1969, among a total of 19,534 neutralizations, fewer than 150 were of senior Liberation Front cadres. Of these, only 23 were from COSVN, and just *1* cadre who had been specifically targeted and who was from the policymaking inner sanctum of the NLF current affairs committee was eliminated. The neutralization data for 1970 shows major improvement (812 senior cadres, of whom 257 were region or subregion officials, and 17 were from COSVN) but still represented a small fraction of the Viet Cong infrastructure, which the CIA estimated at over 65,000. Achieving these results required an overall level of 22,341 neutralizations.[7]

The annual reports of the Civil Operations and Rural (formerly Revolutionary) Development Support organization (the managers of Phoenix) were obliged to conclude that the Liberation Front could readily replace cadres at such levels of loss. The 1970 report cites evidence that the NLF worried privately about the Phoenix effort and had made disrupting it a priority of its own. Against this improvement, however, one must weigh the political cost of a system of arbitrary neutralizations that swept away many innocents for each apprehended Viet Cong. In South Vietnam, a land at war, these methods caused distress, but in the United States there was rapidly increasing moral revulsion to the excesses of the program. Congress investigated Phoenix in 1971, and the United States ended its open involvement with the program that same year. The program continued under the Saigon government and continued to be arbitrary. In this case a program that had shown promise when implemented on a small scale in one place, when taken to the level of a nationwide panacea, ultimately did harm to the political consensus underpinning the entire U.S. war effort in South Vietnam.

Cultural factors also impinged on the possibilities for success for U.S. intelligence in Vietnam. These factors affected even routine military operations, but two are worth mention in the special context of intelligence. The first is the American refusal to learn from the French, who fought their own war in Vietnam from 1946 to 1954. The second is American denigration of the Vietnamese. There are subsets of these phenomena, and other cultural factors that apply as well, but these two factors should not be overlooked.

Having fought their own war under similar conditions in the same country, the French evolved many of the same solutions that the United States would later come to employ. As France was a military ally of the United States and with American observers in place in French Indochina, Washington had ample opportunity to avail itself of these lessons. Indeed, following the Geneva agreements of 1954, as the French were winding down their Indochina expeditionary corps, their high command actually compiled a three-volume study of lessons learned form their defeat in Indochina. Copies of this study were given to the United States. On the argument that the French war had been a colonial war, that the French had been mistaken in everything they did, and that the United States would never repeat French errors or fight the way the French had, Americans went out of their way to pay no attention to this prior experience.

To take just one example, the French had devised a system of mobile operational administrative groups (GAMOs, by their French initials) to cope with the difficult question of identifying and sequestering guerrilla cadres in villages. The GAMOs operated by entering a village and cordoning it off, then systematically requiring all persons present to identify themselves, checking these identifications against their intelligence files and other data. Americans naturally faced the same problem in their war and found its solution exceedingly difficult. Strategic hamlets were compromised because the VCI moved into the new villages along with the innocent peasants; other pacification initiatives also foundered this way. The concept of census grievance teams first deployed in 1966 was not very different from the GAMOs, except that the U.S.-designed teams lacked the vital security protection elements the French had developed. It is instructive that the census grievance teams and the revolutionary development teams that succeeded them both found themselves increasingly diverted into security activities rather than their primary mission of identifying the enemy.[8]

Cultural differences also inhibited American intelligence learning from the South Vietnamese. Lacking the number of high-technology intelligence collectors available to the Americans, the South Vietnamese were seen by MACV intelligence authorities as useful contributors to American analyses but were not thought capable of producing significant insights on their own. Not even the creation of the joint CICV organization could break down this barrier. Yet Vietnamese society, which was relatively closed, remained much more transparent to Vietnamese than to Americans. This was especially true for the elites—former South Vietnamese General Nguyen Khanh once said that the elite were drawn from only thirteen extended families, the sons of which had known each other from youth, had gone to the same schools together, had married into the same families, and so on. The elite provided leadership for both sides in the war. In effect, given the style of warfare, both

Vietnamese sides were better equipped for intelligence work than was the United States.[9]

An example of this cultural dimension as it favored Hanoi would be the CIA's Project Tiger, followed by the military's Operation Footboy, both of which involved infiltration missions into the North between 1961 and 1968.[10] Hanoi became aware of the initiative from the first foray, compromised the second seaborne mission, and then penetrated the operation so thoroughly that few infiltrators escaped death or capture. One example on the South Vietnamese side would be Saigon's detection in 1967 of secret and very closely held contacts between the U.S. Embassy and the National Liberation Front for possible direct negotiations. Another example would be the Tet Offensive of 1968, where South Vietnamese officers at CICV knew of and expected the attacks throughout the South that Americans did not believe would occur. South Vietnamese police took precautionary measures due to their knowledge, while those RVN policemen supposed to guard the U.S. Embassy in Saigon went absent just before the attack. The Vietnamese knew better than Americans what was going on.[11] Many of the American military policemen lost in Saigon the night the offensive began were killed because they lacked the knowledge possessed by their Vietnamese counterparts. Two related factors that increased the difficulty for Americans who sought to optimize intelligence and produce the most accurate estimates on Vietnam were the emphasis the intelligence community put on keeping up a constant stream of reporting and the perception that intelligence reporting had political meaning.

The pressure for a constant stream of reporting was a pernicious factor that affected both material from the field and finished intelligence, that is, reasoned memoranda and estimates prepared by analysts based on the field reports. Washington developed an insatiable demand for "the latest" on Vietnam. A report on Vietnam, a statistic, remained authoritative only until the arrival of another, perhaps more favorable or more recent. If a military service or intelligence organization feared the implications of some analysis, statistics, or information, the onus was on it to produce a competing product with an alternative view. Thus the system fed upon itself. The constant striving for new ways to look at Vietnam meant increasing the frantic pace that much more as well as opening new fronts in the battle of the memoranda. As the war extended in time and space, the competition only became more frantic. Before the end of 1965, in an effort to reduce the bickering on one facet of the war, Secretary of Defense Robert S. McNamara asked the Central Intelligence Agency and the Defense Intelligence Agency to compile joint periodic reports on the effects of bombing North Vietnam. In 1966, to consolidate intelligence work at the CIA, its director created an office of the Special Assistant for Vietnam Affairs. Such initiatives were helpful but the results were fragmentary and the battle of the memos went on.

At the same time, the CIA judged the value of its clandestine service operators by the number and quality of their cables from the field. With the "TDCS," or telegraphic dissemination communication system, the production of cable reports became a staple of CIA work and an object of admiration or scorn to National Security Council staffers, depending on their opinions of the quality of CIA intelligence. But the pressure for reporting made the incentive the quantity of cables. Indeed, a recent biography of CIA Saigon station chief Theodore Shackley, who led the CIA in Vietnam from December 1968 to January 1972, observes that Shackley preferred his officers to break down their reports so as to generate more cables from a given amount of information. While that may be an exaggeration, it is certainly true that an incentive existed for this kind of activity.[12]

The evils of the breakneck pace of reporting combined with a second factor, a sense in both Washington and Saigon of the political importance of the intelligence. Joint CIA/DIA evaluations of the air war have been mentioned, but the dispute over the aerial campaign attained a true political height in the summer of 1967, when the Senate Armed Services Committee held hearings on the matter. McNamara, generally reliant on the CIA, and the Joint Chiefs of Staff, who relied on DIA and air force assessments, openly split on the potential benefits of bombing North Vietnam.[13]

An equally virulent intelligence dispute concerned the "order of battle," the U.S. assessments of the exact identities of enemy units and their numbers on the battlefield. A CIA analyst in 1966 developed information indicating that Liberation Front guerrilla strengths were significantly greater than those carried in the agency's enemy order of battle, an estimate periodically revised to stay current. By early 1967 the CIA sought MACV's concurrence on a revised set of figures. Meanwhile the Joint Chiefs of Staff had informed MACV that upward revision of numbers of NLF attacks in secret records "would, literally, blow the lid off Washington," and similar changes in the order of battle could by extension do the same thing. As a result, military intelligence dug in its heels during the preparation of a special national intelligence estimate on the Vietnam situation as well as at a series of conferences in Washington, Honolulu, and Saigon. After intervention at the highest levels of CIA, the agency went along with lower estimates.[14]

This dispute was much more than an argument over some arcane technical matter. When the North Vietnamese and Liberation Front forces attacked throughout South Vietnam in the Tet Offensive of 1968, failure to accurately assess the number of guerrillas and the VCI infrastructure contributed to the U.S. surprise. In addition, MACV claimed to have inflicted massive losses during Tet, losses that would have been crippling had the NLF forces been at the lower strength in which the military believed. At the higher level the losses were serious but not devastating. The continued activity in the field of National Liberation Front forces after Tet demonstrated the falsehood of the military intelligence statistics.[15]

Arguments about how strong the National Liberation Front really was also illustrate another intelligence problem in Vietnam—the difficulty of collecting information. This has already been alluded to in comments regarding high-technology intelligence gathering. The guerrilla strength dispute actually hinged on captured documents, the old-fashioned kind of intelligence. High-technology spying, with wiretaps, radio interception, aerial photos, electronic sensors, and the like, had a certain applicability to North Vietnamese regular forces, but the difficulty was and remained access. Where the United States had ready access to was actually the *South* Vietnamese. Spying on the U.S. ally not only was easier but seemed justified because Saigon constantly provided the United States with incomplete or inaccurate information, things Washington wanted to hear but that were not necessarily what it needed to know. It is not accidental that the offices of both South Vietnamese President Nguyen Van Thieu and Vice President Nguyen Cao Ky were bugged. The CIA also developed sources in the offices of both Ky and South Vietnamese Prime Minister Tran Thien Khiem. Washington also enlisted former CIA operative Edward G. Lansdale, who had friendly relationships with many South Vietnamese, as a sounding board for his friends who could then report the information derived about Vietnamese political maneuvers to superiors in Washington. The American advisory structure in South Vietnam, with U.S. counterparts at every level of government and military, also produced masses of intelligence. By contrast, the CIA never achieved a penetration of Hanoi's Politburo, and the highest-level agent known to have been recruited (but by China, not the United States) was the North Vietnamese ambassador to the People's Republic of China, Hoang Van Hoan.[16]

Efforts to gain requisite intelligence on the Vietnam situation were complicated additionally by the slow development of intelligence entities. Not only would time be lost through this slow development but so would a crucial opportunity to impede the growth of the National Liberation Front during its earliest, most vulnerable, stages. Moreover, the problem existed on both the South Vietnamese and United States sides.

For Saigon, politics posed major problems. South Vietnamese leader Ngo Dinh Diem formed several intelligence and security services beginning in 1956, including the Political and Social Studies Service (SEPES by its French language initials), the Military Security Service, and the 1st Observation Group. Diem used the former units primarily to keep tabs on his Saigon political opponents; the latter, part of the South Vietnamese Special Forces, were diverted as elite bodyguards and security detachments. As of 1962 the CIA station in Saigon rated SEPES as ineffective for collecting intelligence on the National Liberation Front. In 1961 Saigon formed a new umbrella unit in the image of the CIA, called the Central Intelligence Organization (CIO). It would be 1964 before the CIO was really in the field. Meanwhile, Saigon's communications intelligence entity, the Special Exploitation Service, was tiny during the earliest period and reached a peak strength late in the war of only about 3,500. (Radio interception is a major consumer of staffing resources, and U.S. services worldwide during this same period employed upward of 95,000 people.) Meanwhile, the National Police evolved their own Security Service (Special Branch) to add to that of the military. All told, the South Vietnamese intelligence community came to somewhere around 11,000 specialists, but not until roughly 1967. By that time, Hanoi and the Liberation Front were increasingly fighting a large-unit war with the Americans and South Vietnamese and were well on their way toward launching the Tet Offensive.[17]

For the Americans with their global commitments, the question was less whether intelligence capability was lacking than it was at what point was the intelligence challenge in Vietnam to be taken seriously. As of 1960, the CIA station in Saigon numbered some 40 intelligence officers, at a time when perhaps 400 worked on Cuban operations and the agency's largest stations were in Taiwan and West German, both in the neighborhood of 1,000 CIA officers. Saigon personnel doubled in 1961 with new programs, including cooperation with the Vietnamese CIO, commando forays into North Vietnam, and the beginnings of several paramilitary initiatives. By 1963, with about 300 officers, the Saigon station rivaled Miami's CIA station, which was devoted to Cuban operations. By 1967 the CIA's Vietnam strength was up to some 600, and Saigon station eventually became the agency's largest. Again, as with the South Vietnamese, the buildup took place over a long period of time and never got ahead of the increasing intensity of the Vietnam war.[18]

On the U.S. military side, the staff intelligence unit (G-2) of the Military Assistance and Advisory Group (MAAG) also existed as a very small unit early in the 1960s. In fact, in 1962, when the MAAG G-2 began a project to compile and formalize an order of battle to better estimate National Liberation Front strength, the project required bringing in additional specialists from both the Pacific Command (in Hawaii) and the Defense Intelligence Agency (in Washington). In 1963, with MAAG strength accelerating from 11,000 to over 15,000 by midyear, the size of U.S. military intelligence (excluding communications intelligence elements) remained smaller than the CIA station. In 1965, with the United States on the brink of major escalation and the dispatch of ground forces, the G-2 section of the restyled Military Assistance Command Vietnam (MACV) stood at 300. Exponential growth then began, and MACV intelligence (as a "joint" command, MACV's G-2 became "J-2") rose to a strength of 3,000 with arrival of the

525th Military Intelligence Battalion. The addition of Americans to the multinational Combined Intelligence Center Vietnam beginning in 1967 put the cap on the intelligence system.[19]

On the communications intelligence side, the first U.S. unit went to South Vietnam as a provisional detachment (called "Whitebirch") of 77 officers and men in 1961. In addition were 15 ("Sabertooth") specialists to train South Vietnamese radiomen who, since April 1957, had operated two intercept sites with 67 personnel. By June 1964 there were about 950 specialists in U.S. radio intelligence units alone. There is not yet an exact figure for peak strength, but from partial returns it would appear that in 1968 there were perhaps 5,000 Americans in radio intelligence in Vietnam. Adding those contributing from Thailand, Laos, on naval vessels, and aboard aircraft, the total figure may be about 10,000.[20]

In terms of size, the allied intelligence effort in South Vietnam dwarfed that of the North Vietnamese and National Liberation Front. Of course the same held true for the technical sophistication of U.S. and South Vietnamese collection mechanisms versus those of the enemy. Why were they not correspondingly more effective? There must be problems in the system is the short answer that intuition gives. It is, however, very likely that the failure was due to the slow buildup of U.S.-South Vietnamese intelligence systems, such that the Liberation Front had become entrenched before the allies managed to build their intelligence capability against it. The U.S.-South Vietnamese effort was too little, too late, oriented at the wrong collection targets and crippled by reporting pressure.

Complicating further every effort to assemble an accurate picture of the reality of Vietnam was a factor endemic to intelligence work, the conflict between operations and collection. In CIA history this problem goes back at least as far as the era of competition between the Office of Policy Coordination and Office of Special Operations in the late 1940s, in other words, to the beginning of the agency. It is hardly surprising that the competition continued in Vietnam. Two examples of intelligence practice and a hypothetical one will serve to illuminate this factor.[21]

Consider the National Liberation Front's political structure, with officials and committees from the village and hamlet to districts, provinces, and what the NLF called subregions and regions, capped by the elusive Central Office for South Vietnam (COSVN), the overall headquarters. The allies had a prime interest in developing sources within the NLF hierarchy such that they could have intelligence on NLF intentions and maneuvers. Certainly a real effort was made to recruit agents like these. During the phase of the preparatory work that went into creation of the Phoenix program, the chief of intelligence at CIA's Saigon station reported to superiors that he had some 330 agents among the NLF. The Phoenix program was itself aimed at neutralizing the NLF hierarchy, which meant the CIA's agents were targets of Phoenix activities like everyone else. The CIA also had priority on recruitments, which meant that as Phoenix advisors recruited agents of their own, when the CIA heard of them it had free rein to take over the agents developed. In Saigon there were twice-weekly coordination meetings where all agencies were to report what they were up to, so that things like Phoenix neutralization of active agents could be prevented. But the CIA used the reports to identify agents it could take over. This created an incentive for other agencies to avoid reporting their best intelligence to prevent their agents being taken away by CIA. Meanwhile, the daily arguments over preserving agents by refusing authorization for certain Phoenix missions reduced the impact of the program. Part of the explanation for the small numbers of truly significant neutralizations in Phoenix mentioned earlier may lie here.

A technical intelligence example of the conflict between collection and operations can be cited from 1968, during the battle of Khe Sanh. In the course of that battle, the U.S. intercepted certain radio transmissions that it interpreted as indicating that the North Vietnamese high command had taken to the field and was physically present in the Khe Sanh sector. A logical counter was to plan an air strike against the headquarters in the hope of killing General Vo Nguyen Giap and other senior enemy commanders. The instant counterargument was that using this information would reveal to Hanoi the flaws in its security that had enabled the Americans to learn of the headquarters. The enemy would then close off this intelligence source. The MACV command and Ambassador Ellsworth Bunker dismissed that argument and went ahead with the air attack, conducted by B-52 bombers on January 30, 1968. Although the attack was considered successful, General Giap was never threatened, and the radio emitters were back on the air within thirty-six hours. In 1970, when the United States made an attempt to destroy COSVN, the adversary's radio practice had become considerably more sophisticated, with alternating transmitters that took turns and then displaced to new locations, all remote from the actual command center.[22]

Now let us take up the hypothetical example of an American spy on the North Vietnamese Politburo. Perhaps Hoang Van Hoan would be recruited by the CIA and promoted to that exalted level, or someone else whom the CIA recruited and controlled successfully would have been similarly able to give the agency the inside story on Hanoi's decisions. This eventuality would have posed the huge question of whether U.S. intelligence could ever have *used* that knowledge, for fear of giving away their source. Again, collection and operations would have been in each other's way. Ironically, on those occasions when sources related to the National Liberation Front and the Politburo did provide what may have been critical intelligence, such as before Tet in 1968, it was often rejected due to operational concerns. The warnings these materials provided were dismissed on the grounds that it was in too great a contradiction of prevailing assumptions at MACV about the enemy's strength, which was believed insufficient to support a major campaign. The dilemmas of collection versus operations are not easy ones, nor were they resolved before Hanoi's eventual victory.[23]

For all these problems, it remains true that intelligence in Vietnam ultimately functioned with considerable effectiveness. Major military offensives were known on both sides. The Americans and South Vietnamese had warning indicators that could have led them to anticipate the Tet Offensive. Whether the indicators were correctly interpreted is another matter,[24] but as far as intelligence analysis is concerned, that is a failure in what is generally a good track record in the Vietnam War. In 1972, at the time of the North Vietnamese Easter Offensive, enemy action was expected and the only surprises concerned the scale, location of initial attacks, and timing of the maneuver. On Hanoi's side, the North Vietnamese correctly anticipated the U.S.-South Vietnamese 1970 invasion of Cambodia and were able to move their COSVN headquarters, which survived to fight another day. The following year they had warning of the South Vietnamese invasion of Laos and were able to destroy many of the forces sent against them. On the whole, intelligence on both sides proved able to furnish warning of major moves, if not details of plans. However, the tactical and political impacts of the Tet Offensive and the Cambodian and Laotian operations were major setbacks to the U.S. war effort while Hanoi, even when its forces were hurt, was able to rebound.

This brings back the question of the asymmetrical requirements of intelligence in Vietnam. American and South Vietnamese problems in terms of intelligence were deeper and of more consequence. Hanoi's difficulties were offset by lesser requirements and particular advantages. As a practical matter, the United States could not resolve its fundamental problems on intelligence in the war. For the United States this meant intelligence could not be the panacea some had expected, and which was necessary for victory, and over time the confidence of war managers eroded. In contrast, Hanoi's good intelligence helped pave its way to victory in 1975.

## Notes

1. There is no overall history of the intelligence war in Vietnam. Some material on the U.S. side is contained in Harold P. Ford, *CIA and the Vietnam Policymakers: Three Episodes, 1962–1968* (Washington, DC: CIA Center for the Study of Intelligence, 1998). For the South Vietnamese, see Colonel Hoang Ngoc Lung, *Indochina Monograph: Intelligence* (Washington, DC: Center for Military History, 1981).

2. Declassified documents, especially MACV Command History, 1971, Vol. I, III- 63–67.
3. *Newsweek,* November 2, 1970, 65.
4. See Richard A. Hunt, *Pacification* (Boulder, CO: Westview Press, 1995); and Jeffrey Race, *The War Comes to Long An* (Berkeley: University of California, 1972).
5. See John Prados, *The Lost Crusader: William E. Colby and the CIA* (New York: Oxford University Press, in press).
6. Gregory L. Vistica, "One Awful Night in Thanh Phong," *New York Times Magazine,* April 29, 2001, 50–57, 66–68, 133, Rajiv Chandrasekaran, "Villagers Dispute Kerrey's Account," *Washington Post,* May 7, 2001, A: 1, 13.
7. Declassified documents, especially Phung Hoang year-end reports for 1969 and 1970 (completed February 28, 1970, and May 11, 1971 respectively). See also Douglas Valentine, *Phoenix* (New York: William Morrow, 1990); Dale Andradé, *Ashes to Ashes* (Lexington, MA: D.C. Heath, 1990); Orrin DeForest and David Chanoff, *Slow Burn* (New York: Simon & Schuster, 1990).
8. GAMO by its French name was the *Groupement Administratif Mobile Operationel.* See Bernard B. Fall, *The Political Development of Vietnam: VJ Day to the Geneva Cease Fire,* Ph.D. dissertation, Syracuse University 1955.
9. Interview by author with General Nguyen Khanh, April 17, 2000, Lubbock, Texas.
10. See Sedgwick Tourison, *Secret Army, Secret War* (Annapolis, MD: Naval Institute Press, 1996).
11. Bruce Jones, *War Without Windows* (New York: Vanguard Press, 1987). See also CIA Tet Offensive Postmortem, Interim Report (c. April 1, 1968), Lyndon B. Johnson Library, Papers of Capitol Legal Foundation, Box 1, Folder: "Fact Sheets (April-May 1968)."
12. See David Corn, *Blond Ghost* (New York: Simon & Schuster, 1998).
13. United States Senate, 90th Congress, 1st Session, Foreign Relations Committee, *Hearings: Bombing of North Vietnam,* 1967.
14. See Sam Adams, *War of Numbers* (South Royalton, VT: Steerforth Press, 1994; General Philip B. Davidson, *Secrets of the Vietnam War* (Novato, CA: Presidio Press, 1990. Joint Chiefs of Staff cable quoted in John Prados, *The Hidden History of the Vietnam War* (Chicago: Ivan R. Dee Publishers, 1995), 124.
15. See Ronald H. Spector, *After Tet: The Bloodiest Year in Vietnam* (New York: Macmillan, 1993).
16. Hoang Van Hoan, *A Drop in the Ocean* (Beijing: Foreign Language Press, 1988), 326–336.
17. Hoang Ngoc Lung, *Indochina Monograph,* 12–14, 36–39, 46–48, 55–65. SEPES by its French name was the *Service D'Etudes Politique et Sociales.*
18. John Prados, *President's Secret Wars* (Chicago: Ivan R. Dee Publishers, 1996), 211.
19. Major General Joseph A. McChristian, *Vietnam Studies: The Role of Intelligence, 1965–1967* (Washington, DC: Department of the Army, 1974).

20. Declassified documents furnish the earlier figures; peak numbers are the author's estimates.
21. Prados, *President's Secret Wars,* 32–34, 71, 79–88.
22. John Prados and Ray W. Stubbe, *Valley of Decision* (New York: Dell Books, 1993), 338–339.
23. Marc J. Gilbert and William Head, eds., *The Tet Offensive* (Westport, CT: Praeger, 1996), 144–153.
24. Ibid.,143–180, 231–265.

Chapter Six

# The Cost of Losing the "Other War" in Vietnam

MARC JASON GILBERT

Since the mid-1980s, much of the discourse on why the United States lost the Second Indochina War has focused on the strategy employed by American forces. This discourse has often served to divide American public opinion on the war, but also marks an even greater divide between American and Vietnamese students of the war. For many Americans and chiefly those Vietnamese who championed the cause of the Republic of Vietnam, defeat came as a result of the failure of the United States to correctly identify what kind of war they were fighting, the Clausewitzian prerequisite for all successful military doctrine, let alone a land war in Asia. These students of the war look to its political dimensions as an outside variable that worked to inhibit battlefield success. Some go so far as to decry the fact that, towards the close of the war, when they claim conditions "in country" turned in America's favor, war-weariness and a lack of political will in the United States brought an end to the conflict just when the war held the greatest promise for victory. Such postmortems on the war are viewed with considerable skepticism by most of those Americans who regard the war for the defense of the Republic of Vietnam as unnecessary or unwinnable under the circumstances that governed American intervention. Sharing their skepticism are many Vietnamese on the winning side. They fail to see how any victory would have emerged from a strategy more attuned to the war Hanoi and the Viet Cong were waging, for it was designed, at least in part, to alter the nature of the war to best frustrate the chosen strategy of their much stronger opponent. As for the political and battlefield dimensions of the war, they also see some irony in the argument that war and politics are somehow distinct. The Vietnamese people, following their own chosen master of war, the Chinese philosopher Sun

Tzu, have always understood the two to be integral to victory in war, as did Carl von Clausewitz, Sun Tzu's counterpart in the West. The frustration of many Americans and allied Vietnamese who saw a perennial light at the end of the tunnel is reasonable, but the goal of protracted war is to insure that this light remains beyond reach until the enemy comes to accept that the quest is futile and abandons his attempt to reach it. The gulf that separates differing views of the strategic dimensions of the war is thus very wide. However, the chapter that follows argues that they can be bridged. It seeks to do so through a narrative that attempts to reconcile the greatest divide separating Americans in their own debate over American strategy in the war, commonly known as the Summers-Colby debate.

## The Summers-Colby Debate

The late Harry Summers, Jr., a veteran of the war who was an influential commentator on military affairs in the 1980s and 1990s, contended that America was mistaken in what he alleged to have been its preoccupation both with the enemy's conduct of revolutionary warfare and with its antidote, a counterinsurgency-pacification campaign. He argued that the war was an invasion of one country by another along conventional lines. Had America recognized this truth, according to Summers, it would have been better able to anticipate, prevent, or meet the cross-border assault by the enemy's regular forces that ultimately brought the war to a close. Summers criticized Washington's limited war posture and concluded that an invasion of the Democratic Republic of Vietnam and/or Laos in 1965 conducted along the lines of 1991's Gulf War would have isolated the battlefield in Vietnam, facilitating so rapid a defeat of the Viet Cong as to allow American troops to return home in time for Woodstock.[1]

The premises of what has come to be called the Summers thesis have won favor among many members of the American military establishment, particularly among those who held command rank in Vietnam. Yet his arguments are fraught with errors of fact as well as interpretation. The devotees of the Summers thesis insist, admittedly without foundation, that Washington's fears of a Soviet and/or Chinese intervention in the war that precluded a wider war in Southeast Asia were groundless. However, Sinologists such as John Garver have proven that Washington's concerns were justified. At the same time, military historians such as Peter Dunn have demonstrated that an invasion of the Laos and/or the southern DRV would under any circumstances have proven to be more costly and no more successful than Johnson's limited war strategy.[2] Even advocates of the Summers thesis, like General William Westmoreland, have angrily denounced those post–Gulf War hawks who have apparently forgotten that the campaign in Iraq occurred after the collapse of the Soviet Union eliminated the type of interventionist threat that had limited the scope of Westmoreland's operations in Vietnam.[3] Roger Hilsman and Douglas Pike, two of the State Department's wartime experts on the enemy's strategy, seemingly demolish the central element of the Summers thesis by pointing out that guerrilla revolutionaries, acting with only limited support from North Vietnamese regular forces, would have overwhelmed the Saigon regime as early as 1965 had it not been for the introduction of U.S. combat forces. An invasion of the North in that year would thus, strategically speaking, have been meaningless, a point Summers himself concedes.[4] As for the post-1965 period, which both Summers and Westmoreland tout as a strictly conventional war, the testimony of Vietnam era counterinsurgency veteran Colonel Stuart Herrington and the late General Tran Van Tra, a commander of enemy forces in the South, leaves little doubt that guerrilla forces remained an integral part of Hanoi's strategy after the Tet Offensive of 1968 and right up to the fall of Saigon in 1975.[5] Colonel Herrington has concluded that "those who suggest that the United States erred by focusing its power on the Viet Cong when we should have known all along that Hanoi was the enemy and 'gone for the jugular' simply do not understand the nature of revolutionary warfare and the key role played by Hanoi's Southern organization."[6]

Perhaps an even more serious challenge to the Summers approach has come from the late William Colby, Andrew Krepinevitch, Guenter Lewy, and, most recently, Michael Lind and Lewis Sorley. They argue that while the American defeat in Vietnam was, indeed, traceable to the failures of its counterinsurgency campaign, this failure occurred not because America invested too much in such programs but because it invested too little, too late. They point out that, due to U.S. superiority in conventional warfare, American leaders in Vietnam were slow to apply the lessons learned by successful American counterinsurgency efforts elsewhere. They contend that when these lessons were correctly employed, a marked improvement in pacification was noted even in the face of the distortions of policy that followed in the wake of the death of Ngo Dinh Diem and, later, the Tet Offensive. They maintain that after the Tet Offensive, when U.S. conventional forces were withdrawn and pacification programs finally were given priority and backed by South Vietnamese economic and primary political reforms, the effort to win the hearts and minds of the South Vietnamese people quickly built toward a triumphant success. They maintain that this success was thwarted by domestic turmoil in the United States that led to America's abandonment of its increasingly viable Vietnamese ally. In his own initial account of the war (*Lost Victory*, 1989), Colby, chief of pacification in Vietnam after 1970 and later director of the Central Intelligence Agency, concluded that after the Tet Offensive America had succeeded in achieving what only a few counterinsurgency visionaries like

Edward Lansdale had believed to be possible—nation-building abroad in the face of a campaign of terror and subversion—only to throw that achievement away through a lack of political will at home.[7]

The so-called Colby alternative thesis possesses its own weaknesses. Its charge that the United States failed to support counterinsurgency and pacification measures in Vietnam is belied by the enormous effort that was devoted to this "other war" before and after Tet. It discounts the possibility that the slow response of the American decision-making process to innovative pacification techniques, such as those favored by counterinsurgency specialist Edward Lansdale, may have been tied to unalterable characteristics of American policy in Vietnam. It also fails to consider that even the best American pacification efforts destabilized much of rural Vietnam and so undermined the psychological independence and political sovereignty of the Saigon regime as to contribute to its collapse.[8] Further, the Colby thesis, like the Summers thesis, often relies on faulty evidence selectively employed to support the kind of stab-in-the-back rhetoric that has in the past proven more firmly rooted in contemporary political agendas than in historical reality.[9] The most serious flaw in the Colby thesis, however, can be found in its central counterfactual components. Colby believed that the pacification program might have had a better chance to succeed if Diem had not been killed, if the sudden impact of the Tet Offensive had not undermined American public support for the war, or if economic reforms such as Thieu's Land to the Tiller program had been introduced earlier or had been given more time to succeed. Yet Colby himself seems to have come to understand that if the success or failure of American policy in Southeast Asia depended on avoiding the moral and political implications of the murder of a favored if obstreperous son, on the reversal of the domestic ramifications of an unexpected military debacle, and on the staying of the hands of time, then what was needed for victory in Vietnam was not Edward Lansdale but the biblical Joshua and King David.[10]

The attractions and pitfalls inherent in each side of the Summers-Colby debate render a final judgment on the conventional-unconventional warfare issue elusive, but many scholars believe that a definitive analysis may emerge from closer study of American and Vietnamese perceptions and actions during the pivotal year of 1965 and their ramifications for the later Tet Offensive of 1968.[11] It is argued here that a close study of the revived American advisory effort of 1965 and its post-Tet fate illuminates fundamental aspects of war that appear to have been obscured by the Summers and Colby theses. The focus of this analysis is on the strategic contradictions between American conventional military operations and the war's goals, and between the unique brand of idealism inherent in American nation-building and the realities of Vietnamese political culture. Only an Americanization of the war could preserve the independence of the Republic of Vietnam (RVN), and the Americanization of the war held the potential to fatally undermine the RVN's independence. This was understood from the very moment the United States dispatched combat troops to Vietnam, but the variables of time and the tide of events that had so often favored America in its foreign wars, and were expected to favor it again in Indochina, worked to the enemy's advantage. Yet the outcome of the war and the pattern of ideas or events behind it were not the result of blind fate nor the result of incidental failures of American or RVN leadership or strategy that could have been avoided easily by more prudence or probity. It was the result of enemy action based on what Vietnamese communist leaders would call a "correct" assessment of history and a war-fighting strategy suited to it. Their view of history, however flawed it came to be seen in the aftermath of the war, was sufficiently correct to win it.

## The "Good Americans"

In the spring of 1965, the U.S. government confronted an unprecedented crisis in its conduct of its war in Vietnam. It was becoming locked into a rapidly escalating conflict that appeared both unavoidable and necessary, but that was, in President Johnson's and in many of the president's advisor's own words, most likely unwinnable. This pessimism was derived from the fact that although a variety of options were before the United States, including stepped-up bombing of the North and large U.S. troop deployments "in country," none was as yet thought to guarantee victory and all contained the seeds of an embarrassing defeat or, in the event U.S. troops were deployed, something worse—a "quagmire" that "could turn into an open end commitment on our part that would take more and more ground troops, without a realistic hope of ultimate victory."[12] According to John McNaughton, the most brutally pragmatic of Johnson's wartime advisors, only one aspect of the war effort was not a double-edged sword and held out real promise for long-term success: America's effort to achieve progress within South Vietnam toward building a stronger pro-government infrastructure and improving its spirit, effectiveness, stability, and physical security. In March McNaughton told President Johnson that while such efforts might not "pay off quickly enough to affect the present ominous deterioration, some may, and we are dealing here in small critical margins. Furthermore, such investment [was] essential to provide a foundation for the longer run."[13]

McNaughton was referencing a nation-building strategy that had been devised some years before by Edward Lansdale with the advice and support of British counterinsurgency expert Sir Robert Thompson and Roger Hilsman, a former American guerrilla in Burma and the director of intelligence for the Department of State in the Kennedy administration.[14] Lansdale had argued that it would do no good to pursue an anticommunist crusade in Vietnam if it made the Vietnamese dependent on the United States, as this would

> place the U.S. in a position of continuing major help [there] for endless years, on the basis that if our aid were lessened then the enemy would win . . .
>
> Thus I would like to see our efforts here geared as completely as possible to the operating philosophy of helping the Vietnamese to help themselves, not only Vietnamese government or army, but the people themselves. It will mean insisting on more extensive and effective use of our help by the Vietnamese-and our acceptance of workable Vietnamese standards rather than our own perhaps to a greater extent. This will increase proprietary interest in what is constructed (whether it be army division or individual farm), build the muscularity of national abilities, and start giving the Free Vietnamese the confidence in their own competence which the Vietminh have demonstrated so remarkably on their side.[15]

Lansdale's role in the creation of the Republic of South Vietnam had earned him praise as well as blame for interfering in Vietnamese affairs, but Lansdale was adamant that the advisory effort he now recommended would not be led by meddling "ugly Americans" who would themselves direct military and rural development operations. It would be led by "Good Americans"[16] who would merely assist South Vietnamese authorities in the conduct of antiguerrilla tactics that were of necessity tied to bridging the gap between the people and their government. To Lansdale and later to Roger Hilsman, political legitimacy and hence victory in a revolutionary war would fall to those indigenous forces best capable of providing local security and advancing the cause of nation-building. The interests of local security would, in terms of resource allocation, always vie with nation-building efforts. The warriors would always prefer the former to the latter, but for the embattled government as well as for the insurgents, there was no other road to take.[17]

Drawing on his own successful implementation of this strategy in the face of the Huk Rebellion in post–World War II central Luzon, Lansdale knew that it worked best when supported by a strong indigenous leader. He hoped Ngo Dinh Diem would be the man who would do for Vietnam what former Defense Minister and later President Ramon Magsaysay had done for the Philippines.[18] Unfortunately, Vietnamese political and cultural currents that ran as deep as Diem's mandarin psyche combined to thwart Lansdale's program. Whereas Magsaysay's populist touch and the nature of Filipino political culture permitted him to defer to American advice and to launch effective antiguerrilla operations supported by "mass-line" economic reforms,

Diem's greater personal and political need to stand aloof from the Americans and his inability to reach out to the majority of his own people stifled allied cooperation as well as his nation's political development. Further, Diem's need to service a power base far narrower and less democratic than Magsaysay's led to mismanagement and corruption that undermined the key element of the early pacification effort, the Strategic Hamlet program designed by Sir Robert Thompson. Diem's counterterror operations were, moreover, aimed at his noncommunist domestic opponents as much as at those he labeled as Viet Cong insurgents. His version of nation-building included the abolition of traditional village elections for posts he intended to fill with his own appointees and land reform policies that ultimately reduced the quality and amount of land previously placed in peasant hands by the Viet Minh.[19] Perhaps just as important, he sought to abolish what many consider the most universal cultural practice of Southeast Asians: cockfighting. In so doing, Diem fulfilled a dream of the Roman Catholic and Mandarin establishment but also secured for himself in the eyes of the masses the best possible credentials as an interloper/elitist unworthy of the Mandate of Heaven.

The assassination of Diem in November 1963 and the subsequent chronic instability of the Republic of Vietnam created conditions favoring a quick communist victory, but Lansdale and Hilsman remained convinced it was not too late to implement a nation-building strategy. Shortly before John F. Kennedy's assassination that same month, Hilsman urged the president to resist the temptation to view the insurgency in Vietnam as a military problem, a warning he continually repeated for the benefit of the Johnson administration until his resignation in March 1964. His last significant memoranda urged reform within South Vietnam and stressed Robert Thompson's belief that "Vietnam was a political problem of winning the allegiance of the people rather than a military problem of killing Viet Cong," and that the latter "had no more than a limited need for outside resources."[20] Johnson ultimately replaced Hilsman not with Lansdale but with William Bundy, who had little interest in the Lansdale-Hilsman tradition. Like his brother McGeorge Bundy (a National Security Adviser), William Bundy was a believer in both the domino theory and its Vietnamese corollary: the war was, at the very least, part of "Chicom imperialism" that the Democratic Republic of Vietnam (DRV) served by their aggression against the Republic of Vietnam. The problem in Vietnam was foreign aggression, not internal unrest. Nonetheless, at the end of 1963, Military Assistance Command, Vietnam (MACV) concluded that in "no amount of military effort or capability can compensate for poor politics,"[21] and many within Johnson's inner circle of advisors, including General Maxwell Taylor, his ambassador in Saigon, had at the beginning of 1965 come to agree with that assessment. This was also the view of the military advisors who were arriving in Vietnam in increasing numbers during

1964. In his last letter home before he was killed, Captain Norman W. Heck of Advisory Team 51 in Rach Gia wrote that he was "certain that the war can be won, but it is going to be a difficult task. A fairly effective program of improving the economic and political situation is, in effect, the whole key to success in winning the whole hearted support of the people, and not in the number of Viet Cong killed."[22]

Unfortunately, the coordinator of the U.S. rural affairs program in Vietnam, James Killen, a career foreign service officer, never lent the full force of his office to nation-building. Experts such as Rufus Phillips, Lansdale's right-hand man, and George Tanham, a retired vice president of RAND Corporation who had been its first student of warfare in Indochina, could not get Killen to leave Saigon to see conditions in the provinces. Tanham eventually went home, his health broken by the stress and disappointment brought on by seeing America losing a war on his watch. He left convinced that unless the Vietnamese accomplished it for themselves,

> the war could not be won. . . . Even if we won militarily for a time, the guerrillas would take to the hills again and recommence guerilla warfare. . . . Once we took over, I could not foresee victory for our side. . . . the Americans were not incompetent, but they really didn't understand the war and that they could never replace the Vietnamese as leaders of South Vietnam."[23]

A promising reorganization of the South Vietnamese leadership in the spring of 1965 may have given McNaughton hope that the nation-building model might yet achieve what he told the president a bombing campaign of the North and an American-led conventional war in the South might not: a quick victory and an early disengagement from a potential Southeast Asian quagmire. Johnson and his advisors were desperate to match military strategy to its strategic goals, and none of those goals, McNaughton warned, would be served by the long-term American military occupation of Vietnam. Like Tanham, McNaughton believed that only a strong Republic of Vietnam could ensure that the country remained independent, undivided, and not aligned with the communist bloc. This was America's minimum, irreducible measure of victory, and nothing short of victory was worth the dangers inherent in risking a protracted war in a place as likely to deliver one as Indochina.[24]

McNaughton's opinion that "progress inside SVN [South Vietnam] is our main aim" was shared by staff within the Department of Defense who had had long since recognized that, while Hanoi was then active in strengthening the forces facing the Saigon regime, the latter remained primarily indigenous. They also admitted that while "the introduction of limited ground forces into the northern area of South Vietnam . . . would have a real stiffening effect in Saigon and a strong signal effect to Hanoi . . . such forces would be possible attrition targets for the Viet Cong."[25] As a result, the United States had to remain committed to assisting the Vietnamese government to improve its standing with its own people and revive its pacification effort. In the end, McNaughton had no difficulty in moving the government in the direction he desired. Chester L. Cooper of the National Security Council had, on March 10, 1965, advised the president to launch a "crash pacification program" later worked with the head of the United States Information Agency, Carl Rowan, to advance the latter's plan that would mobilize the State Department, USAID and USIA to upgrade its political and civic action in South Vietnam so as to "match and even out-match" increases in ground forces then under consideration. Cooper eventually concluded that "positional" warfare alone could not win the war and that victory "was dependent on the success of our non-military efforts." The antiguerrilla "political-economic-psychwar" steps he and Rowan favored were quickly given presidential sanction.[26] In keeping with Edward Lansdale's repeated recommendations that this effort be led as much as possible by independent, specially trained civilians, much of the responsibility for reinvigorating this aspect of the war fell to the Agency for International Development (AID, later USAID), whose programs in Vietnam were placed under Killen's successor, Charles Mann, who was eager to lead the counterinsurgency-pacification effort.

In early 1965 AID widely publicized the need for volunteers for its mission in Vietnam. It secured dozens of old hands at rural development as well as military officers and police administrators who understood the difference between military and civilian approaches to social control and also recognized the central role Vietnamese hamlets and villages would play in both the theory and application of counterinsurgency doctrine. AID's prize catch was John Paul Vann, who had served in Vietnam as a military advisor in 1962 and was surpassed by no American in his understanding of the need for a nation-building strategy. Vann, however, saw that the AID effort's greatest triumph was not the recruitment of professionals like himself but in its successful courting of the International Voluntary Services (IVS), the nongovernmental organization that had provided the template for the Peace Corps.

The IVS, a nonsectarian organization sponsored by the Church of the Bretheren, Mennonites, Quakers, and other secular as well as religious organizations, had been providing apolitical people-to-people development assistance in Indochina since 1957. Yet one of its early volunteers, former Iowa farmer Edgar "Pop" Buell, had left IVS in Laos to become the standard-bearer of the CIA-AID counterinsurgency policy in that country.[27] It may have thus been with some optimism that, as part of the ramp-up of the advisory program, AID successfully approached IVS with an offer to channel funds through ministries in Saigon and Vientiane that would permit IVS to expand the number of its volunteers in Indochina. Several hundred were to serve in Vietnam. Such was their success that military officials wrote to draft boards in the United States claiming that IVSers were far more valuable to the war effort as development workers than they ever could be as soldiers. The Viet Cong so respected the devoted service and political independence of individual workers that sometimes attacks on AID centers were postponed until visiting IVSers had departed. Vann never stopped praising IVS performance or results. Trained in the Vietnamese language, living as the Vietnamese did wherever they were stationed, IVSers were, in Vann's view, the only Americans in-country with hands on the "pulse" of what he considered the real war.[28]

The Vietnam that America's renewed advisory program faced in the summer of 1965 was dangerous ground. In Hau Nghia, a province created by Diem as an advertisement for pacification, Viet Cong ambushes kept the road to the nearby capital impassable. The province was also home to the famous tunnels at Cu Chi, which, long undiscovered, bedeviled allied military operations in the region. After a visit to Hau Nghia in 1965, one-time marine and policy analyst Daniel Ellsberg, then a staunch supporter of the war, was told by a local official that, out of the 220,000 people in the province, 200,000 were directly ruled by the Viet Cong.[29] This province was Vann's responsibility. Within a few short months, his AID team's security chief was ambushed and killed and his own chief assistant, Douglas Ramsey, was captured by the Viet Cong.

Nonetheless, by the end of 1965, the "Good Americans" had settled into their work. Few Americans had a better command of conditions in the field or were better respected by the Vietnamese they served. None was in a better position to evaluate the overall tenor and prospects of the renewed effort to win hearts and minds of Vietnamese people. How then did they evaluate that effort? They believed that the entire pacification campaign and the American cause in Vietnam seemed headed for defeat, insofar as victory was measured by the ability of the United States to effect a withdrawal from Indochina that would leave in its wake a Republic of South Vietnam able to stand on its own.[30]

Most of the new wave of advisors shared in Lansdale's recognition that America's exit from Vietnam was predicated not on Saigon's ability to deny the Viet Cong access to or control over the Vietnamese peasantry but on the ability of the Saigon regime to win the active support of that peasantry. This it could not easily do for reasons arising as much from the Viet Cong's own strengths as from the government's weaknesses. As the U.S. Embassy staff already knew, the Viet Cong were able to project a commitment not only to national unification but to nation-building far beyond the capacity of Saigon because the Viet Cong cadre lived among the people and could co-opt, discredit, or eliminate those members of the Saigon-based South Vietnamese ruling elite who willingly ventured into the countryside. It quickly became clear that the Saigon government had lost control of rural Vietnam in the years after Ngo Dinh Diem's assassination and that only a radical transformation of that government and its delivery of services in the rural areas could even hope to retrieve the situation. They ultimately concluded that such a transformation was unlikely given the political culture of South Vietnam and its interplay with the culture of its American ally.

Few advisors believed that the military leaders who had come to control the government in Saigon had to be paragons of the American democratic tradition to introduce the economic reforms that could have lifted the peasantry out of poverty and out of the hands of the Viet Cong. They feared, however, that the resources that should have been devoted to this vital task were being siphoned off by the attachment of these leaders to a traditional system of patronage that had turned predatory down to the village level by the pressure of war. They understood that, while many of Saigon's officials were honest men devoted to their country, Vietnam's myriad patron-client arrangements—arrangements that involved all-important family and wider social ties—ensured that such men had to purchase their positions, accept bribes, and overlook criminal exploitation of state resources if they and their families were to survive, let alone prosper.[31] It was this system as much as the individual moral failings or a lack of concern for the people that was responsible for the nondelivery of social services, such as relief supplies for refugees, the illicit transfer of basic rural development commodities like concrete to the black market,[32] and the seeming intransigence of government officials assigned to investigate or correct abuses of power.[33]

This same system impeded the performance of the Army of the Republic of Vietnam (ARVN) and the Republic's administrative personnel. These officers were college-educated urbanites who often exhibited the worst characteristics of Vietnamese feudal elitism when addressing their overwhelmingly poor, illiterate, and rural rank and file soldiers and the masses of farmers from which the latter were recruited. The distribution of military, police, provincial, and district assignments according to political and financial criteria or family or feudal obligation not only impeded the government's ability to defeat the Viet Cong but also forced and/or condoned counterproductive behavior, from the taking of bribes to petty harassment for personal gain. These inequities turned the government's officials into living propaganda for the Viet Cong. Weapons, medical supplies, and other equipment were routinely sold on the black market: ARVN troopers could see in the marketplace the supplies they had been promised but that they never received. ARVN's functioning also was severely impaired by the politics of its masters. The chief duty of the general in command of 25th ARVN division was not to interdict enemy operations but to watch over the neighboring 5th ARVN division, whose commander was tied to his patron's rivals in the Saigon military cabal. Suborned into defending their patrons' interests and forced to seek sources of revenue to offset the purchase price of their positions, the Republic of Vietnam's province and district chiefs, field commanders, and police officers functioned more effectively as intimidators of the regime's opponents and the exploiters of the common people than as legitimate defenders of the nation. ARVN and the republic's American-trained National Police were thus ill-suited to the antiguerilla role required by classical counterinsurgency theory, mirroring the inability of South Vietnam's leaders to shape themselves into popular, stable, and broad-based nation-builders as was required by American counterinsurgency tradition.[34]

The best of the new civilian advisors, however, at least tried to resist indulging in what today would be called "blaming the victim." If the political culture of the Republic of Vietnam was becoming increasingly vile by American standards, these advisors were convinced that the United States was itself contributing mightily to this decline. Accusations such as the charge of Saigon's newspaper *Cong Chung* that "American aid is entirely responsible for the current corruption in Viet Nam"[35] may have been something of an exaggeration, but it was not that far from the truth. None could deny the corrupting influence of U.S. cash and goods that accompanied the increased U.S. presence in Vietnam. The Americanization of the Vietnamese economy dangled a temptation of riches before struggling Vietnamese that few could resist and for which they blamed the Americans. U.S. civilian advisors could see clearly that U.S. contractors had a major role in the Vietnamese black market and that this greatly angered the Vietnamese.[36] American authorities in Saigon failed to account for the corrupting influence of American aid, if only by condoning even the most visible and, to westerners, the most venial practices, such as the sale of key military and civilian posts, through what today would be called a "don't ask, don't tell" posture. What raised the advisors' ire was that such conditions were fatal to both American and South Vietnamese public interests. Even some among the Vietnamese elite understood that the corrupting influence of American aid undermined the legitimacy and hence fighting spirit of the government's forces and imperiled the careers of would-be reformers in both the American and South Vietnamese camps,[37] but so long as the South Vietnamese political elite believed that the United States would never abandon them as long as they were even marginally effective, there was no incentive for them to challenge the status quo that had hitherto sustained them. The arrival of more Americans only worsened this situation and created a vicious circle. The more responsibilities the

Americans took on, the less the Vietnamese did, and the less they did, the more advisors would be sent. It became commonplace to hear Vietnamese say to them: "It's your war, you fight it."[38]

McNaughton's new wave of civilian advisors in 1965 was prepared to endorse steps such as the republic's new constitution and election procedures introduced from 1965 to 1967 under pressure from President Johnson, but they quickly came to see that most Vietnamese "saw it as the same old regime."[39] Most believed that unless the will was found for truly revolutionary development, the war was already lost, for until the coup-making military power brokers were removed, real change was unlikely, and, without it, rural pacification and an early and victorious American withdrawal was impossible.[40] These advisors urged their superiors to create the needed leverage to effect such changes, but they were thwarted at the embassy level and above. These officials already were on such poor terms with Vietnamese leaders that changes such as those favored by American advisory personnel were rejected out of hand in Vietnam and Washington as unacceptable interference in the internal affairs of Vietnam. The advisory mission was, nonetheless, able to make some headway, but its limited gains in pacification against a robust Viet Cong were not enough to halt the major change in strategy then contemplated by MACV.

## More Bombs and Big Battalions

The failure of the advisory effort to rapidly reverse the deterioration of the Republic of Vietnam's popularity and military security compelled General Westmoreland to offer another solution to the problems posed by the failings of America's Vietnamese ally: more direct American participation in the war. After assuming control of Military Assistance Command in October of 1964, Westmoreland had strongly supported the buildup of the American advisory program, and his initial monthly reports stressed the importance of the pacification campaign. Yet by the spring of 1965, the slow pace of low-level civil operations and mounting enemy opposition left him frustrated and eager to try a more traditional approach.[41] Since Ulysses S. Grant's Wilderness Campaign of 1964, the United States Army had equated victory with the destruction of its opponent's armed forces. In June 1965, Westmoreland decided to do the same. He requested forty-four American maneuver battalions that would take the war directly to the enemy, forcing it into a faster tempo of operations that would exhaust its reserves of manpower and expose its logistical train to crushing interdiction.

After the war, Westmoreland felt that the (by then) much-criticized failed war of attrition[42] he pursued had not worked because he never had adequate forces to meet the enemy in the field and to provide the local security necessary for the required progress in nation-building. Expanding the war geographically in order to better interdict the enemy's supplies and reinforcements, he then remarked, was the only alternative, even though this also might be a losing strategy.[43] Fatefully, he never placed these opinions squarely before his commander in chief. When Westmoreland had accepted his appointment, President Johnson had made it clear that any strategy he might devise to secure America's national interests in Southeast Asia had to be limited to Vietnam because a wider war was contrary to those interests. Westmoreland had assured the president that he would so limit his strategy. Today Westmoreland credits Johnson "for not allowing the war to expand geographically" while still complaining that his hands were tied and victory was prevented by such restrictions. Such concerns were shared by the Joint Chiefs of Staff (JCS), but they, like Westmoreland, preferred to conceal from or compromise their professional judgment in conversations with their commander in chief rather than admit that the thing could not be done. This can-do philosophy ultimately moved Westmoreland to advise Johnson that a call-up of the reserves in support of his attrition strategy, while perhaps useful as means of intimidation, was unnecessary. Only after Tet would Westmoreland argue forcefully that the enemy had to be interdicted before they arrived in Vietnam, that is, in Laos, in Cambodia and in North Vietnam, thereby opening the door to an international conflict neither Westmoreland nor the Joints Chiefs of Staff may have wanted and Westmoreland himself now praises Johnson for preventing.[44] Such duplicity and contradiction are all too human, but in Westmoreland's case it clouded his own mind and that of the president, in whose hands the lives of thousands were entrusted.

When making his request for the introduction of large-scale American combat forces in 1965, Westmoreland had been buoyant over the inevitable success of the new strategy he favored. Neither he nor his superiors at the JCS ever seriously considered a scenario in which the enemy might refuse the challenge of a war of attrition and either remain in dispersed formations until conditions were more favorable to what they called "concentrated" formations or retreat deeper into their international sanctuaries. Even when the president put such an outcome clearly before them, they confidently dismissed it. This failure of judgment was not necessarily dishonorable. Like most army officers who reached command rank after the Korean War, Westmoreland regarded guerrillas merely as partisans, whose activities heralded, as they had in Northeast Asia, a conventional cross-border enemy strike.[45] Nothing in Westmoreland's personality or training—or in that of his superiors—predisposed him to seriously consider how faulty the application of the "Korea analogy" was to Vietnam. The chairman of the JCS and Westmoreland could not conceive of a circumstance in which the enemy might succeed in using hit-and-run and other guerrilla-style tactics to exhaust the military and political reserves that sustained Westmoreland's command until it was forced to withdraw, leaving the field free for conventional operations such as a large-scale invasion.

Upon receipt of Westmoreland's request for forty-four maneuver battalions, the JCS, which had hitherto expressed a decade-old aversion to land wars in Asia, told the president that "putting more men in will turn the tide and let us know what further we need to do." When President Johnson asked what would happen if a more aggressive posture led to Chinese intervention, Army Chief of Staff Harold Johnson angered the president by saying, "Well, that would be a whole new ball game." The President asked how many men would turn the tide; Marine General Wallace M. Greene opined that "five years, plus 500,000 troops. I think the American people would back you."[46] Johnson then voiced skepticism that the American people would support an investment of so many men for so long a time and the billions of dollars their operations would cost,[47] but he so feared that failure in Vietnam would turn the conservative dogs loose upon his Great Society programs that he could not reject the military's formulations outright. He leaned toward what he himself recognized as an uncomfortable and potentially fatal middle ground. Rather than approve of a sudden call-up of reserves recommended by the Joint Chiefs, Johnson favored a gradual buildup and incremental escalation approved by a temporizing Westmoreland. This course had the advantage of avoiding a widening of the war into an international conflict, but it "eroded my popularity from two directions—with those who wanted me to do more in the war and with those who wished me to more at home."[48]

Johnson then asked his civilian advisors to comment on the wisdom of responding to Westmoreland's appeals for additional resources by authorizing the dispatch to Vietnam of over 100,000 more American troops to bring the total to more than 185,000 before the end of 1965. It is widely known that Undersecretary of State George Ball, one of Johnson's most trusted personal friends, stridently resisted this proposal. He was convinced the large-scale introduction of conventional American ground forces into Vietnam was certain to lead to a prolonged, dirty, costly, and ultimately futile American war in the midst of a population that would refuse to cooperate with any Western forces or their Vietnamese allies. Ball also believed the war would last five years, but accurately predicted it would end in defeat at the cost of over 50,000 American lives. He told Johnson what American defense analysts had been saying for some time: "The Viet Cong—while supported and guided from the North—is largely an indigenous movement," and that "although we have emphasized its Cold War aspects, the conflict in South Vietnam is essentially a civil war within that country."[49]

Johnson measured these views against more encouraging advice and the press of both positive and negative events. These included the success of the recent American intervention in the Dominican Republic, General Westmoreland's and Secretary of Defense Robert S. McNamara's current optimistic assessments of conventional warfare's capacity to bring a quick end to the war, and the likelihood of a Viet Cong victory within weeks rather than months. John McNaughton, McNamara's deputy, was given the job of delivering the good/bad news. McNaughton, who friends say never espoused such views himself but was merely expressing those of his department (i.e., McNamara), argued effectively that the Vietnam adventure, however ill starred, should not be allowed to sully America's reputation as the guarantor of the sovereignty of allies facing communist subversion. The United States should be prepared to support any strategy that would avoid this outcome, even one that meant the abandonment of McNaughton's own effort to ensure that America would not be bogged down in a land war in Asia. Even a quagmire was better than humiliation.[50] When Johnson asked Ball to address these concerns, Ball replied that a withdrawal from Vietnam could not deal a blow to America's reputation, because "our commitment to the South Vietnamese is of a wholly different order from our major commitments elsewhere—to Berlin, to NATO, to South Korea, etc."[51] Ball was convinced that the worst humiliation America could experience in Vietnam was precisely what the recommended course of action would produce: a protracted conflict seemingly in which "the mightiest power on earth is unable to defeat a handful of guerrillas."[52]

Robert McNamara undercut Ball's views and made his colleagues' decision to escalate the war easier by convincing them that the quagmire they supposedly were hazarding was entirely ephemeral. Hanoi would tire of the war if it saw that American troop commitments in the South would deprive it of an early victory and if "North Vietnam itself was under continuing and increasingly damaging punitive attack."[53] This argument denied the validity of Ball's contention that there was, in addition, a potentially self-sustaining revolutionary force in the South that sought to overthrow the South Vietnamese oligarchy by force of arms. It also assumed that the Viet Cong—as agents of international communism—were incapable of representing themselves effectively as the true champions of Vietnamese nationalism, whether they were or not. It was an argument, however, consistent with the longstanding belief in official circles, both political and military, that the Vietnam conflict was little more than Soviet and Chinese communist aggression in disguise and that Vietnam was the place where superior American strength could be brought to bear most effectively to halt it.

McNamara won his case, but this was never really in doubt. Johnson and the Bundys had from the beginning decided that there was more to be lost at home and abroad by an outright abandonment of the war effort than in risking the dispatch of troops. Much has been made of Johnson's concerns over the domestic political ramifications of "losing" Vietnam, but the record indicates that Cold War fears over the international ramifications were just as great. The chairman of the JCS let the president know that the United States could simply not afford to lose the first "war of National Liberation" lest it encourage others elsewhere.[54] Thus emerged a decision-making process that H. R. McMaster (*Dereliction of Duty,* 1997) would later judge to be so full of self-deception, "arrogance, weakness and lying in the pursuit of self interest" as to constitute "dereliction of duty" to the American people. It was, however, not much different from the venalities that shadowed civilian and military decision making during all of America's wars. It was probably less than that which attended the American Civil War when measured against Jefferson Davis's back-channel assaults on Robert E. Lee and the North's George B. McClellan and Benjamin Butler debacles. The problem in 1965 was that it served to commit America deeper into a war that McMaster contends "it could not win at a politically acceptable level of commitment,"[55] and that was the only level of commitment that mattered or has ever mattered in war. On July 28, 1965, Johnson announced the sending of American combat forces to Vietnam, professing the achievement of a consensus that, in reality, reflected only the dismal state of Cold War civil-military relations and domestic politics that had by then clouded the policies of four presidential administrations.

The selective demonization of McNamara, the Joints Chiefs, and Lyndon Johnson by some writers who are looking for scapegoats for the subsequent American defeat may be emotionally satisfying. It may even help explain, in part, the failure of the American war effort. But as senior military historian Ronald Spector notes in his review of McMaster's attempt to hold Washington responsible for America's defeat, this narrow focus "displays some of the same ethnocentrism, the same assumption of American omnipotence, for which McMaster pillories the leaders of that era. It largely leaves out of account the ideas, plans and actions of the Vietnamese."[56] Spector does not dismiss the role of American decision making, but he comes close to suggesting what is here considered the other major flaw in McMaster's still-impressive work. Cold War politics and strategic assumptions held by successive American administrations, its military advisors, and its intellectual elites, conservative and liberal, paved the road of good intentions in Vietnam, not just those of the Johnson administration, and all such roads had only one destination.

## Vann and PROVN

The U.S. civilian advisory teams witnessed the influx of U.S. troops in Vietnam that followed the decision of July 28, 1965. They saw clearly that their nation's solution to the war's lack of progress was to take upon itself the task of liberating Vietnam from subversion. At first, some welcomed the quickened pace of both the American air campaign against the North and the introduction of American ground forces in the South, but it soon became obvious that these efforts would fail. They feared that too large an expression of American power and too great a number of American troops would only further weaken the Saigon regime in the eyes of its own people and destroy whatever morale existed in ARVN, turning the South into a hollow shell that could be crushed at will when conditions favored the enemy.

They were certain that the American way of war also would result in the needless and counterproductive devastation of Vietnam. Like so many other observers in Vietnam's villages, the "Good Americans" noted that, following their initial contact with the Viet Cong, ARVN and American military units were prone to "call for an air strike and kill women and children."[57] Such tactics were designed to minimize their own casualties and might inflict heavy casualties on the enemy: however, they could generate more guerrillas than they killed. Even if they did not, they would certainly not make the people of the Republic of Vietnam better love their dysfunctional government, the sine qua non of the war effort. Further, always short of men and fearing an "enclave" outcome equated with defeat, instead of Roger Hilsman's "clear and hold strategy," MACV favored a search-and-destroy strategy that in practice (if also not in theory) placed little value on local security. Few advisors could understand how even a conventional war could be won by forces that returned time after time to the same killings zones but, in the interim, stayed close to their own support bases. True, American advisors were now also taking up more civic action duties so that the counter-insurgent war could hardly have said to be abandoned. Yet only a very few sought to get to know the people, hardly any spoke Vietnamese beyond the IVS cadre (whose Vietnamese was often rudimentary), and most stayed as much as possible in base camps, unconsciously doing exactly what the Viet Cong wanted them to—surrender the day-to-day administration of villages to them and, at best, turn a blind eye to the embezzlement of rural development resources by America's Vietnamese allies. Even casual observers saw this truth.[58]

In sum, every aspect of the Lansdale-Thompson-Hilsman program, from self-reliance through rural security to the winning of peasant loyalty, was being abandoned by the Americans and the South Vietnamese in favor of a strategy that relied on firepower alone.[59] Was there an alternative to this march of folly? In the late fall of 1965, a fresh team of Americans appeared in the provinces of Hau Nghia and Phouc Long to see if there was.

As part of the early 1965 policy review that had occasioned McNaughton's announcement of official support for a revived nation-building effort, President Johnson had criticized the military for talking only of bombs and more bombs and failing to give him "any solutions for this damn little piss-ant country."[60] Army Chief of Staff Harold Johnson responded to the president's comments by creating a team charged with "developing new sources of action to be taken in South Vietnam by the United States and its allies which will . . . lead in due time to successful accomplishment of U.S. aims and objectives."[61] This study, ultimately entitled *PROVN: The Program for the Pacification and Long-term Development of South Vietnam,* was based on an evaluation of the war in Hau Nghia on the grounds that a survey of an extreme worst case would best suit the purpose of gaining a fresh look at the problem. The study concluded that as "the problems facing the GVN [the Republic of Vietnam] were due more to deeply rooted social and political difficulties than to communist subversion or North Vietnamese aggression," the war against communism in Vietnam could be won only by reforms in the delivery of government services and other efforts that secured the goodwill of the peasantry. Referring to both the stated U.S. war aims in Vietnam and a U.S. General Military Order of 1863, which established that the American military must focus on the objective of the belligerent that lies beyond the war, PROVN warned that:

> People are the decisive elements of that "object which lies beyond" this war. The GVN, with U.S. support, must orient on this point of decision. This fact, too often mouthed without real understanding in the now trite phrase 'winning the hearts and minds of the people,' must guide all our future actions . . . all other military aspects of the war are secondary.[62]

To drive home this point, PROVN explicitly cautioned against any tendency to allow military operations, even those conducted ostensibly to provide local security, to obscure the fact that rural reconstruction or pacification efforts would ultimately decide the outcome of the struggle. While PROVN conceded that the bulk of American and South Vietnamese forces would be directed against formations of enemy troops, the remainder would have to sustain the momentum of development in Rural Reconstruction areas. PROVN identified specific steps that had to be taken to achieve its goals. It recommended, for example, that the office of the South Vietnamese province chief be strengthened and empowered to punish or remove underperforming or corrupt Vietnamese soldiers and officials and to reward or promote those Vietnamese judged best suited to the task before them. The three great questions PROVN hoped to resolve were daunting: First, could the necessary socioeconomic reforms be implemented in Vietnam without violating both the spirit and the letter of the Lansdale-Thompson-Hilsman tradition by short-circuiting and thereby undermining both the authority and sovereignty of the Saigon regime? Second, could these reforms be achieved without converting America's limited advisory mission into a "powerful American presence in Vietnam for an indefinite period"? Third, could the requisite local security for pacification operations be achieved without militarizing rural development operations thus rendering them counterproductive? PROVN analysts were pessimistic but believed that the effort had to be made. The only alternative—the one PROVN said was always a possibility when fighting with and within a weak client state—was to accept defeat.[63]

Coincidentally, John Paul Vann was working on a proposal parallel to the PROVN study, which, after all, was basing its conclusions largely on the study of his situation in Hau Nghia. The results of Vann's work, a report entitled "Harnessing the Revolution,"[64] cleverly cast PROVN's provincial reorganization, which the JCS ultimately believed would "downgrade the role of the Government of Vietnam . . . and involve the United States too directly in [its] governmental structures at all levels,"[65] into what appeared to be little more than an experimental streamlining of command and service elements in select provinces whose success could be repeated under Saigon's aegis. But what Vann's proposal and PROVN shared was the conviction that the major problem in the countryside was that "the present leaders, bureaucrats, and province and district officials do not come from, think like, know much about or respond to the wishes of the rural majority of the population." As this circumstance was largely beyond the RVN's ability to change, both proposals argued that "the U.S. Government should accept *responsibility* for actual governmental performance in South Vietnam and act upon it." It remained entirely problematic how long the "facade" of Vietnamese authority could survive such an arrangement and how able the United States would be to overcome the charges, "not only from the VC, that we had taken on a colonialist role."[66]

The authors of the PROVN report and Vann need not have bothered struggling with these questions. Vann got "Harnessing the Revolution" into the hands of Ambassador Taylor's successor, Henry Cabot Lodge, in September 1965, long before PROVN was published. But Lodge had, by then, already been apprised by Washington that Westmoreland's buildup and war of attrition was ascendant. Henceforth Lodge, an advocate of pacification in his first tour as ambassador, placed priority on destroying "the main force enemy first, pacify, second."[67] Accordingly, he joined Westmoreland in politely filing away for the duration of their tenures in Vietnam both Vann's program and the subsequent PROVN report. Lodge would later regret his failure to understand how divorced Westmoreland's command was from the political realities of Vietnam.[68] PROVN so discomfited Westmoreland that he refused even to mention it in his memoirs. As it "forthrightly attacked [Westmoreland's] search-and-destroy concept,"[69] he and/or his allies in the Pentagon ensured that PROVN itself was destined to be "treated with such delicacy that Army officers were forbidden even to discuss its existence outside DoD [Department of Defense]."[70]

Edward Lansdale, then in Saigon as an advisor to Ambassador Lodge, but isolated from the embassy by wide political and personal disagreements, continued to urge anyone who would listen "to do something for the folks" and to never forget that Vietnamese culture and society held the key to the war.[71] However, as PROVN's coordinator, Lieutenant Colonel Donald Marshall, observed at the time, the pressure for results generated by the then-growing number of enemy victories in the field overrode any remaining value his own or Lansdale's advice might have had.[72] The time of Roger Hilsman's "fighting the guerrilla by adopting the tactics of the guerrilla"[73] had passed, and the day of the big battalions had arrived. This point cannot be overemphasized. A reorganized American counterinsurgency effort may or may not have been successful, but the enemy's continuing pressure derailed it. This was no matter of "if only" or "what could have been." It was not an accident. It was a result of enemy action.

## The Way of the Tiger

The beginning of this new era came on a Sunday morning, November 14, 1965, when a few battalion-size units of the First Cavalry Division (Air Mobile) did battle with the North Vietnamese 33rd and 66th regiments in the Ia Drang Valley. By dint of the uncommon valor so commonly displayed by U.S. forces facing overwhelming odds in Vietnam, the enemy's initial assaults were repelled, to their own great cost. However, this same PAVN force then ambushed and overran other First Cavalry units, killing approximately 200 troopers, bringing the total U.S. casualties to almost a third of the forces committed (more than 70 had died earlier in the battle). This engagement was thus less than the overwhelming victory touted by Westmoreland. Still, MACV happily interpreted it to mean that the revolution in Vietnam had reached its third and decisive stage—a main-force, nonguerrilla struggle—for which traditional American conventional warfare tactics were ideally suited. President Johnson was not entirely convinced of this, and even Robert McNamara, suddenly less sanguine about the war as a result of this battle and several dismal reports from the field, doubted that the enemy would complete its rush to destruction before American public opinion tired of the war's lack of results and turned against it. Nonetheless, the fear of failure that had led to the July decision to commit American combat troops ultimately drove Johnson and McNamara to accept Westmoreland's assertions that America was not about to get bogged down in George Ball's dirty war that would end in humiliation but was about to fight its way into a relatively clean conventional struggle it could not fail to win.[74] In Hanoi, the lessons of the battle of the Ia Drang Valley were interpreted differently.

The expansion of the American presence in the South that occurred in the spring and summer of 1965 had led to a reevaluation of Hanoi's war effort. For Hanoi, the war's tripartite goals of national reunification, social revolution, and independence were immutable: It would remain a revolutionary struggle against what many Vietnamese, communist and noncommunists alike, regarded as an unjust, foreign-backed regime. The success of the war in the villages from 1963 to 1965 had convinced the North that, while hope of a quick victory faded with the arrival of the Americans, Saigon had no hope of winning the hearts and minds of the Vietnamese people and continued to exist only because of the presence of foreign military forces. It was thus deemed proper that their principal target should shift from undermining Saigon's army and sociopolitical infrastructure to the destruction of the political support and martial resources of fresh American and allied foreign forces. It was judged that, like the French before them, American troops would prove highly vulnerable to protracted warfare. It only remained to be determined which combination of elements of the Vietnamese version of protracted war and associated political-military struggle was most appropriate to the task of compelling an American withdrawal. These elements were arranged in a seeming parallel to the Maoist three stages of revolutionary warfare—from political struggle to political struggle gradually supplemented by armed guerrilla struggle, and hence to large-scale operations combined with mass action. The elements of Vietnamese war-fighting strategy, however, were at once more complex and interchangeable than their Chinese counterparts. The Vietnamese were to prove as adept at using guerrilla formations to draw enemy conventional forces away from their own endangered regular forces as they were at using conventional formations to tie down opposing regular forces so that their guerrillas could mount a campaign of their own, as at Tet in 1968.[75]

After the battle of the Ia Drang Valley, General Nguyen Chi Thanh, the Politburo's own Westmoreland in the South, had pushed for the all-out commencement of third-stage, main-force operations. North Vietnamese casualties in that battle had been high, but Thanh believed that the more than 250 Americans lives taken in the "Valley of Death" proved the utility of his strategy. He correctly judged that the more than 1,800 men of his own command killed in action had bled the Americans more than he believed the American war machine could sustain over a long period of time or, rather, would be allowed to sustain by an American public whose latent antipathy for imperialist interventionism was expected to be awakened by the war's increasing costs. The Politburo itself had recognized that the American intervention had raised the ante beyond the victories in the guerrilla war, but Senior General Vo Nguyen Giap and Ho Chi Minh were able to use the losses in battle to encourage their commander in the field to preserve the strategic flexibility that had served them so well against the French and, thus far, against the Americans.

Nguyen Chi Thanh and his lieutenants proved agreeable to the pursuit of big-unit operations only when favorable terms of battle could be secured. They acknowledged the strengths of small-unit operations and had never underestimated the advantage of minimizing the superior U.S. firepower and their own casualties by the Vietnamese traditional guerrilla cling-to-their-cartridge- belt strategy. Their forces would also henceforth pursue "the way a tiger leaps at it prey," employing their full strength only when success was within their reach.[76] When the odds ran in favor of the Americans, their forces would rely on guerrilla formations, whose casualties, when necessary, could be made up from regular army units detailed for training in the South by guerrilla cadres. Wherever possible, regular and guerrilla units would be brigaded together to optimize operational unity and flexibility. The capacity for syncretism that had enabled the Vietnamese people to blend Taoism, Confucianism, and Buddhism with indigenous folk culture and to shift smoothly between main-force and guerrillas units in their long struggles against the Chinese enabled Hanoi to leaven ideologically rigid modern revolutionary theory with its own time-tested pragmatic war-fighting strategy and decision making during its struggle with the French, with Diem, and with the Americans.

Advisors like Vann, who understood that the war rested on understanding and exploiting the enemy's mind-set, were adamant that the war would always be a social revolution that could be best achieved by delivering the fruits of that revolution through government-sponsored democratic, nonviolent socioeconomic change. Politics mattered more than body counts, and the civil war in Vietnam had to take priority over the international dimensions of the war. So long as the revolution remained unfinished in Vietnam, the menace of communist subversion from within and invasion from without would persist.

These concerns, continually voiced by Lansdale in Saigon and Hilsman in Washington, were shared by Daniel Ellsberg, who had worked in Hau Nghia with Vann and was then was filing increasingly pessimistic reports with Robert McNamara and National Security Advisor Walt W. Rostow.[77] Ultimately, such views were also expressed by the third highest-ranking general in the Marine Corps, Victor "Brute" Krulak, formerly a bitter critic of the "other war."[78] After the Ia Drang campaign, Krulak accurately diagnosed that the enemy would henceforth "seek to attrit U.S. forces through the process of violent close-quarters combat, which tends to diminish the effectiveness of our supporting arms." He also accurately assessed Giap's thinking: that the cost of protracted war, which had led the French to gamble and lose at Dien Bien Phu and to surrender at Geneva, also would produce an American withdrawal. Only by winning the war in the villages by its own small-unit operations in support of an aggressive pacification program did

America stand any chance of success. With the help of Marine Commandant Lewis Walt, Krulak managed to present his views to President Johnson and the Joint Chiefs of Staff.[79]

The command position in Washington and at Westmoreland's headquarters, however, was unshakable. The war was merely the result of an extension of the Asian tentacle of the Soviet communist octopus. The so-called social revolution seemingly sought by the guerrillas, like their publicly touted goals of anti-imperialism, unification, and independence, was a mere figment of communist propaganda. The only value associated in mastering the communist tactics of the so-called Vietnamese people's war national liberation was to detect and exploit weaknesses in what were assumed to be typically communist and thus rigid modus operandi, such as the seeming shift toward third-stage warfare in 1965. In their view, the moment regular forces of the People's Army of North Vietnam began to shoulder more combat responsibilities than the guerrillas, the war ceased to be a revolutionary struggle and became a conventional war in which guerrillas were irrelevant. This confusion of the enemy's ends with its means led Westmoreland, President Johnson, and Robert McNamara to believe that bombing the North and the Ho Chi Minh Trail could bring the war to a halt, for they erroneously assumed that the enemy in the South, like any conventional American force, could not long survive with its supply lines severed. It also locked Westmoreland into a search-and-destroy campaign against a force that used guerrilla tactics to avoid his searches and employed conventional forces when the terms of engagement enabled it, not the Americans, to be the destroyer.

Westmoreland announced his war of attrition by declaring that "we'll just go on bleeding them until Hanoi wakes up to the fact that they have bled their country to the point of national disaster for generations."[80] Yet it was his command, as Krulak predicted, that was the first to be forced to scramble for resources. The costs of the war of attrition had virtually put an end to all alternative strategies. MACV had little choice but to relegate the ostensibly parallel nation-building campaign to oblivion, despite President Johnson's and McNaughton's continued pressure to expand the pacification effort in 1966–1967. Westmoreland was not immune to their concerns and tried to support the "accelerated pacification program" they urged upon him. However, he needed the men and he did not need an alternative policy distracting his subordinates or his superiors from the increasingly arduous task at hand. Attrition had worked in World War I and, he believed, it would work in Vietnam if given enough chance. Under Westmoreland's authority, the counterinsurgency-pacification campaign was largely handed over to Saigon's forces, where it no doubt properly belonged. Unfortunately, ARVN's past poor performance in the "other war" had only worsened with exposure to recent American operations in the villages. Also, as Robert Brigham points out in chapter 4, the relegation of ARVN to such defensive operations signaled to both ARVN and Hanoi that the RVN was fulfilling its destiny as a weak American puppet. Further, the major legatee of America's classical counterinsurgency tradition, the relatively successful marine Combined Action Platoon (CAP) program, was radically curtailed.[81] Finally, the chief hard-won legacy of PROVN, the American Civil Operations and Revolutionary Development Support program (CORDS) was militarized and placed directly under MACV. The Phoenix program, tasked with coordinating operations against the Vietnamese revolutionary cadre, shared the same fate. When directed by hand-picked American and Vietnamese officers, Phoenix may have been as legitimate in its tactics and as effective as some of its early practitioners claim. Once rapidly expanded and militarized to meet MACV's push for higher body counts, however, it clearly ceased to be either.[82] In the end, according to the U.S. Army's official history of the war, the advisory effort was relegated to "a permanent back seat in the American war effort."[83]

The coup de grâce to nation-building was delivered by Robert McNamara, though he would almost immediately regret it. As mentioned earlier, McNamara returned from a visit to Vietnam in early November of 1965 with little hope of a "favorable outcome" as defined by McNaughton earlier that year, but he nonetheless endorsed Westmoreland's view that the failure of the South Vietnamese to achieve any permanent gains in local security could be made up by more American troops and more bombing.[84] By the end of that month, with new reports in hand, he began to realize that the results of America's emphasis on a big-unit war of attrition supported by a stepped-up aerial campaign were exactly what the American civilian advisors had long feared: The peasants were betrayed into the hands of forces better calculated to generate refugees and guerrillas than supporters of the government in Saigon. The campaign certainly undermined the RVN's authority in the countryside without which the war effort, as originally defined, was doomed to fail.

One year later, in December of 1966, four-year Vietnam Rural Affairs bureau veteran Richard Holbrooke (later a U.S. ambassador to the United Nations) had an opportunity to bring the most serious ramifications of the Americanization of the war directly to the attention of the White House. Returning from a visit to Vietnam, Holbrooke noted the usual claims of progress—some of it real—but also confirmed what critics of an Americanized war had long feared: It was fatally undermining not only Vietnamese society, but the RVN itself, turning the United States into a colonial power:

> There is the growing [negative] chorus of urban Vietnamese who see their cities being changed by the American presence. . . . On the other hand, there are many other Vietnamese who are consciously deciding to cast their lot with

> the Americans, and [to] become "our Vietnamese." . . . By our very presence, we are therefore creating a group of people . . . who are making a commitment to the American Marines, or the Army, or the "Embassy." Despite the theories VIPs get in briefings, this commitment cannot be transferred from the Americans to the GVN . . . they are choosing the Americans, not the GVN. . . . So if the war drags on, we may find ourselves cast increasingly . . . into a strange sort of "revolutionary colonialism"—our ends are "revolutionary," our means quasi-colonial. . . . Thus, our very presence may prevent the emergence of a new leadership which would be willing to carry out the revolutionary programs which we are advocating and which are vital to our success. . . ."[85]

By 1967 the IVS country team sickened of watching the American way of war destroy the very fabric of Vietnamese life. Some had witnessed friendly villages being napalmed in front of them as they arrived for work. Others were demoralized by being forced to administer one of the new centerpieces of the big-unit war's view of pacification, the strategically bankrupt and fiscally corrupt "Refugee Generation Program."[86] The final straw for some was that even their closest Vietnamese friends told them that their presence was simply prolonging the killing of Vietnamese and that the United States would better serve the country if it withdrew, no matter what its political outcome.[87]

IVSer Don Cohon arrived in Vietnam so committed to the American mission that John Paul Vann had singled him out as someone with whom he enjoyed sharing his plans for winning the war. By 1966 Cohon and many of his cohort who arrived in Vietnam in 1965 saw the war only as a means of bringing destruction upon the people they served without the benefit of any real hope of "saving" them from communism.[88] In 1967 the most experienced leaders of IVS in-country resigned and joined with forty-nine rank-and-file-volunteers—most of whom, like Cohon, had arrived in Vietnam in 1965–1966 as American idealists and ardent anticommunists—in petitioning President Johnson to deescalate the war at any cost.[89]

Secretary of State Dean Rusk told the discontented IVS workers that the views of war-weary Vietnamese they cited in their petition reflected the opinions of only a small minority and that the vast majority were all for continuing the military effort. William Bundy told those who had resigned—all of whom had been closest to the Vietnamese and to the implementation of American policy—could not see the Vietnam issue in its "proper perspective."[90] Lower-echelon pacification officials privately reassured IVS leaders that they, too, had been unable to make any headway in convincing their superiors that the Americanization of the war was losing it.[91] Thereafter, an increasing number of IVS recruits were pacifists or young people coming to see the war with their own eyes. When these recruits took even less time to become war critics and joined the antiwar movement upon their return home, the U.S. government responded by telling the officials of the Republic of Vietnam, under whose authority IVS officially operated, to close the program down. They did so with alacrity, although they were somewhat puzzled, having assumed the IVS was a successful covert CIA program.

Stifling criticism from those who had their hands on the "pulse" of the Vietnamese people could not change the realities of conditions in the field. As Robert McNamara himself had begun to fear after Ia Drang, the American war effort could not annihilate the enemy fast enough to both over-match its ability to produce more soldiers or co-opt the growing antiwar movement at home. As Hanoi anticipated, America would withdraw bleeding, leaving the field at last clear for a military offensive that would bring about the final victory exactly as Le Loi had done in 1427 against the Chinese, the very model Ho Chi Minh said he would follow against Vietnam's enemies as early as 1945.[92] Only the brightest and most shining lies could conceal these truths, but they were plentiful well before the expulsion of the IVS country team.

The depth of the subsequent cover-up of the failure of Westmoreland's war of attrition was put on display between June 13 and July 4, 1966, when the 2nd Brigade of U.S. 25th Infantry Division swept through Hau Nghia during Operation Santa Fe. Its targets were the local Viet Cong militia that had for years kept the road closed between that province and Saigon, less than 30 miles away. These units were then, as always, seriously harassing local military formations and road travel. The results of the operation: four Viet Cong killed at the cost of fourteen American lives. Thirty Americans were wounded. The villagers swept up into the maelstrom of the fighting were judged pacified by handouts of medical supplies and toothpaste. The after-action report concluded that this successful search-and-destroy operation "through balanced combination of tactical operations and civic action programs was able to dominate the terrain and population."[93] The Santa Fe after-action report was but a single example of the delusional reporting that helped keep the Johnson administration wedded to big-unit warfare long after its failure was apparent.[94] There were many other examples, as one of the heroes of the Ia Drang, Lieutenant General Harold Moore, reminds us in his deeply moving account of the operations of the First Cavalry on the Bong Son plain in early 1966.[95] The much-heralded subsequent "County Fair" pacification operations raised this delusional process to the level of high art.[96]

Glowing reports of the success of the war of attrition from 1965 to 1967 did not fool Robert Komer, a Johnson aide assigned first to monitor and then to direct the pacification effort. Komer, a staunch supporter of the war, immediately warned that the overall effect of up-tempo conventional U.S. military operations would be to obliterate the pacification program and increase anti-American attitudes. He was virtually alone in this belief. As noted, even

Lodge, who had once championed pacification, knew a bandwagon when he saw one and advised the president that a war of attrition and pacification operations could go hand-in-hand. This optimism remained even after Westmoreland's war turned 4 million South Vietnamese into refugees and fatally undermined the social and economic fabric of the country.[97]

After the war, Komer observed that, while the counterinsurgency-pacification effort suffered a slow death in 1966, it was resurrected after the Tet Offensive in 1968. America and its Vietnamese ally had little choice but to do so. The magnitude of Westmoreland's error of misreading the enemy's operational flexibility was revealed at the onset of that offensive. In 1965 he claimed that the enemy had, at Ia Drang, begun to abandon protracted war. This statement was conveniently forgotten at Tet, when he announced, as if for the first time, that the enemy had finally abandoned their protracted war in favor of the "third-stage" main-force operations. In fact, he was facing concentrations of guerrillas acting without the reserves and logistics of main-force units. The infuriatingly flexible enemy had temporarily shelved protracted war in favor of a general offensive/general uprising associated with "third phase" operations but employed concentrations of guerrillas, rather than abandoning them in favor of regular units, as was typical of Maoist strategy as perceived by MACV. Westmoreland tried to translate the heavy casualties his forces claimed to have inflicted upon such troops as proof of the correctness of his strategic posture. He was correct in believing that, after Tet, the burden of the war would fall on regular North Vietnamese units. The enemy's performance at Tet, however, rendered these new conditions irrelevant. The Tet Offensive may have had catastrophic costs for the NLF, but its effort constituted the ultimate proof of the effectiveness of the union of the political and military objectives always sought by the Vietnamese foe.

The meaning and impact of Tet was hotly debated in Hanoi. A mea culpa was offered by the Le Duan-Troung Chinh clique that favored its most disastrous element—the push for a general uprising. This was accompanied by an expression of deep regret from Vo Nguyen Giap, who planned it reluctantly under duress from the Le Duan–dominated Politburo. This debate, however, has obscured the actual plans and purposes of the offensive. According to General Tran Van Tra, the Tet Offensive harnessed the energies of all forces at all levels and had two objectives, one political and the other military. The political objective, fully achieved, was aimed at breaking the mutually painful deadlock of the war of attrition and pushing the already wavering Washington war-making elite into doing what Robert McNamara had by then already recommended: admit its failure to win a quick military victory and seek a negotiated settlement. The military objective, aimed at unmanning if not overwhelming U.S. forces, was designed to support the political objective with the added benefit that movement toward the desired negotiated settlement might be accelerated or even obviated by a successful general uprising. Thousands of guerrillas had died and the general uprising failed, but the offensive's purpose was realized: the demoralization of the enemy's leadership, the achievement of a much-desired American bombing halt and the resultant opening of serious negotiations to end the war. Decades after the war, Tran Van Tra remained amazed that Tet was considered in America as a "military failure" that was, at best, a freak political success. He bridled at the "blind xenophobia" of those American writers who claim that Washington was "forced to withdraw due to internal conflicts and psychological panic" unrelated to any intentional act of the Vietnamese people. He admonished the "smug" devotees of these arguments to remember that, while the offensive was, indeed, a political victory, "there is never an easy 'political victory' won by the grace of Heaven or through an enemy's mercy without first having to shed blood and scatter bones on the battlefield, particularly in a big war such as ours."[98] For Tran Van Tra, as for Carl von Clausewitz, war was the extension of politics. In 1965 PROVN tried to remind its audience of this, but with no success. Yet, the PROVN team would have one more chance to prescribe for allied forces the enemy's formula for success.

## Too Little, Too Late?

The imperatives arising from the need to reassess the war effort in light of the Tet Offensive permitted Westmoreland's successor, General Creighton Abrams, to try to return the army's focus to rural security in support of political and economic reforms, an approach then being touted by analyst Francis West.[99] The Tet Offensive also permitted Komer to free CORDS from MACV control and attempt to finally implement PROVN's recommendations. PROVN's Lieutenant Colonel Donald Marshall was brought back to Vietnam to assist in this effort.[100] More important, the Tet debacle seemed finally to galvanize the South Vietnamese government to devote more resources to its own Revolutionary Development Program and to accept the American-sponsored managerial and economic reforms, including Thieu's Land to the Tiller program.

Yet, according to Komer, while Tet had led to a reduction of the chief traditional obstacles of the pacification program, the divisions, corruption, and disinterest rife among the South Vietnamese ruling elites compounded by U.S. mismanagement had not been eradicated. Worse, a RAND Corporation study of Saigon's urban elite indicated that, while overjoyed at the punishment meted out to the Viet Cong in Saigon at Tet, they had no doubt that the enemy's forces were repelled and could in the future be repelled only by U.S. forces. In their view, the republic was sure to perish if American combat troops were ever withdrawn. This report concluded that any movement toward

"Vietnamization" was counterproductive, as it would demoralize the republic's core supporters.[101]

In the aftermath of Tet, President Thieu told his ambassador to the United States, Bui Diem, that the war had not been going well because his civilian and military advisors were too weak to be of any assistance. Ambassador Diem then asked why the president did not purge the government of such men. Thieu gestured helplessly and replied, "because they are the government."[102] Although knowledgeable American analysts such as Gerald Cannon Hickey warned as early as 1967 that Thieu had to clean up, strengthen, and broaden the Republic of Vietnam's political base, Thieu himself proved too wedded to the existing political power structure and too confident in Nixon's support of his autocratic leadership to abandon the kind of elections during which peasants were told that "no one could belong to any party but [Thieu's] Democracy [Party]."[103] His Saigon elite orientation inhibited his interest in political and land reform, while his obsession with that elite's and his own security delayed accelerated pacification efforts until he felt his capital was fully secure. The weak reeds Thieu leaned upon were home grown.

Concerns such as Hickey's had led to Edward Lansdale's return to Vietnam to assist in making the Vietnamese election process more honest and fair. Upon his arrival, however, he found little real support in Saigon or Washington for any substantive change in Vietnamese politics. In desperation, Lansdale tried to enlist in this cause an old friend then visiting Saigon: Richard Nixon. Nixon, however, reportedly responded to Lansdale's election reforms by winking and saying "Oh sure, honest yes, that's right, as long as you win," a remark he punctuated by driving his elbow into Lansdale's side and slapping his own knee.[104] As president, Nixon was to turn a blind eye to Thieu's rigged elections until the bitter end.[105]

To Bui Diem, this story has special meaning. He has written extensively on how Nixon and Kissinger's need for stability in Saigon favored strongmen like Thieu and thereby thwarted anticorruption efforts and democratic reform, which, as a result of pressure from President Johnson, had at least produced a constitution and regular, if not pristine, elections. Without further progress in this direction, the South Vietnamese were easily stigmatized as undemocratic and corrupt, thus rendering them "unworthy of support by an ever-increasing percentage of the American public and Congress."[106] More immediately, the unpopular nature of the American-backed regime produced only "apathy, cynicism and, finally, in the [Vietnamese] anti-corruption movement, outrage."[107] Some Americans writing on the war, particularly those who served in it, complain that they "cannot understand why Congress abandoned the war." Apparently, Vietnamese like Bui Diem understood what they do not; so did President Johnson and his advisors, who feared this outcome from the very beginning. Democracies can fight prolonged conflicts, but will not support indefinitely those that fail to demonstrate real progress in defense of an ally even its own citizens have reason to despise.

Thus, the most pernicious internal obstacles to pacification embedded in Vietnamese politics and in U.S. - South Vietnamese relations survived the Tet scare intact. At the same time, the equally serious external obstacles remained. Although battered during the offensive, the Viet Cong's own pacification apparatus remained potent. The Viet Cong retained the capacity to terminate government rural development personnel and could, whenever they wished to do so, undermine the ability of any allied authority to provide reliable local security. Komer himself acknowledges that whatever advances in rural security and development occurred after Tet, it was not because of any renewed allied efforts, but because Hanoi's losses in rural cadre during the Tet Offensive had created a vacuum that CORDS and parallel South Vietnamese efforts, "as slow as we were," were able to exploit.[108] Eric Bergerud's study of post-Tet Viet Cong strength in Hau Nghia, extended by Ngo Vinh Long's research to apply across much of the Republic of Vietnam, suggests that Viet Cong losses at Tet were so quickly made up as to deny these achievements any semblance of permanence.[109]

Whether or not they were ultimately ephemeral, the allies' post-Tet achievements were dramatic enough to convince Abrams and Komer that a full-fledged revival of the "other war" could bring victory in Vietnam. Time, however, was running out. The enemy's so-called political victory at Tet had not only demoralized America's political leadership but, as was intended, had shaken the confidence of chairman of the Joint Chiefs of Staff, General Earl Wheeler, and other key figures of the American military establishment.[110] After meeting with these men, McNamara's successor, Clark M. Clifford, determined that America's only course in Vietnam was disengagement.[111] The Nixon administration may never have had a strategy for victory, just confidence that the United States and its Vietnamized ally could hold on until face-saving terms could be achieved. Henry Kissinger had long since decided that the war could not be won by military means and was "extremely cautious about committing himself to anything that might be called a 'victory.'"[112] Abrams and Komer thus were forced to devise a plan to win the war not with renewed support from home but while covering an American withdrawal. In 1969 they made PROVN's recommendations part of such a plan, one they believed so potent with regard to rural development and local security as to convince Abrams that the independence of South Vietnam still might be preserved. Unfortunately, this new plan had to acknowledge that this objective "would take a couple of decades and that far less time would be available."[113] PROVN advocates had, moreover, always known that this objective could be achieved only "through bringing the individual Vietnamese to support willingly the GVN," and, for all the hopelessly flawed American Hamlet Evaluation Surveys that showed quiescence after Tet and all the Phoenix program depredations, there was only limited anecdotal evidence that such progress was being made in this direction.[114]

The enemy knew this as well as MACV. Whether Hanoi and the National Liberation Front had the forces in place to vigorously contest rural development through guerrilla operations after 1969 or not, they had the luxury of not having to do so. The Viet Cong may not have completed the effort to win the hearts and minds of the South Vietnamese, but they had achieved the dual political purposes of the village war. They had driven out the Americans and prevented the Saigon regime from establishing itself as a legitimate rival to champion Vietnamese nationalism. Once the South Vietnamese government was deprived of the shield provided by American forces in the field, Hanoi was convinced that no amount of renewed indirect American aid in the "other war" or belated land reform could save Saigon.[115]

In the end, Abrams and Komer faced what Summers and his fellow revisionists have yet to appreciate—that in losing the insurgent war through a failed war of attrition resting on an inadequately popular local base, America and its Vietnamese allies had paved the way for Hanoi's more conventional offensive campaigns of 1972 and 1975.[116] Komer's summary explanation of the American failure to grasp the true nature of the war addresses why America failed in its objectives in Vietnam: "Politically, we failed to give due weight to the popular appeal of the Viet Cong . . . or the dearth of factionalism among traditional South Vietnamese elites. We only grasped belatedly the significance of the steady attrition of GVN [Government of Vietnam's] authority . . . in the countryside . . . which was directly linked to how the Viet Cong conducted the war."[117]

Komer concludes that as the war ultimately hinged on the ability of the South Vietnamese government to combat insurgents and halt this erosion, a battle the United States could only assist, but not itself fight, it is not true that America lost the war in Vietnam but that "the Saigon government and its army lost their own war with some help from us."[118] Henry Kissinger entertained the possibility of this outcome as early as 1963. His fears were confirmed by his visits to Vietnam in October-November of 1965 and in July of 1966. He has since written that the failure of Saigon's inability to develop, and U.S. military strategy to sustain, "a political program to which non-communists South Vietnamese could rally" figured prominently in his decision to cut the best deal he could to extract America from Vietnam.[119] Kissinger the diplomat thus washes his hands of his actions as policymaker: His support of Thieu, while pragmatically aimed at promoting the stability necessary to cover an American withdrawal, severely inhibited the development of the required popular political program.

William Colby, who succeeded Komer as pacification chief in Vietnam in 1970, stated that the post-Tet gains in pacification under Abrams's leadership were so substantial as to finally place success in the "other war" within America's grasp. Yet even he conceded that Saigon waited too long to begin its own social revolution and that American forces in Vietnam failed to deliver to an understandably frustrated American public what was ultimately needed for victory: steady, demonstrable progress sufficient to justify an unlimited commitment such as that provided the Republic of Korea.[120] Colby was well aware that not only did American forces in Vietnam fail to produce such progress from 1964 to 1970, but the Korea-style commitment he believed was required for victory was alien to both the original terms of engagement in Vietnam and those that governed MACV's final comprehensive plan in 1969, which, in part, defined Colby's own field of action.[121]

Harry Summers had similarly qualified much of his evaluation of the overall tenor of American strategy in Vietnam. He openly admitted that his suppositions were based on his experiences in Korea, not Vietnam, and that his views were untainted by close knowledge of Hanoi's policymaking process or strategic calculations.[122] He never doubted that the South would have fallen in 1965 to guerrillas, not main force units, if the United States had not intervened. He undoubtedly would have agreed with his critics' assertion that his own criticism of the failure of post-1965 and post-Tet American military operations to destroy the supposed "real enemy," the North Vietnamese regular army, is designed more as a much needed reminder of how far these operations departed from classical Clausewitzian military tradition than as practical suggestions as to how America could have won the war.[123] The Colby and Summers theses thus offer counsels of perfection that ignore the boundaries of historical analysis and transcend wartime political and military realities.

## Conclusion

In Vietnam, the U.S. government felt compelled to win a quick victory against historical forces that had been gestating for generations. It pursued what seemed to be the only politically acceptable course before it: an American war of attrition supported by a pacification program managed by the South Vietnamese. Unfortunately, Hanoi could win the pacification war merely by not losing to Saigon's less adept forces, and it possessed the political will, human resources, and battlefield strategy (by controlling the tempo of engagement and thus its own casualties) to win the war of attrition. The United States grew increasingly aware of the enemy's strengths, but it was overburdened by the liabilities of reforming its ally, appeasing New Left and traditional American anti-imperialism at home, and pursuing a limited war strategy that kept potential Soviet and Chinese interventionists at bay. Hanoi might have played into Westmoreland's hands if it inflexibly pursued Maoist revolutionary strategy—as it came close to doing so during the Tet Offensive—but this would have required the enemy to think in stereotypes, and, even at Tet, that was not the Vietnamese way. America's interests might have been better served if it had not thought in stereotypes, but that was the American way in Vietnam. The field reports of civilian advisors like Vann, the advice of analysts as diverse as Ellsberg and Krulak, and, above all, the formal investigations embodied in PROVN and similar studies should have equipped America's leaders with an early understanding of the conflict's unique dimensions. These materials would have made clear the political requirements that would have to be met by the Saigon regime and the sacrifices that America would have to make to secure victory in Vietnam. They were, however, ignored or suppressed by American officials, who, in their rush to keep up with the often overwhelmingly rapid pace of events in Southeast Asia, attributed their own inflexible behavior to enemy. In the end, Kissinger angrily denounced Hanoi's peace negotiators for holding out for the overthrow of the RVN instead of letting the United States off the hook by accepting slightly less so as to salvage America's pride of place in the emerging new world order. Kissinger described this posture of sticking to one's war aims as "dishonorable" and typical of the stubborness of the communists.[124]

In a sense, the enemy's strategy *had* to fit America's image of Red Tide expansionism and ideological rigidity. To have believed otherwise would have been to throw doubt on the prevailing monolithic model of communism, the bulwark of contemporary American foreign policy, and require a rethinking of the superior firepower doctrine that lay at the basis of the prevailing American Korea-model anticommunist military strategy, which denied the enemy a legitimate indigenous political motivation. As a result, even ameliorative efforts, such the post-1968 Vietnamization program, were doomed to failure. As a contemporary RAND Corporation study concluded even before that program began:

> The Army's entire repertoire of warfare was designed for conventional war in Europe. In Vietnam, the Army simply performed its repertoire though it was frequently irrelevant to the situation. Although changes were repeatedly proposed, few were made. The Army seemed to be prevented by its own doctrinal and organizational rigidity from understanding the nature of this war and from making the necessary modifications to apply power more relevantly. Vietnamization is not a solution to our own problem of rigidity. The danger exists that in transferring the war to the Vietnamese, we will also transfer also

> our organization, our style of fighting, and our mistakes . . . thus rendering the Vietnamese incapable of doing anything different from what we have done.[125]

The accuracy of this analysis may be measured in the outcomes of the enemy's Spring or Easter Offensive of 1972 against America's Vietnamized ally. Colby and others have called the 1972 offensive a triumph for Saigon's conventional forces. These claims, however, have been refuted as mere propaganda by the after-action analysis published by the U.S. Army Command and General Staff College.[126] The valor of ARVN troops at An Loc at the height of that offensive had been remarkable, but at its conclusion key areas of the country were in enemy hands and much of its population had been conditioned to accept Saigon's defeat.[127] Those like Harry Summers Jr., who tout the conventional nature of Hanoi's 1975 offensive, ignore the revolutionary political dimensions of the final campaign evidenced by the lack of resistance in the countryside and the relatively easy seizure of Saigon, which fell like "an overripe fruit."[128] Neither the rapid consolidation of the enemy's post-1972 gains nor the sudden collapse of the RVN would have been possible had the latter regime been able to match the political and revolutionary agenda of their opponents and the comparatively efficient cadre and staff that ran the DRV/NLF war machine. The leaders of the Republic of Vietnam indulged themselves too long in its ally's largess and, whether out of self-interest or naïveté, pursued its meddling ally's example to the very last, and there proved to be no light at that end of that tunnel.

Those who support the Colby "Lost Victory" thesis make much of Henry Kissinger's assertion that ARVN collapsed in 1975 due to a decline in (and finally, the sudden cutoff) of American aid by the U.S. Congress and not because of enemy action supported by their more generous and loyal backers in Russia and China. Yet, the United States was then providing the Republic of Vietnam with more than three times the amount of aid than that supplied by the DRV's socialist allies ($3.3 billion to $730 million between 1973 and 1974).[129] At the time of its fall, Saigon is reputed to have yet to expend the money provided in the previous funding cycle, though it was so malfeasant in what it did spend that its troops ran short of ammunition in their final campaign.

Compounding the failures during the war's endgame was the inablity of the United States to crack Vietnamese feudalism to the point that ARVN could develop a large, effective staff corps. As the end approached, some Vietnamese generals committed suicide, others deserted. But in either case, in elitist fashion, these officers, patriot martyrs and cowards like, left their men in the field and their nation to fend for themselves. As historian Patrick Hearden has unsparingly observed:

> The hard fact of the matter is that the South Vietnamese army suffered more from a lack of leadership than from a shortage of supplies. ARVN soldiers did not desert to take care of their families until after their units had been abandoned by their senior officers. Despite many years of indoctrination and training, American military advisers had failed to build a professional army in South Vietnam. The military forces supporting Thieu remained rotten from top to bottom, and in 1975 the day of reckoning had come.[130]

Tragically, almost a decade earlier, Robert McNamara sensed that American policy was out of joint with Vietnamese realities and American limitations, but his loyalty to prevailing American political formulas and military traditions was just as strong as Westmoreland's and, at the most critical juncture, just as immovable.[131] America in Vietnam was thus stabbed in the front, not in the back, betrayed not by the media, or civilian decision makers, or a misguided Congress, but by its own collective limited vision of the nature of the war and the requirements for victory. This limited vision, which also helped obscure the mounting empirical evidence of the fatal policy errors it occasioned, has been variously attributed to an arrogance of power, to an obsessive anticommunism, to the nightmare of appeasement, to an imperial presidency, to a "can do/group think" mentality, or to an overly bureaucratic war-making machine.[132] We must take care, however, that we do not, when enumerating these causes, increase the likelihood that the failure of the American War in Vietnam will be viewed as the product of American mistakes that might have been avoided and the war won, as Summers, Colby, and Komer have seemingly suggested. These masters of war and realpolitik do us a service by seeking to ascertain what America failed to do during the war, but a close reading of their work shows that even they would not wish to prevent us from recognizing that the outcome of that war was determined less at MACV and Washington than by the persistence of the enemy on the battlefield and in the political cultures of the Saigon regime, the National Liberation Front, and its partners in Hanoi.

## Notes

1. See Harry G. Summers, Jr. *On Strategy: A Critical Analysis of the Vietnam War* (Novato, CA: Presidio Press, 1982). For similar views see John N. Moore, ed., *The Vietnam Debate* (Lanham, MD: University Press of America, 1990).
2. John Garver, "The Tet Offensive and Sino-Vietnamese Relations," in William Head and Lawrence Grinter, eds., *Looking Back on the Vietnam War: A 1990s Perspective on the Decisions, Combat and Legacies* (Westport, CT: Greenwood Press, 1993), 105–117; and Peter M. Dunn, "*On Strategy* Revisited: Clausewitz and Revolutionary War," in Lawrence E. Grinter and

William Head, eds., *The American War in Vietnam: Lessons, Legacies, and Implications for Future Conflicts* (Westport, CT: Greenwood Press, 1987), 104–105.

3. Remarks by General William Westmoreland at the Seminar on Military History, United States Military Academy, West Point, New York, June 15, 1993. For the different parameters under which the Persian Gulf and Vietnam wars were fought, see William Head, "Air Power in the Persian Gulf: An Initial Search for the Right Lessons," *Air Force Logistics* 15, no. 1 (Winter 1992): 10–19 and Mark Clodfelter, "Of Demons Storms and Thunder," in Head and Grinter eds., *Looking Back on the Vietnam Wars,* 145–160.
4. Douglas Pike, "Conduct of the Vietnam War: Strategic Factors, 1965–1968," in John Schlight, *The Second Indochina War Symposium: Papers and Commentary* (Washington, DC: United States Army Center for Military History, 1986), 107; and Roger Hilsman, Jean Reisen, and Frank McCarthy, "Vietnam Was Lost Before Hanoi's Infiltrations," letter in the *New York Times,* May 7, 1985, sec. A: 30.
5. General Tran Van Tra, "The 1968 General Offensive and General Uprising," in Jayne Werner and Luu Doan Huynh eds., *The Vietnam War: Vietnamese and American Perspectives* (Armonk, NY: M. E. Sharp, 1993), 37–63.
6. Herrington's remarks can be found in his introduction to Orrin DeForest and David Chanoff, *Slow Burn: The Rise and Bitter Fall of American Intelligence in Vietnam* (New York, NY: Simon & Schuster, 1990), 13. The best single critique of this aspect of the Summers thesis can be found in John M. Gates, "If First You Don't Succeed, Try to Rewrite History: Revisionism and the Vietnam War," in Grinter and Head eds., *American War in Vietnam,* 177–189.
7. See William Colby with James McCarger, *Lost Victory: A Firsthand Account of America's Sixteen Year Involvement in Vietnam* (Chicago: Contemporary Books, 1989); Andrew Krepinevich, *The Army in Vietnam* (Baltimore, MD: The Johns Hopkins University Press, 1986); Guenter Lewey, *America in Vietnam* (New York: Oxford, 1978); Michael Lind, Vietnam: *The Necessary War: Grand Strategy, Domestic Politics, and the American War for Indochina* (New York:Simon & Schuster, 1999); and Lewis Sorley, *A Better War: The Unexamined Victories and Final Tragedy of America's Last Years in Vietnam* (New York: Harcourt,1999).
8. See David G. Marr, "The Rise and Fall of 'Counterinsurgency,' in The Senator Gravel Edition, *The Pentagon Papers: The Defense Department History of the United States Decisionmaking on Vietnam: 1945–1967,* 5 vols, (Boston: Beacon, Press, 1971) [hereafter referred to as *The Pentagon Papers*], Vol. 5, 202–209; and Bui Diem with David Chanoff, *The Jaws of History* (Boston: Houghton Mifflin, 1987), 155–156, 190.
9. Jeffrey P. Kimball, "Stab-in-the-Back Legend and the Vietnam War," *Armed Forces and Society* 14 (Spring 1988): 433–458.
10. Colby did not abandon the idea that the situation in Vietnam was improving after 1970, but he offered that the failure of the war managers, himself

included, to offer anything that could be perceived as progress after many years of war, fully justified the decision of the people of the United states to terminate it. Colby made these remarks at "Paris+20," a conference sponsored by the Center for the Study of Vietnam at Texas Tech University, Lubbock, TX, April 24, 1993. Due to the volatility of these remarks, the author asked him to confirm them at the Center's next triennial conference on Vietnam at the same locale. Both events were videotaped by the Center.

11. These scholars range from Larry Berman, author of *Planning a Tragedy: The Americanization of the War in Vietnam* (New York: Norton, 1982), to George Herring, who addressed this question in "'Cold Blood': LBJ's Conduct of Limited War in Vietnam," in Dennis E. Showalter and John G. Albert, eds. *An American Dilemma: Vietnam, 1964–1973* (Chicago: Imprint Publications, 1993), 63. See also Lieutenant General Harold Moore (Ret.) and Joseph L. Galloway, *We Were Soldiers Once . . . and Young: Ia Drang-The Battle that Changed the War* (New York: Random House, 1992).
12. Clark M. Clifford to President Johnson, May 17, 1965, Johnson Library, National Security File, NSC History of the Deployment of Major U.S. Forces to Vietnam, no. 307, in *Foreign Relations of the United States, 1964–1968, Volume II, Vietnam, January-June 1965,* no. 307, *www.state.gov/www/about_state/ history/vol_ii/301_310.html.*
13. John T. McNaughton to McNamara, March 24, 1965, and William Bundy and John T. McNaughton, "Courses of Action in Southeast Asia," in *The Pentagon Papers,* Vol. 3, 660, 696–697.
14. The best discussion of the evolution of the Lansdale-Thompson-Hilsman tradition can be found in Hilsman's *To Move a Nation: The Politics of Foreign Policy in the Administration of John F. Kennedy* (New York: Doubleday, 1967), 413–439.
15. "Edward G. Lansdale on the Importance of the South Vietnamese Experiment, 1955," in Robert McMahon, *Major Problems in the History of the Vietnam War* (New York: D.C. Heath, 1991), 125–126.
16. David Halberstam, *The Best and the Brightest* (New York: Penguin, 1972), 155–156.
17. See Hilsman, *To Move a Nation,* 417–439 and Nguyen Thi Dinh, trans. Mai Van Elliot, No Other Road To Take (Ithaca, NY: Cornell University Press, 1979).
18. However, Rufus Phillips, Lansdale's close associate, has denied categorically that Lansdale expected Diem to be another Magsaysay. Lansdale knew that Vietnam was not the Philippines; the only parallel was that, for any counterinsurgency doctrine to work, the nation's leadership would have to be committed to its support. Lansdale hoped Diem would see the wisdom of this. Author interview with Rufus Phillips, Austin, Texas, October 10, 1994.
19. Hilsman, *To Move a Nation,* 418, and Ngo Vinh Long, "Vietnam," in Douglas Allen and Ngo Vinh Long, eds., *Coming to Terms: Indochina, the United States and the War* (Boulder, CO: Westview Press, 1991), 33–34.
20. Hilsman, *To Move a Nation,* 525.

21. *The Pentagon Papers,* Vol. 4, 169–175.
22. Letter by Norman "Rusty" Heck to John McLaney, November 28, 1964, published in Ray Bows, *Vietnam Military Lore: Legends, Shadows and Heroes* (Hanover, ME: Bows and Sons, 1997), 722.
23. George K. Tanham, "Defeating Insurgency in South Vietnam: My Early Efforts," in Harvey Neese and John O'Donnell, eds., *Prelude to Tragedy: Vietnam, 1960–1965* (Annapolis, MD: Naval Institute Press, 2001), 155–179.
24. During the war, many minimum and maximum outcomes were discussed, but America's war goals were formally embodied in National Security Action Memorandum 288, as "a free and independent, non-communist South Vietnam," and this was the goal pursued by its military forces as the war progressed. See, for example, Memorandum from the Joint Chiefs of Staff to Secretary of Defense, August 27, 1965, Washington National Records Center RG 330, OSD/ADMIN Files: FRC 70 A 1265, Viet 381, in *Foreign Relations of the United States, 1964–1968, Volume III, Vietnam, June-December 1965,* no. 130, *www.state.gov/www/about_state/ history/vol_iii/130.html.*
25. McNaughton to McNamara, "Proposed Course of Action Re: Vietnam," March 24, 1965, *The Pentagon Papers,* Vol. 3, 696 and William P. Bundy, "Memorandum for the Secretary of Defense," January 6, 1965, *The Pentagon Papers,* Vol. 3, 686.
26. See Chester C. Cooper, National Security Council Staff, to Presidential Special Assistant for National Security Affairs (Bundy), March 10, 1965 in *Foreign Relations of the United States, 1964–1968, Volume II, Vietnam, January-June 1965,* no. 194, *www.state.gov/www/about_state/ history/vol_ii/192_194.html* and Cooper's further exchange with Bundy on July 21, 1965, in *Foreign Relations of the United States, 1964–1968, Volume III, Vietnam, June-December 1965,* no. 73, www.state.gov/www/about_ state/history/vol_iii/070.html.
27. John Lewallen, "Reluctant Counterinsurgents: International Voluntary Services in Laos," in Nina S. Adams and Alfred W. McCoy, *Laos: War and Revolution* (New York: Colophon Books, 1970), 357–371.
28. Author interview with Don Cohon, April 16, 1995.
29. Daniel Ellsberg, *Papers on the War* (New York: Simon & Schuster, 1972), 155.
30. The following account of the civilian advisory program in Vietnam is based largely on over 100 interviews with IVS and USAID advisors collected as part of the IVS Indochina Oral History Project conducted by this writer and Dr. Paul Rodell of Georgia Southern University (hereafter referred to as IVSOHP). Transcripts of the interviews cited are available to scholars upon application to the Librarian, Stewart Library, North Georgia College and State University, Dahlonega, Georgia, 30597. The contents of these interviews regarding the subject under review do not differ from the analysis of rural development programs in Vietnam found in Don Luce and John Sommer, *Vietnam—The Unheard Voices* (Ithaca, NY: Cornell University Press, 1969). Much of the data presented here is confirmed by U.S. Army official histories

of the war, including Jeffrey L. Clarke's *Advice and Support: The Final Years, 1965–1973* (Washington, DC: Center for Military History, 1988) and John M. Carland's *Stemming the Tide: May 1965 to October 1965* (Washington, DC: Center for Military History, 2000), as well as Richard Hunt's *Pacification: The Americans Struggle for Vietnam's Hearts and Minds* (Boulder, CO: Westview Press, 1995).

31. Luce and Sommer, *Vietnam—The Unheard Voices,* 97–100.
32. James Hamilton-Paterson, *The Greedy War* (New York: McKay, 1972).
33. This system is sympathetically described in a memory piece by Keyes Beach, "Christ Almighty, How Can They Do This," in Larry Englemann, ed., *Tears Before Rain: An Oral History of the Fall of South Vietnam* (New York: Oxford, 1990), 187–188. See also Jeffrey J. Clarke, *Advice and Support,* 22.
34. Ellsberg, *Papers on the War,* 149–150, 162–167.
35. Luce and Sommer, *Vietnam—The Unheard Voices,* 97
36. Ibid., 99–101.
37. Bui Diem with David Chanoff, *Jaws of History,* 156–399.
38. Luce and Sommer, *Vietnam—The Unheard Voices,* 215.
39. Ibid., 63.
40. Ibid., 55–64.
41. See *The Pentagon Papers,* Vol. 2, 547.
42. See, for example, Summers, *On Strategy,* 86–88.
43. Westmoreland, *A Soldier Reports* (Garden City, NJ: Doubleday, 1976), 153.
44. See comments of Westmoreland and General Bruce Palmer in Ted Gettinger, *The Johnson Years: A Vietnam Roundtable* (Austin, TX: Lyndon Baines Johnson Library, 1993), 76–77; 100–101, 159–161.
45. For Westmoreland's strategy and tactics, see Andrew Krepinevich, "Vietnam: Evaluating the Ground War, 1965–1968," in Showalter and Albert, eds., *An American Dilemma,* 87–107. For the Korean precedent, see Larry Cable, *Conflict of Myths: The Development of American Counterinsurgency Doctrine and the Vietnam War* (New York: New York University Press, 1986).
46. Notes of Meeting, July 22, 1965, Meeting Notes File, Box 1, Johnson Library, in the *Foreign Relations of the United States, 1964–1968,* Volume III, Vietnam June-December 1965, no. 76, *www.state.gov/www/about_state/ history/vol_iii/070.htm.*
47. Ibid.
48. Lyndon Baines Johnson, *Vantage Point: Perspectives on the Presidency, 1963–1969* (New York: Henry Holt, 1971), 323.
49. See Ball to Rusk, McNamara, McGeorge Bundy, William Bundy, McNamara, McNaughton, and Unger, June 29, 1965, in *The Pentagon Papers,* Vol. 4, 609–610, and George Ball, Memorandum for the President, July 1, 1965, in *The Pentagon Papers,* Vol. 4, 615–17.
50. See George McTurnan Kahin and John W. Lewis, *The United States and Vietnam* (New York: Dial Press, rev. ed., 1967), 310–311, 356–357.
51. Ball to Rusk, etc., June 29, 1965, in *The Pentagon Papers,* Vol. 4, 609–610.

52. For the authoritative account of this debate, see Berman, *Planning a Tragedy,* 109–110.
53. See Johnson, *Vantage Point,* 134–136; and Memoranda prepared for President Johnson by Robert McNamara, dated July 1 and July 20, 1965, in George C. Herring ed., *The Pentagon Papers: Abridged Edition* (New York: McGraw-Hill, 1993), 129–131.
54. Memorandum for the Record (prepared by Chester Cooper), July 21, 1965. National Security File, Vietnam, 2E, 1965 Troop Decision, Meeting Notes, File Box 1, Johnson Library, in the *Foreign Relations of the United States, 1964–1968,* Volume III, Vietnam June-December 1965, no. 75, *www.state.gov/www/about_state/ history/vol_iii/070.htm.*
55. H. R. McMaster, *Dereliction of Duty: Lyndon Johnson, Robert McNamara, the Joint Chiefs of Staff, and the Lies That Led to Vietnam* (New York: HarperCollins, 1997), 334
56. Ronald Spector, "Cooking Up a Quagmire," in the *New York Times,* July 20, 1997, sec. 7, col. 1, 31.
57. David G. Marr, "The Rise and Fall of 'Counterinsurgency': 1961–1964," in *The Pentagon Papers,* Vol. 5, 203, 205. See also Daniel Ellsberg, *Some Lessons from Failure in Vietnam* (Santa Monica, CA: RAND Corporation, 1969).
58. "The V. C. are hurting but they still control things because we are afraid to get out of our forts on other than temporary patrols or sweeps. We need to devote fully 50% of our effort to psychological operations and civic action." Entry for August 6, 1965, Diary of U.S. Air Force Colonel Robert Sexton, Bolling Air Force Base, Washington DC, Project CHECO, microfilm.
59. The writers of the *Pentagon Papers* confirm that pacification, which once figured prominently in the monthly reports filed by Military Assistance Command, Vietnam, "fades away to virtually nothing in the months of the build-up." See *The Pentagon Papers,* Vol. 2, 545–48.
60. David Halberstam, *The Best and the Brightest* (New York: Penguin, Reprint, 1985*),* 684.
61. *A Program for the Pacification and Long-term Development of South Vietnam* (PROVN), 2 vols., prepared by the Office of the Deputy Chief of Staff for Military Operations, Department of the Army, March, 1966, Histories Section (Vietnam), U.S Army Center for Military History (CMH) (Hereafter referred to as PROVN). For the eleven-page summary of PROVN and a fairly accurate assessment of the report's policy implications, see Joint Chiefs of Staff, to Secretary of Defense, August 24, 1966 (JSM-538–66), Washington National Records Center, RG 330, OASD/ISA Files: FRC 70 A 6649, 381 Vietnam, Secret, in the *Foreign Relations of the United States, 1964–68, Vol. 4 Vietnam,* no. 216, *www.state.gov/www/about_state/history/vol_iv/16_ 233.html.* However, the following discussion of PROVN is also based on the briefing given by its chief author, Lieutenant Colonel Don Marshall, to the Vice-Chief of Staff (acting chief) General Creighton Abrams; the Secretary of the Army, Stanley Resor; and the Joint Chiefs of Staff in Executive session,

chaired by General Wheeler. According to Marshall, this briefing formed the basis of virtually all subsequent discussions of PROVN. This briefing was described and the briefing script shown to the author by Marshall during an interview in Salem, Massachusetts. It was also discussed further in an interview by telephone on February 1, 1994.

62. PROVN, Vol. 1, v.
63. Ibid., 1, 1–102, chaps 1–4, passim. For further discussion of PROVN's significance, see Eric Bergerud, *The Dynamics of Defeat* (Boulder, CO: Westview Press, 1991), chaps. 2–3; and Lewis Sorley, *Thunderbolt from the Battle of the Bulge to Vietnam and Beyond: General Creighton Abrams and the Army of His Times* (New York: Simon & Schuster, 1992), 192–193, and 232–241.
64. See Sheehan, *A Bright and Shining Lie,* 527–546.
65. Joint Chiefs of Staff, to Secretary of Defense, August 24, 1966 (JSM-538–66), OASD/ISA Files: FRC 70 A 6649, 381 Vietnam. Secret, Washington National Records Center, RG 330, in the *Foreign Relations of the United States, 1964–68, Vol. IV, Vietnam,* no. 216, www. state.gov/www/about_state/history/vol_iv/216_233.html
66. Ellsberg, *Papers on the War,* 144–145. Ellsberg, a friend of Vann's, was privy to Vann's plan of reform and wrote a formal critique of "Harnessing the Revolution."
67. See *The Pentagon Papers,* Vol. 2, 532.
68. By the summer of 1966, Lodge went so far as to conspire with Marine Commandant General Wallace Green to challenge Westmoreland's conduct of the war. See George Herring, "The Johnson's Administration's Limited War in Vietnam," in Head and Grinter eds., *Looking Back on the Vietnam War,* 83.
69. Phillip B. Davidson, *Vietnam at War: The History, 1946–1975* (Novato, CA: Presidio Press, 1988), 410–411.
70. See also *The Pentagon Papers,* Vol. 2, 576.
71. Author interview with Ben Fordney, formerly on the staff of the U.S. Embassy in Saigon, January 12, 1994.
72. Donald Marshall, in an interview with author by telephone, February 1, 1994.
73. Roger Hilsman, Memorandum to the Secretary of State, March 14, 1964, *The Pentagon Papers,* Vol. 3, 43–44.
74. See the memorandum prepared by Robert McNamara for President Johnson, November 1965, in Herring ed., *The Pentagon Papers,* 134–136.
75. See Training Committee of South Vietnam, *Tinh Hinh Moi, Nheim Vu Moi [new situation, new tasks],* published as "Lao Dong Party Study Document for Political Reorientation, March 5, 1965," in Gareth Porter ed. and trans., *Vietnam: A History in Documents* (New York: New American Library, 1981), 304–305 and Le Duan, *Ta Nhat Dinh Thang (We will certainly win, the enemy will certainly lose),*" published as "Speech by Lao Dong Party Secretary Le Duan to a Cadre Conference, July 6–8, 1965," in Porter ed. and trans., *Vietnam,* 315–317. The line established in these documents is discussed in William Duiker, "Waging Revolutionary War: The Evolution of Hanoi's Strategy in the South, 1959–1965," in Werner and Doan Huynh eds., *The*

*Vietnam War,* 124–135. For a discussion of the various forms of *dau tranh,* see Douglas Pike, *Viet Cong: The Organization and Techniques of the National Liberation Front of South Vietnam* (Cambridge: MIT Press, 1966), 85–108, and, by the same author, *PAVN: People's Army of Vietnam* (Novato, CA: Presidio, 1986), 213–252.

76. Patrick J. McGarvey, ed. and trans., *Visions of Victory: Selected Vietnamese Communist Military Writings, 1964–1968* (Stanford, CA: Hoover Institution, 1969), 72–149.
77. For Hilsman, see *To Move a Nation,* 12, 434–435. For Ellsberg, see Halberstam, *The Best and the Brightest,* 207, 266–267; and Daniel Ellsberg, *The Day Loc Tein Was Pacified* (Santa Monica, CA: RAND Corporation, 1968). See also David W. P. Elliot, *Documents of an Elite Viet Cong Delta Demolition Platoon of the 514th Brigade-Part Four: Political and Military Training* (Santa Monica, CA: RAND Corporation, 1969).
78. Pike remarks that "Early on I wrote that victory in Vietnam in the long run will go to the side that . . . can most successfully disorganize the other side. I kept thinking, what [Saigon] needed is a Ho Chi Minh. That was the one ability he did have—to create organizations, drown little ones in big ones, and use one to slay the other," in Harry Mauer, *Strange Ground: Americans in Vietnam, 1945–1975: An Oral History* (New York: Henry Holt, 1989), 98, 121–123.
79. Sheehan, *A Bright and Shining Lie,* 630–643.
80. Ibid., 643.
81. According to a thorough study of the CAP program, even if MACV had been employed nationwide, the United States would not have won the war. See Michael Peterson, *The Combined Action Platoons* (New York: Praeger, 1989), 125.
82. Harry S. Summers, Jr., comments at a symposia on the American counterinsurgency tradition conducted and recorded under the auspices of the United States Air Force Special Operations Command School, Hurlburt Field, Florida, May 16, 1993. Summers closed the discussion of the Phoenix Program with the remark that "There are some things the American people do not want done in their name."
83. Jeffrey J. Clarke, *Advice and Support: The Final Years, 1965–1973* (Washington, DC: U.S. Army Center of Military History, 1988), 209.
84. See Robert McNamara's "Report on Visit to Vietnam, November 30, 1965," in *The Pentagon Papers,* Vol. 4, 622–623.
85. Richard Holbrooke, Memorandum of the White House Staff to the President's Special Assistant (Robert Komer), December 1, 1966, Washington National Records Center RG 330, McNamara Vietnam Files: FRC 77–0075, Vietnam—1966, Foreign Relations of the United States, Volume IV, Vietnam 1966, no. 321, www. state.gov/www/about_state/history/vol_iv/321 _335.html.
86. Searching for a means to defeat the enemy, the U.S. Army and ARVN had sought to create free-fire zones from which Vietnamese peasants were

ostensibly relocated so that allied forces could operate in their former terrain without killing civilians. However, these zones were established not merely to facilitate the telling of friend from foe, but with the express purpose of cutting off the Viet Cong from their bases of supply: the Vietnamese people. The program was never a strategic success. Thousands of Vietnamese civilians rebuilt their homes inside the zones despite the risks, and the Viet Cong quickly resumed their exploitation of these resources. It did succeed, however, in transforming Vietnam from a largely rural country to a country in which the majority of the population lived in urban areas. Unfortunately, the rural poor were herded into urban "relocation camps" where there were few resources. To remedy this situation, the United States poured thousands of dollars into accounts that were to be disbursed by the Republic of Vietnam to the refugees. Vietnamese administrators promptly created fictional refugees, and most of the money was disbursed to themselves via a variety of such subterfuges. IVS workers were expected to turn a blind eye to such affairs, but it became harder to do so as the pace of the war increased and IVS rural development and refugee resettlement workers realized, via accidental radio intercepts, that village clearances were undertaken by U.S. forces because IVS workers were "in place" and could be expected to coordinate the relocation process. Author interview with David Nesmith, IVSOHP, April 16, 1996. This unofficially labeled "Refugee Generation Program" may have eliminated large segments of the Vietnamese population as sources for Viet Cong recruitment, but it is doubtful it bred support for the Republic of Vietnam, as the lack of urban resistance in Saigon and Hue in 1975 indicates.

87. Author interview with Jerry Kliever, IVSOHP, April 23, 1999.
88. Author interview with Don Cohon, IVSOHP, April 16, 1996.
89. Letter to President Johnson, dated September 19, 1967, text in Luce and Sommer, *Vietnam: The Unheard Voices,* 315–321.
90. Ibid., 22.
91. Ibid.
92. See John M. Gates, "People's War in Vietnam," *Journal of Military History* 54 (July 1990): 324–344.
93. Cited in Larry E. Cable, "Everything Is Perfect and Getting Better," in Head and Grinter, eds., *Looking Back at the Vietnam War,* 205–206. Cable has been accused of being a nonveteran claiming veteran status. No one has, however, ever doubted his scholarship. In this case, it is confirmed by Lieutenant General Harold Moore, a hero of the Battle of Ia Drang (see fn. 95).
94. Ibid., 217–219.
95. Moore and Galloway, *We Were Soldiers Once,* 142–143. Moore recalls that the "next hint that something was wrong" was when he led many of the same troops he commanded at Ia Drang into battle in the Bong Son plain where his first contact was with civilians wounded in his air assault. They included a child the same age as his daughter, a sight that made him "heartsick." Then came the bitter loss of 82 men killed and 318 wounded in a clearing operation

seemingly so successful that Nguyen Cao Ky and his wife, Mai, personally came to his headquarters for a celebratory briefing. Yet, "within one week after we pulled out, the North Vietnamese and Viet Cong Main Force units had returned," as they did even after two more costly operations by his brigade. The last failure led Moore to remark that, "If they couldn't make it work in Bong Son—where the most powerful American division available had cleared the countryside—how could they possibly hope to reestablish South Vietnamese control in the other contested regions where the American military presence was much weaker." This was offered as a statement, not a question.

96. "How would you feel," one Vietnamese villager remarked, "if a bunch of burly foreigners invaded your hamlet, took away your men, and played weird music to 'entertain' you." See Luce and Sommer, *Vietnam: The Unheard Voices,* 213–214.
97. *The Pentagon Papers,* Vol. 2, 516–517, 530–531.
98. Tran Van Tra, "Tet: The General Offensive and General Uprising," in Werner and Doan Huynh, *Vietnam War,* 37–65.
99. Francis West, *Area Security* (Santa Monica, CA: RAND Corporation, 1969).
100. Sorley, *Thunderbolt,* 232–241.
101. Victoria Pohle, *The Viet Cong in Saigon: Tactics and Objectives during the Tet Offensive* (Santa Monica, CA: RAND Corporation, 1969).
102. Author interview with Bui Diem, April 24, 1992.
103. See Gerald Canon Hickey, *Accommodation in South Vietnam: The Key to Sociopolitical Solidarity* (Santa Monica, CA: RAND Corporation, 1967). For the impact of Thieu's election policies on support for the government, see James W. Trullinger, *Village at War: An Account of Revolution in Vietnam* (Stanford, CA: Stanford University, new ed., 1994), 156–162.
104. Halberstam, *The Best and the Brightest,* 256.
105. Stanley Karnow, *Vietnam: A History* (New York: Penguin, 1984), 365–366.
106. Bui Diem with David Chanoff, *The Jaws of History,* 339.
107. Ibid., 339–340.
108. Robert Komer, "Commentary," in John Schlight ed., *The Second Indochina War Symposium: Papers and Commentary,* 162–163.
109. During an interview conducted by the author, Jeff Doyle, one of the authors of the official history of Australia's involvement in Southeast Asian conflicts, remarked that despite the best counterinsurgency training methods and practices, when the Australian forces in Vietnam were withdrawn from their assigned areas, more villages were under Viet Cong control than when they arrived.
110. Robert Komer, quoted in Kim Willenson et al., *The Bad War: An Oral History of the Vietnam War* (New York: New American Library, 1979), 95–97.
111. Clark M. Clifford, "A Vietnam Reappraisal: The Personal History of One Man's View and How It Evolved," *Foreign Affairs* (July 1969): 609–613.
112. See Theodore Draper, "Ghosts of Vietnam," in *Dissent* 26 (Winter 1979): 31.
113. The "MACV Strategic Objectives Plan" is discussed in Sorley, *Thunderbolt,* 234–237.

114. *The Pentagon Papers,* Vol. 2, 576.
115. The impact of this strategy is revealed with particular clarity in Trullinger, *Village at War,* 150–201.
116. Colonel Stuart Herrington notes that "Like us, Hanoi failed to win the hearts and minds of the South Vietnamese peasantry. Unlike us, Hanoi's leaders were able to compensate for this failure by playing their trump card—they overwhelmed South Vietnam with a twenty-two division force." See Stuart Herrington, *Silence Was a Weapon: The Vietnam War in the Villages* (Novato, CA: Presidio, 1982), 203. Summers cites this statement as support for his assertion that the primary enemy America faced in Vietnam was the North Vietnamese regular army. Summers forgets that during the years of the cross-border assaults, 1972 to 1975, the North Vietnamese were the primary enemy of the South Vietnamese army, not the American army. The guerrilla sacrifices of 1964 to 1968 had insured that there were precious few Americans still around to confront it. For Summers's use of Herrington, see Harry Summers, "A Strategic Perception of the Vietnam War," in Grinter and Dunn, eds., *The American War in Vietnam,* 92.
117. Komer, "Commentary," in Schlight, *Second Indochina War Symposium:,* 161–165.
118. Ibid.
119. Henry Kissinger, *The White House Years* (Boston: Little, Brown, 1979), 230–234.
120. See note 10.
121. See Sorley, *Thunderbolt,* 235. MACV's "Objectives Plan" was published in 1969. It stated that the ultimate objective for South Vietnam, "a free, independent and viable nation which is not hostile to the United States," would take twenty years or more to achieve and that much less time was going to be available to achieve it.
122. See also Douglas Pike's recollection of a conversation with Harry Summers in Harry Mauer, *Strange Ground,* 122. When asked by Pike how he could write a book analyzing the strategy of the Vietnam war "and not have one chapter in which you talk about the enemy," Summers replied, "Well, that is very hard to do, hard to understand. Anyway, this is about American strategy." Pike responded by asking "Well, would you write a book about fighting Rommel in the desert and not go into what Rommel was doing and thinking? Doesn't that escape you, the logic of it?"
123. See Dunn, "On Strategy Revisited," 96–108. Dunn concludes that "had Clausewitz been alive in our time and serving as an American general during the Vietnam years, he too probably would have lost the war. His theory demands a target, and enemy to destroy, and the Communists would not have offered him such a target."
124. Henry Kissinger, *The White House Years* (Boston: Little Brown, 1979), 281–282.
125. B. Jenkins, *The Unchangeable War* (Santa Monica, CA: RAND Corporation, 1970), 1–15. This position is echoed in Robert Komer, *Bureaucracy at War:*

*U.S. Performance in the Vietnam War Conflict* (Boulder, CO: Westview, 1986).

126. Lieutenant General James H. Willibanks, *Thiet Giap! The Battle of An Loc, April 1972* (Fort Leavenworth, KS: Combat Studies Institute, U.S. Command and General Staff College, 1993), 75–77.
127. See Trullinger, *Village at War,* 177–179.
128. Ngo Vinh Long, "Post-Paris Agreement Struggles and the Fall of Saigon," in Werner and Doan Huynh, *The Vietnam War,* 206.
129. Patrick J. Hearden, *The Tragedy of Vietnam* (New York: HarperCollins Publishers, 1991), 173–174.
130. Ibid., 174. For the fate of ARVN's commanders, see David Bulter, The Fall of Saigon (New York: Simon and Schuster, 1985), 483–489.
131. See George Herring, "The Strange 'Dissent' of Robert McNamara," in Werner and Doan Huynh, *The Vietnam War,* 140–150.
132. See for example Robert Komer, *Bureaucracy Does Its Thing: Institutional Constraints on U.S.-GVN Performance in Vietnam* (Santa Monica, CA: RAND Corporation, 1972).

CHAPTER SEVEN

# THE ROLE OF ECONOMIC CULTURE IN VICTORY AND DEFEAT IN VIETNAM

ANDREW J. ROTTER

"*Ah, les statistisques!*" a South Vietnamese general once exclaimed to an American friend. "Your Secretary of Defense loves statistics. We Vietnamese can give him all he wants. If you want them to go up, they will go up. If you want them to go down, they will go down."[1] Apart from fulfilling a longstanding authorial desire to begin an essay in French, the quotation (more significantly) suggests that economics, the grand name we give *statistiques,* was found in the fiber of the American and Vietnamese war. Economic analysis, properly done, can illustrate why the North won, and the United States lost, the Vietnam War.

This chapter begins by examining the role played by economics in the origins and progress of the Vietnam War and starts, more specifically, by looking at Vietnam, South and North. Were there economic reasons for the failure of South Vietnam? On the other side, to what extent did economics shape Vietnamese resistance, to the French and then to the Americans? Did the United States have economic reasons for making a commitment to a noncommunist Vietnam, or part of Vietnam? Were economic considerations present when Dwight Eisenhower embarked on his experiment in nation-building south of the seventeenth parallel, when John F. Kennedy sent in the Green Berets, when Lyndon Johnson began bombing North Vietnam and put soldiers ashore at Danang, or when Richard Nixon and Henry Kissinger decided they had no choice but to withdraw U.S. troops? The chapter ends with remarks concerning the economic consequences of the war for both sides, on the assumption that even short-run consequences have much to do with determining ultimate winners and losers.

But in between exploring economic causes and consequences—and forgiveness is begged for both the use of passive voice and this slightly unorthodox organization—the chapter lingers over perhaps more controversial matters hinted at by the American interest in *statistiques,* and the ironic response to it by the Vietnamese. This, the core of the chapter, explores the American infatuation with numbers as a symbolic indication of a deep culture of economics. Let us understand that economics is not merely the keeping of accounts; it is instead a cultural system, a network of significance people invent to give meaning to the process of exchange, to money, and to production and consumption of goods and services. In this sense, the Vietnam War was profoundly economic in nature. Among the most fundamental differences between Americans and Vietnamese was their understanding of economics. The images and stereotypes Americans formed of their Vietnamese allies and enemies were frequently the product of American economic culture. The vocabulary used by Americans and Vietnamese to describe their war was often economic in its origin. Economic culture strongly influenced the way each side made war: The Americans relied heavily on technology, machinery, and ordinance, while the National Liberation Front (NLF) and North Vietnamese mobilized people to work and fight together for the common causes of nationalism and socialism. The economic assumptions each side brought to the war had much to do with determining its outcome.

Economics—more precisely, the economic relationship between the United States and South Vietnam—offers a persuasive explanation for the failure of any government in Saigon to gain popular legitimacy. Beginning in the 1950s, the United States seemed intent on giving southern Vietnam a complete economic makeover. Much rice had always been grown south of the seventeenth parallel, but maldistribution of land and the growing conflict in the countryside meant that by 1965 South Vietnam relied on the United States for food. Efforts to create industrial zones and to encourage foreign investment in the South were largely unavailing. Fearful that growing demand and slumping production would trigger runaway inflation, the Americans created the Commodity Import Program, under which the U.S. Agency for International Development (AID) made loans to South Vietnamese firms to import American consumer goods. The idea was to put modern conveniences—refrigerators, stereos, motorcycles, and the like—into the hands of South Vietnam's middle class while soaking up the excess money supply. The program, combined of course with the increasing U.S. military presence in Vietnam, had several unintended results. William Duiker, who served in the economic section of the U.S. embassy in Saigon, has described the emergence of a well-heeled middle class "amid a swelling urban population of poor workers, beggars, and refugees flooding into refugee camps in the suburbs."[2] The South Vietnamese finance minister complained in 1965 that the growing number of U.S. soldiers had caused "a vertiginous rise in the cost of labor (100%) and the prices of some products."[3] The effect of U.S. intervention was practically surreal. The Saigon sanitation system failed when its workers abandoned their posts for construction jobs on U.S. military bases, where the pay was much better than in the city. Corruption was rampant. Construction materials, intended for housing and commercial building projects, were siphoned off by South Vietnamese generals for sale on the black market. (Enough nevertheless got through for the construction of forty ice cream plants for U.S. soldiers. And residents of Saigon improvised, flattening discarded beer and soda cans and nailing them to scraps of wood to make walls and roofs.)

Prostitution grew to keep pace with the rate of U.S. troop commitment. Brothels appeared around the military bases. Saigon alone had 56,000 registered prostitutes; no one knew how many remained unregistered. Political officials in Saigon, allegedly including Nguyen Cao Ky and Nguyen Van Thieu, were involved in heroin trafficking.[4] Begging, theft, and violence on city streets were the fallout of South Vietnam's social and economic degradation. Garbage and filth formed mountains in Saigon. At night, journalist Neil Sheehan noted, the piles of garbage would move as one walked by; they were crawling with rats. One day Sheehan saw a Vietnamese phrase scrawled on the pavement in front of a garbage pile. A companion translated for him: "This is the fruit of American aid."[5]

The Americans hoped to strengthen South Vietnam's resolve by pumping the country full of aid. Instead, the aid spoiled the country, and in doing so destroyed any hope that a regime in Saigon could gain popular support. The plenty provided by the United States told the South Vietnamese all they needed to know about the inability of their government to manage its own affairs, for any government that depended so heavily on outsiders for its sustenance must be weak, and any government that required the luxurious provender of the Americans surely needed an enormous fig leaf to cover its inadequacies. Bui Diem, a South Vietnamese politician and diplomat, thought the American war was absurdly out of scale. "The Americans," he said when it was all over, "made the war too expensive by the way they fought it. It was a kind of 'affluent war' never seen before or even thought of by the Vietnamese. They opened their eyes in bewilderment when they looked at the helicopters bringing hot food to the fighting men. They saw the thousands of gadgets piled up in huge PXs for the use of the GIs, the hundreds of planes flying back and forth across the Pacific for the transport of US troops and supplies."[6] Many no doubt wondered why it was necessary. South Vietnam lost the war because it was dependent on the United States, economically and in every other way.

North Vietnam's war also had an economic basis. Ho Chi Minh's Vietminh had some success organizing the northern Vietnamese countryside during World War II. But the Vietminh's breakthrough came in the summer and fall of 1945, when flooding destroyed much of northern Vietnam's rice crop. Relief from the south proved to not be forthcoming, in part because the transportation system was disrupted, in greater part because the French and Japanese hoarded rice for their own nationals. The result was a famine, in which northern Vietnam lost 1.5 to 2 million people. It might have been worse, had the Vietminh not acted swiftly. They seized and distributed rice held by the Japanese in warehouses, and they promised meaningful land reform once they had the power to effect it. The Vietminh's revolution of August 1945, leading to the declaration of independence by the Democratic Republic of Vietnam (DRV) on September 2, was thus born in economic crisis and sustained by popular gratitude to Ho Chi Minh for having combated it.

Ho recognized that land redistribution in the north would not be enough to keep his people fed. The Mekong River rice bowl was vital to all of Vietnam. Jean Lacouture, Ho's perceptive biographer, was relatively sanguine at the prospect of Vietnam dividing politically and culturally—the country had not always been unified, after all—but, he wrote, "to break up Viet-Nam's economic unity was to attempt the irrational."[7] No simple churlishness, nor even some sentimental notion that Vietnam should be whole, sustained Ho's struggle to unite the country following its division at Geneva in 1954. For a Western reporter in 1955, Hanoi's foreign trade minister, Phan Anh, wielded a pair of chopsticks and declared: "Rice! First and foremost there must be enough rice. This country must be unified. They need each other economically, the North and the South. There can be no question of continued partition."[8] As late as October 1960, Ho's government asked to buy rice from the South "at a reasonable price."[9] Saigon ignored the request; the National Liberation Front (NLF) was formed two months later.

For the United States too, the Vietnam War had economic roots. The U.S. commitment to a noncommunist Vietnam, or part of Vietnam, originated with the decision of the Harry S. Truman administration to grant a small amount of economic and military aid to the French-backed Bao Dai government in the spring of 1950. This decision was based on the administration's understanding of the post - World War II international economy. By mid-1949, the Americans saw their plans for stabilizing the noncommunist world unraveling at an alarming rate—this in spite of the Marshall Plan. West Germany, though by then destined to become a building block of the anti-Soviet alliance, remained militarily impotent, strategically isolated, and economically unsound. France was not quite so badly off. Still, no one was yet betting on French political stability, especially given the increasing amounts of blood and treasure the nation was spending to hold its Vietnamese colony against the Vietminh. Apparently in better shape, Great Britain underwent, in the late spring of 1949, a shocking dollar drain to the United States, which Marshall Plan aid proved insufficient to stanch and which resulted, in the fall, in a humiliating devaluation of the sterling pound. Things were even worse in Asia. While the French war in Vietnam intensified, the communists were close to victory in the Chinese civil war. Japan, the United States' choice to replace China as the bastion of Western interests in East Asia, had not yet recovered from its devastating defeat of four years before, nor from the economic defibrillation treatment of its American occupiers between 1945 and 1947.

The Americans now came to a sequence of revelations about what was needed to revive and protect their most important allies. Economic aid, even the billions showered on the fortunate under the Marshall Plan, was not enough to stimulate permanent economic recovery in the noncommunist world; this would require a dramatic increase in world trade. The scope of trade could not be limited to developed, noncommunist nations but must include the colonies and former colonies of the powers—small and allegedly primitive countries, perhaps, but places frequently rich in cheap labor, natural resources, and agricultural goods. And U.S. policymakers discovered that the most important places fitting this description were in Southeast Asia. Indonesia had oil; British Malaya was the world's leading producer of rubber and smelted tin; Thailand and Burma were traditional exporters of rice. Everyone wanted oil; U.S. dollars spent on Malayan rubber and tin could be recouped by dollar-hungry Great Britain; Japan needed rice as well as raw materials in exchange for its (potential) industrial exports, especially after the communization of China. The United States hoped to encourage the growth of these trading relationships, and hoped as well to protect Southeast Asia by aiding the French in their conflict with Vietnamese nationalism. If the Americans pulled French chestnuts from the Indochinese fire, they would assist in stabilizing conditions in Paris, while at the same time opening the possibility that the return of French military assets to the European continent might at last allow the restoration of West German military influence, under the aegis of the North Atlantic Treaty. Thus did a sophisticated understanding of international economics carry the United States into confrontation with the forces of nationalism in Vietnam.[10]

Concerns for the future of the Southeast Asian economy continued during the Dwight Eisenhower administration. Even more firmly than his predecessor did Eisenhower believe that the nations of Southeast Asia were like dominoes, certain to topple if the first of them, Vietnam, fell to the communists. Secretary of State John Foster Dulles told a New York audience in late March 1954 that Southeast Asia was the "'rice bowl' which helps to feed the densely populated region that extends from India to Japan. It is rich [he continued] in many raw materials, such as tin, oil, rubber, and iron ore. It offers industrial Japan potentially important markets and sources of raw materials."[11] High-level statements like this suggest that there were economic reasons why the Eisenhower administration greatly expanded the U.S. role in Vietnam, providing advisors, aid, and Central Intelligence Agency (CIA) dirty tricks to the South Vietnamese government of Ngo Dinh Diem, flouting the Geneva agreement, and in general making a going concern of a regime that lacked popular support even its own precincts.

At this point—say 1961—the economic trail seemingly goes cold. There is not much in the documentary record to sustain an economic interpretation of the U.S. escalation of the war during the 1960s, nor much evidence that Richard Nixon's decision to reverse course and withdraw U.S. troops was impelled by economic factors. To be sure, there are intriguing hints that economic thinking persisted among American policymakers, among them President Lyndon Johnson's private eruption in March 1968: "Our fiscal situation is abominable. We have a deficit running over 20 [billion dollars]. We are not getting the tax bill. The deficit could be over 30. If it does [exceed that], the interest rate will rise. The British pound may fall. The Canadian pound may fall. The dollar will be in danger." And he went on in this vein.[12]

The most subtle economic interpretation of the Vietnam War is the historian Gabriel Kolko's. Slightly adapted, it goes like this: U.S. policymakers believed in the domino theory, and did so presumably when they escalated the war in 1965. If Vietnam was not by itself valuable, the rest of Southeast Asia certainly was. Or even if Southeast Asia was not of overwhelming economic significance, Vietnam was a test case of America's willingness to protect its economic interests in all other Third World countries; the United States could not afford to withdraw from Vietnam because doing so would encourage other revolutions. The sound of helicopters ferrying soldiers into the jungle of South Vietnam was also the death rattle of U.S. imperialism.[13]

This is one of those arguments that is difficult to disprove. While key decision makers never put things quite this way—that is, we had better hold the line in Vietnam or our interests in Central America will be threatened—it is plausible that the commitment to Vietnam would be connected to predicaments elsewhere; the Vietnam War did not occur in a vacuum. Still, by the mid-1960s, a modicum of reality had settled in Washington, and the economic case for escalating the war could not have been compelling. Most U.S. policymakers had at last recognized the Sino-Soviet split, which made talk of world communism extending its reach throughout Southeast Asia pretty much meaningless. The economically valuable Southeast Asian dominoes also seemed less likely to fall. British Malaya, that rich repository of rubber and tin, had survived the Emergency of 1948–1955 and in 1957 had become the independent nation that would be called Malaysia, more, not less, stable than previously. Singapore had emerged in 1959, under the Asian values capitalism of Lee Kuan Yew. Lee, a fierce anticommunist, would prove himself a satisfactory associate of the United States. Looking very little like a domino, Thailand was by the mid-1960s floating in a sea of U.S. military aid. Hong Kong, still a British colony, and Taiwan, periodically shaken by threats from the People's Republic of China (PRC) but evidently immune to out-and-out attack, were safely noncommunist and increasingly prosperous. And while U.S. policymakers had worried incessantly about the radical tendencies of President Sukarno in Indonesia, the coup that toppled his government on September 30, 1965, brought to power a far more cooperative regime, backed by the military and just repressive enough to give the Americans reassurance without unduly offending their taste. U.S. officials labored to establish a connection between the Indonesian coup and the war in Vietnam. They labored in vain; there was none.[14]

Far more important than economics as a reason for U.S. escalation in Vietnam were several other factors, well documented by historians. Anticommunism was to some extent a reflex by the mid-1960s. Lyndon Johnson and his war managers did not need to think about it much—they just knew that a communist victory in Vietnam would be a bad thing. Politics also played a role for LBJ, the consummate politician. Johnson remembered the recrimination that followed the so-called loss of China by the Truman administration in 1949 and suspected the Republicans would repeat their performance, against him, should the United States fail to preserve South Vietnam. And Johnson had personal reasons for seeking victory in Vietnam. Diplomatic historian Robert Dean has argued that a cult of masculinity surrounded President John F. Kennedy, whereby negotiation and compromise were equated with weakness and associated with effeminacy.[15] As much as Kennedy did Johnson wish to avoid being called effeminate. Johnson saw the Vietnam War as a test of his manhood: He would hunt the quarry successfully and "nail the coonskin to the wall," or he would effeminize his enemy, then seduce her—"I'm going up Ho Chi Minh's leg one inch at a time," as he told George McGovern.[16] Most important, by the 1960s the U.S. commitment to a noncommunist South Vietnam had taken on a life of its own, become valuable for its own sake. Policymakers stressed the importance of keeping faith with the South in order to reassure the allies that America's word was good: If the United States would fight for South Vietnam, it would clearly do so for (say) West Germany. The logic was flawed but unfortunately durable.

And yet, in spite of the apparent lack of evidence that U.S. war managers were much moved by economic thinking, there was a way in which America's conflict had a vital economic dimension. It was not, by 1965, a war for tin, tungsten, and oil, nor had it much to do with the maintenance of capitalist hegemony in Asia. Instead, the Vietnam War reflected the fundamental assumptions of American economic culture. It was war conducted according to the logic of advanced corporate capitalism, "technowar" (according to James William Gibson) or, in Jeffrey Record's terminology, "industrial warfare."[17] While economics cannot explain *why* the United States went to war in 1965, surely the confidence policymakers had in the strength of the American economy contributed to their belief that the United States could not lose in Vietnam: our gross national product (GNP), after all, was over thirty times the size of theirs. Economic culture does explain *how* the United States fought the war, and insofar as the American defeat was the result of failed strategy, economics can explain that too.

The realm of culture is a murky one—British cultural critic Raymond Williams once called culture "one of the two or three most complicated words in the English language"[18]—so some precision of definition is important. In the first place, language offers clues about the culture from whence it comes. Words reflect the attitudes, values, and assumptions of those who use them. It is meaningful, for instance, that Johnson did not say to McGovern, "I'm going to try to convince Ho Chi Minh to bargain with me," but instead: "I'm going up Ho's leg an inch at a time." Johnson's language here suggests that he had confidence in his own abilities to seduce an adversary, that Ho was weak and effeminate enough to fall prey to seduction, and that, in the end, guile and not mere force would provide the key to victory in Vietnam.

Gender aside, the language of American war managers, officers, and soldiers was replete with economic references. For intelligence officers, getting reliable information through interrogation was known as "making money."[19] An interrogator made the most money if the information he got resulted in a successful B-52 strike. Policymakers talked of achieving "production quotas." At a meeting in Honolulu in 1966, ambassador to Saigon Henry Cabot Lodge thought his side could increase its level of pacification from 52 percent to 66 percent of South Vietnam's population by the end of the year.[20] The absurd precision of these numbers—why not 50 percent and 65 percent?—brandished a false authority. General Maxwell Taylor once gave President Johnson a paper titled "Assessment and Uses of Negotiation Blue Chips," in which he calculated American "purchasing power" and the "value of our holdings" compared to those of the North Vietnamese. (William Bundy, responding, thought Taylor's opening "asking price" was too low.)[21] Chester Cooper, a senior member of the National Security Council during the war's genesis, found the enumeration of *les statistiques* exhausting. "Numbers!" he complained. "There was a numbers mill in every military . . . installation in Vietnam. Numbers flowed into Saigon and from there to Washington like the Mekong River during flood season. Sometimes the numbers were plucked from the air, sometimes the numbers were not accurate. Sometimes they were accurate but not relevant. Sometimes they were relevant but misinterpreted. . . . By 1967 the numbers may have been accurate, relevant, and correctly interpreted, but few really believed them. The 'briefees' had become numbers numb."[22] But they did not stop using them in a vain attempt to measure U.S. progress in the war.

The ways in which the Americans described the Vietnamese, both allies and enemies, drew on a long tradition of stereotyping Asians as economically backward. "Lazy" is an economic epithet, implying an unwillingness to work hard, to take advantage of opportunities presented; to be lazy is un-American. U.S. representatives in Vietnam often called the Vietnamese lazy. They did so in early 1967, when Vietnamese villagers apparently refused to use water from a newly built canal—a joint project of the Agency for International Development and Saigon government—to irrigate their crops. It turned out that there were several good reasons why they did not. A road bordering the canal, built at the same time, had no culverts underneath it, so farmers on its wrong side could not get to the canal's water. A tenant farmer using a parcel of the adjoining land pointed out that if his fields became too profitable, his landlord would repossess the land and farm it himself. Others observed that the canal walls were so high they could not sufficiently raise the irrigation water with their modest electric pump.[23]

"Dirty" is also an economic epithet, although its valence is wider than economics. The Vietnamese were dirty because they were less prosperous, less advanced, less civilized than westerners. People get dirty, and stay dirty, if they live too close to the land, as most Vietnamese did. "We were fools," decided one bitter GI, "to be ready to die for people who defecated in public, whose food was dirtier than anything in our garbage cans back home."[24] And the Americans simply knew that agrarian societies were more primitive than industrial ones. Only those who readily dismissed the significance of land could believe that uprooting a rural people and removing them to barbed-wire compounds would win the hearts and minds of the displaced. As Marilyn Young has written, American soldiers trampled seedlings in the paddies of South Vietnam because "rice cultivation simply didn't register" with them.[25] Jeffrey Record, who served as an advisor under the Office of Civil Operations and Revolutionary Development Support (CORDS) in the Mekong Delta, once watched U.S. helicopters annihilate a herd of domesticated water buffalo, "apparently for sport."[26] The gunners were doubtless letting off steam. Their victims were the farmers whose livelihood depended on the work the animals provided.

American economic culture was not just expressed in language; it was embedded in the organization of the U.S. military. Like the American corporate world, the armed forces were bureaucratized and stratified. Officers were managers, troops were workers. "[My troops] work, and they work hard," said General William Westmoreland in 1966. "It has been my policy that they're on the job seven days a week, working as many hours as required to get the job done."[27] (Those were the days of time clocks in the jungle, to paraphrase songwriter Paul Simon.) For officers, Westmoreland provided "career management." In order to maintain the morale of his officer corps, the general shortened the time needed to get promoted "up and out" of the combat zone. By 1968, over half his battalion commanders were rotated out in less than six months. More than half the company commanders were sent to the rear before they finished four months. Having received combat command experience, these colonels and captains were eligible for promotion; they had, in military parlance, got their tickets punched.

Ticket punching did not make for better, more prudent officers. Inexperienced commanders—those, that is, with little time in the field—wasted their soldiers, in both traditional and colloquial senses of the verb. The Pentagon's systems analysts found that battalion leaders with less than six months' experience lost an average of 2.5 men a month, while those with more than six months lost 1.6 men a month. In a world of numbers, machines are more valuable than men because they have more killing power. As a colonel reportedly told a lieutenant: "I don't care what happens to your men, but I'm not losing any more God damn tanks." Faced with the detachment and indifference of their managers, the troops formed emotional bonds with their enemies. "I was more at war with the officers there than I was with the Viet Cong," recalled a navy scout.[28]

This was a war of cost accounting, so it was no surprise that success was measured by the number of Vietnamese bodies found after an engagement. "It was as if LBJ's war slogan were We Shall Overwhelm," as the historian Loren Baritz has put it. Many Americans bitterly criticized war by body count, which led, they claimed, inevitably to the dehumanization of the other implicit in the notorious "mere gook" rule: If it's dead, and Vietnamese, it's VC. But how else would the United States conduct war? The lavish use of firepower and the body count measure were logical extensions of American economic culture in the 1960s. Baritz quotes Lieutenant Colonel Zeb B. Bradford: "Highly mechanized and technical warfare reinforces our tendencies and talents and serves as a vehicle for evolutionary advance—counterinsurgency goes against the grain. We are a rich, industrial, urban country. Highly technical forces are compatible with our characteristics and resources."[29]

One of the most heated controversies on the American side of the war stemmed from charges that General Westmoreland suppressed information indicating that the enemy order of battle was considerably larger than official sources had reported. The CIA analyst Sam Adams estimated the Viet Cong's strength by adding in local forces and irregular units previously discounted by military intelligence, and concluded that the brass had sold short the enemy by some 300,000 fighters.[30] Westmoreland's decision regarding the order of battle was widely interpreted as underhanded, but it was not a deliberate deception. Rather, it was consistent with the nature of American warfare, with the assumptions of war managers who patterned their behavior after corporate models. The Viet Cong locals were not real soldiers, not like ours anyway; according to Robert Komer, President Johnson's personal representative in Vietnam, they were "low-grade, part-time hamlet self defense groups, mostly weaponless."[31] They were, in other words, only marginal employees, often women and children, requiring little pay, few benefits—and, from the American standpoint, no regard. They literally did not count.

Technowar is not without its defenders. Those who praise it argue that it allows the substitution of machines for men, long-distance killing for eye-to-eye combat, and thus saves soldiers' lives. An artillery barrage or an air strike maximizes your forces' killing power while minimizing their exposure to the enemy. The problem is, of course, that in putting distance between themselves and the carnage of war, the war makers anesthetized themselves to the pain of battle. The result was the dehumanization of everyone involved. The Americans dehumanized the enemy, whose deaths were so often unseen, statistically recorded but otherwise unremarked. American soldiers dehumanized each other, hoping to avoid attachments that, if sundered, would increase their emotional pain. They could not avoid attachment altogether, and some of their friendships were strong. But the grunts also referred to each other as "meat," as if to acknowledge their mortality by trivializing their value,[32] and they resisted close relationships, especially near the end of their tours.

And technowar caused war managers to dehumanize their own troops. Soldiers—employees—were "assets." One hates to lose assets, but assets have no bodies, no faces, and there are inevitably more to be employed. Many soldiers were convinced that Westmoreland's search-and-destroy strategy meant that they were "bait" for the enemy. Military Assistance Command, Vietnam (MACV) from time to time published "proper terminology" tables, designed to replace candid language with an antiseptic vocabulary of officialese. Thus "Hamburger Hill" became "Hill 937," a "free-fire zone" was really a "pre-cleared firing area," and U.S. troops were never "ambushed" but "engaged the enemy on all sides." The phrase "troops used to bait the enemy" was simply "never to be used."[33]

Self-insulated from battlefield death, the military and the U.S. government could not own up to the terrible human cost of the war. Officials deluded themselves that the price could be kept reasonable, and policymakers, Lyndon Johnson most prominently, failed to explain to the American people that their fellow citizens would have to die to sustain the South Vietnamese regime. Policymakers agonized over the loss of American lives in Southeast Asia. But the American people, not their government, finally rejected the distancing that inured the war managers to the killing, and having seen too many of their husbands and sons come home in body bags, the majority demanded an end to the American war.

So, too, did the economic culture of the Democratic Republic of Vietnam (DRV) shape that nation's war effort, although with dramatically different results. Hanoi's leaders oversaw the "socialist transformation" of the North and the liberated areas of the South. Economic development was to be a collective enterprise undertaken by hardworking citizens who were theoretically equals. When the DRV went to war against the United States, its leadership harnessed the war effort to the struggle for economic development. There was thus no distancing possible: The ideological message (make socialism work) was integral to the practical (keep the economy thriving in order to sustain the combatants). The line between workers and fighters was blurred. The United States fought the war "in cold blood," as Secretary of State Dean Rusk liked to say.[34] For the DRV, the war was total. Addressing a group of Communist Party cadres in Haiphong in early 1970, General Vo Nguyen Giap exhorted his audience to "fight when the enemy comes, continue production and normal life when he has been driven away."[35] The lessons of heroic war were the same as those to be learned in heroic work for the socialist system: "The movement in which the workers take part in the management of their workshops and take their production team as a basis . . . has raised the sense of responsibility of the workers, their love of labour, and their courage in combat, and has taught them to live an organized and disciplined life."[36] Economic success would breed success in battle, and without the first the second would not happen. The Communist Party Central Committee urged the North "to carry out production while fighting to defend itself."[37] Ho Chi Minh appealed to the people to resist the "U.S. imperialists." Thus far, he claimed in 1966, "North Vietnam has not flinched in the least. Our army and people have eagerly emulated one another in production and fighting," with the happy result that over 1,200 U.S. aircraft had been shot down.[38] Propaganda? Of course. But Ho's rhetoric specifically and skillfully reminded Vietnamese that economic culture and war culture were same thing.

One cannot help but admire the ingenuity of the leadership's appeal, and one cannot help but be impressed with its success. It was no accident that the growing collectivization of the economy coincided with an increasing determination to fight the Americans until they withdrew. The North Vietnamese and NLF fighters worked and fought out of the same impulse, and for the same things. But there was a less happy side to the situation. By harnessing the war effort to economic culture, and in linking them both with the rhetoric of sacrifice, the North Vietnamese leadership may have convinced itself that its people would, or should, do anything for the cause. You could work people to the bone in the name of socialism and for the cause of independence, and you could send them off to die for the same purposes. This is what Hanoi did, putting at risk the lives of thousands of soldiers—at Khe Sanh, during the 1968 Tet Offensive, and in the Easter Offensive in 1972. (Giap reportedly opposed the Tet attacks because he feared losing too many fighters. He lost thousands, decimating the NLF.) Blinded by its own propaganda, or coldly convinced that there was no other choice, Hanoi sacrificed lives not because it was distanced emotionally from the war but because it saw no cause as distinct from it.

The Vietnam War had significant economic consequences for all sides; assessing them gives us some measure of victory and defeat in the conflict. The war's economic impact on the United States (to begin there) was at first limited. Even after federal spending for the war increased dramatically in fiscal year 1966, Lyndon Johnson remained in denial concerning its costs. He could not bear to sacrifice his Great Society, "the woman I really loved," to the demands of "that bitch of a war."[39] He refused at first to cut nondefense spending or raise taxes. His denial of economic reality was abetted by Defense Secretary Robert McNamara, who allowed to creep into the budget the assumption that the war would be over by June 30, 1967. What happened, of course, was that the war demanded more resources, not less, in 1967: The budget estimate of $10.2 billion for the war turned out to be roughly half of what the administration finally needed. Belatedly, the president acted. He tried for a 6 percent tax surcharge in 1967, but Congress said no, apparently having been told once too often that the war would not cause economic pain. A temporary 10 percent tax surcharge was passed in June 1968, but in approving the bill Congress demanded that Johnson cut nondefense spending by $6 billion. So much for the Great Society.[40]

The Johnson administration's refusal to recognize economic reality created serious problems. Johnson's commitment to the poor diminished; the new Office of Economic Opportunity had its budget cut in half in 1966. "Losing the Great Society was a terrible thought," Johnson told his biographer Doris Kearns, "but not so terrible as the thought of being responsible for America's losing a war to the Communists."[41] The dollar, supreme among the world's currencies since the Bretton Woods conference in 1944, lost status during the Vietnam War. The balance of payments worsened considerably, and between 1965 and 1967 the United States was forced to finance over half of its payments deficit in gold.

Most of all, the administration's prolonged unwillingness to face the hard economic facts of the Vietnam War resulted in destructive inflation. With employment high and with the economy at nearly full productive capacity in 1965, the increased demand for war matériel administered a terrible shock. As defense expenditures rose, so did the Wholesale and Consumer Price Indexes. What started as "demand-pull" inflation—that is, prices jump skyward by a sudden increase in demand—became, around 1969, inflation of the "cost-push" variety, whereby employers and wage earners alike win pay increases, the costs of which are passed on to consumers as higher prices.[42] Increases in the cost of domestic goods led to more purchases of imports, which exacerbated the balance-of-payments problem and created resentment among American workers. Most of all, the inflationary spiral set off by the Vietnam War shaped the economic thinking of a generation, just as surely as the Great Depression of the 1930s shaped the outlook of the previous one. The nightmare of the depression generation was unemployment and privation. The Vietnam War generation fears an income that cannot keep pace with rising prices for housing, food, and travel to academic conferences. Social critics twit baby boomers for their frantic consumption, their apparent unwillingness to save money. Boomers spend like there is no tomorrow because they are afraid that tomorrow the price of everything will be much higher. This behavior is neither rational nor constructive. It will feed inflation. It is, however, understandable as a legacy of inflationary expectation, set off by the Vietnam War.

The Vietnamese should have problems like this. Estimates of North Vietnamese and NLF war dead, fighters and civilians, for the period 1965 to 1975, range from a half million to more than twice that. The number of South Vietnamese dead, fighters and civilians, seems to have been about 750,000. The destruction of the country itself was terrible: Rural areas had been depopulated as their residents fled the fighting, bombing, and mines; defoliation had torn the land and burned away the jungle; and cities, especially Saigon, were overwhelmed with desperately poor refugees. The workforce had been decimated by the killing, while those in uniform needed to be mustered out or, in the case of many of those who had fought for the South, "reeducated." The foreign aid the victorious North Vietnamese had expected, particularly from the United States, did not materialize. And very quickly the newly united country found itself at war with Kampuchea (Cambodia) and China.

The new regime nevertheless bears responsibility for several of the economic calamities that descended on Vietnam between 1976 and 1986. While the government made some concessions to recent history in the South, it still insisted that the transition to socialism would be substantially completed within the life span of the Five Year Plan of 1976 to 1980. Private enterprise, briefly tolerated by the government, ended abruptly on March 23, 1978, when the state took control of commercial goods and assets. The government subsequently limited the amount of currency an individual could retain outside of a regulated savings account. Land collectivization proceeded rapidly in the countryside, but farmers resisted it and food ran short. A sad exodus of refugees, mostly ethnic Chinese, left Vietnam under dreadful conditions. For all these things, officials bear considerable blame. Their application to the postwar period of the wartime ethos, whereby all citizens were to labor simultaneously to boost production and fight the war, was unfortunate but perhaps inevitable. Healing and building were not the same as warring. The Vietnamese people could be convinced to mobilize against a foreign enemy, but it was too much to ask that they mobilize, on behalf of the state, to secure their postwar well-being.[43]

The compromise was economic reform, called *doi moi.* Launched in 1986, the reform program rolled back socialism, restored private land ownership, and sought foreign investment. The leading economic indicators—GNP, per capita income, agricultural production, and so on—have risen in the years since *doi moi* was announced. It is tempting to assume that Vietnam, like many of its neighbors, is transforming itself entirely into a market economy. But many Vietnamese are troubled by this prospect, afraid that the corruptions of capitalism will damage the nation's spirit and its particular virtues. Interviewed in the spring of 1998, Bui The Giang, a communist member of the National Assembly, stressed the historical pragmatism of Vietnam's communists. Economic renovation and open markets were sensible courses of action. But the government had to proceed with caution. The Asian economic crisis that started the previous year had not yet crested, and while Vietnam had lost some 28,000 jobs in foreign-owned firms as its result, Vietnamese were congratulating themselves that it had not been worse: The remaining public sector had insulated the economy from the most powerful shocks. Besides, with liberalization came a rise in unemployment, higher prices, and pernicious Western exports like drugs and pornography. No one wanted that. And would the reappearance of American businesses in Vietnam be altogether a good thing? In 1994, one day after the Clinton administration lifted the U.S. trade embargo with Vietnam, Pepsi-Cola and Coca-Cola started advertising campaigns designed to win back Vietnamese consumers. Pepsi ran ads proclaiming its cola the "choice of a new generation," and featuring Miss Vietnam. Coke's slogan was "Glad to see you again."[44] One can only imagine what the Vietnamese thought of that.

## Notes

1. James William Gibson, *The Perfect War: The War We Couldn't Lose and How We Did* (New York: Vintage Books, 1986), 314.
2. William J. Duiker, *Vietnam: Revolution in Transition* (Boulder, CO: Westview, 1995), 135.

3. Memorandum of conversation between members of the Government of Vietnam and the United States government, July 16, 1965, Department of State, *Foreign Relations of the United States, 1964–1968, Volume III, June-December, 1965,* no. 60, www. state.gov/www/about_state/history/vol_060.html.
4. Gibson, *The Perfect War,* 266.
5. Neil Sheehan, *A Bright Shining Lie: John Paul Vann and America in Vietnam* (New York, Random House, 1988), 626; Gibson, *The Perfect War,* 266.
6. Bui Diem cited in Loren Baritz, *Backfire: A History of How American Culture Led Us into Vietnam and Made Us Fight the Way We Did* (New York: W. Morrow, 1985), 161.
7. Jean Lacouture cited in G. Nguyen Tien Hung, *Economic Development of Socialist Vietnam, 1955–1980* (New York: Praeger, 1977), 15.
8. Ibid., 33.
9. Ibid., 34.
10. Andrew J. Rotter, *The Path to Vietnam: Origins of the American Commitment to Southeast Asia* (Ithaca, NY: Cornell University Press, 1987); William S. Borden, *The Pacific Alliance: United States Foreign Economic Policy and Japanese Trade Recovery, 1947–1955* (Madison: University of Wisconsin Press, 1984); Michael Schaller, *The American Occupation of Japan: The Origins of the Cold War in Asia* (New York: Oxford University Press, 1985).
11. Address by John Foster Dulles, New York City, March 29, 1954, Department of State *Bulletin,* April 12, 1954, 539–540.
12. Notes of the President's Meeting with General Earle Wheeler, JCS, and General Creighton Abrams (and Secretary Rusk), March 26, 1968, David M. Barrett, ed., *Lyndon Johnson's Vietnam Papers: A Documentary Collection* (College Station: Texas A & M University Press, 1997), 708–09. See also Robert Buzzanco, *Vietnam and the Transformation of American Life* (Malden, MA: Blackwell Publishers, 1999), 98–99.
13. Gabriel Kolko, *The Roots of American Foreign Policy: An Analysis of Power and Purpose* (Boston: Beacon Press, 1969).
14. James C. Thomson, Jr., "How Could Vietnam Happen?: An Autopsy," *The Atlantic Monthly* (April 1968): 47–53.
15. Robert D. Dean, "Masculinity as Ideology: John F. Kennedy and the Domestic Politics of Foreign Policy," *Diplomatic History* 22, no. 1 (1998): 21–62.
16. George McGovern, *Grassroots: The Autobiography of George McGovern* (New York: Random House, 1977), 104.
17. Gibson, *The Perfect War;* Jeffrey Record, *The Wrong War: Why We Lost in Vietnam* (Annapolis: Naval Institute Press, 1998).
18. Raymond Williams, *Keywords: A Vocabulary of Culture and Society* (New York: Oxford University Press, 1983), 87.
19. Gibson, *The Perfect War,* 205.
20. Ibid., 271.
21. Ibid., 345–46.

22. Record, *The Wrong War,* 51.
23. Robert L. Sansom, *The Economics of Insurgency in the Mekong Delta of Vietnam* (Cambridge, MA: MIT Press, 1970), 162.
24. Baritz, *Backfire,* 9.
25. Marilyn B. Young, *The Vietnam Wars, 1945–1990* (New York: Harper Collins, 1991), 175.
26. Record, *The Wrong War,* 87.
27. Baritz, *Backfire,* 295.
28. Ibid., 294, 302, 304.
29. Ibid., 160, 318.
30. Sam Adams, *War of Numbers: An Intelligence Memoir* (South Royalton, VT: Steerforth Press, 1994), 30.
31. Gibson, *The Perfect War,* 160.
32. This sentiment is well expressed in a poem by combat veteran David Connolly entitled,"It Don't Mean Nothin," in his work, *Lost in America* (Woodbridge, CT: Vietnam Generation, Inc. & Burning Cities Press, 1994), 10
33. Gibson, *The Perfect War,* 188.
34. George C. Herring, *LBJ and Vietnam: A Different Kind of War* (Austin: University of Texas Press, 1994), 2.
35. Vo Nguyen Giap, *People's War Against U.S. Aero-Naval War* (Hanoi: Foreign Languages Publishing House, 1975), 113–114.
36. Ibid., 115.
37. Ibid., 53.
38. Ho Chi Minh, "Appeal to Compatriots and Fighters Throughout the Country," July 17, 1966, Ho Chi Minh, *Selected Writings 1920–1969* (Hanoi: Foreign Languages Publishing House, 1973), 307–08.
39. Doris Kearns Goodwin, *Lyndon Johnson and the American Dream* (New York: Harper & Row, 1976), 251.
40. Anthony S. Campagna, *The Economic Consequences of the Vietnam War* (New York: Praeger, 1991), 32–42.
41. Kearns Goodwin, *Lyndon Johnson,* 259–260.
42. Robert Warren Stevens, *Vain Hopes, Grim Realities: The Economic Consequences of the Vietnam War* (New York: New Viewpoints, 1976), 4–8.
43. Studies of the wartime and postwar Vietnamese economy include Duiker, *Vietnam;* Murray Hiebert, *Chasing the Tigers: A Portrait of the New Vietnam* (New York: Kodansha International, 1996); Sansom, *Economics of Insurgency;* Neil Sheehan, *After the War Was Over: Hanoi and Saigon* (New York: Random House, 1991); and Nancy Wiegersma, *Vietnam: Peasant Land, Peasant Revolution* (New York: St. Martin's Press, 1988).
44. Hiebert, *Chasing the Tigers,* 43.

CHAPTER EIGHT

# "HO, HO, HO CHI MINH, HO CHI MINH IS GONNA WIN!"

MARILYN YOUNG

The notion that North Vietnam won the American War in Vietnam because of the actions of the American peace movement pleases both the left and the right. The left because it testifies to its own efficacy: Never before in the history of warfare has a domestic peace movement forced the government to call a halt to war. The right because it means that U.S. arms remain invincible; only betrayal can explain American defeat.[1] Judgments about whether the antiwar movement was responsible for U.S. defeat are, of necessity, post facto. A quite different task is to look forward from the event: to understand what role the U.S. antiwar movement played over the course of the war. Did it shorten or prolong its length? Demoralize U.S. fighting forces? Influence military tactics? Give essential aid and comfort to the enemy?

The first question, the antiwar movement's impact on the war's outcome, is enigmatic because it cannot be answered historically. There is no way to know whether the antiwar movement prolonged, shortened, or was irrelevant to the length of the war. Adam Garfinkle, in his book *Telltale Hearts: The Origins and Impact of the Vietnam Antiwar Movement,* offers a somewhat idiosyncratic version of the proposition that the movement prolonged the war. His argument rests on a set of interdependent counterfactual propositions. Antiwar public opinion, Garfinkle believes, would have appeared earlier and increased massively had the movement not aroused so much hostility by its militant behavior. In partial consequence, so would the "impulse" of Democratic Party members to "betray their party leadership and their president. . . ." Had that impulse been allowed free rein, rather than resign from the presidency in 1968, Johnson would have yielded to pressure, reversed the course of the war, and gone on to win the presidential election. The antiwar movement gave Johnson "more time to fail" and in so doing "contributed at least something to the conditions under which American soldiers were being killed by the thousands each and every year."[2] Thus, the antiwar movement was culpable because it was ineffective.

However, had the movement been effective, it also would have been guilty. Assuming the war was winnable, as Garfinkle, like many of those who blame the movement do, "then a hypothetically effective antiwar movement was the agent of unnecessary catastrophe in Vietnam, and worse, mocked the purposes for which more than 58,000 American soldiers died." The analysis does not consider that, for many, perhaps for most, protesters, the problem was not winning the war but fighting it at all. Nor does Garfinkle question the implication that victory in war ipso facto makes the war itself just, the lives lost in its pursuit meaningful.[3]

There are two further problems with Garfinkle's judgments of the antiwar movement, problems common to all those who believe that but for the protest movement, the United States would have won. First, like many others, Garfinkle separates "public opinion" from the antiwar movement, reading protesters out of the American body politic in much the same way the U.S. government defined the National Liberation Front as somehow not South Vietnamese. Whatever figures measuring public opinion Gallup may have gathered over the years, the fact remains that hundreds of thousands of ordinary citizens took to the streets in unprecedented opposition to an ongoing war. Those who participated were the public; not all of it, certainly, but not outside of it either. Second, there is the notion that the domestic political impact of the war on the United States can be separated from its the military course. "If only there were no protests and if only those protests had not influenced Congress," this line of analysis suggests, "we could have won." Such a separation makes little historical sense. No war is a purely military endeavor. The domestic response to the war was not an independent variable, open to government manipulation, but a direct response by Americans of every variety, including politicians and soldiers in the field, to the escalating violence in Vietnam.

Lecturing to a college audience after the publication of his most recent reconsideration of the war, former Secretary of Defense Robert McNamara reminded an aging veteran of the antiwar movement that "your people weren't in the majority. Most Americans supported the war [here he pounded the table with the flat of his hand], supported escalation [another pound], supported the bombing [a final, yet more decisive pound that made the water glasses jump]. "At least until 1968," he added-and his hand was still.[4] And he may be right. Depending on how you read the statistics, the public remained committed to the Vietnam War throughout much of its course. Benjamin Schwartz, of the RAND Corporation, has argued that while figures indicating public disapproval for having gotten into Vietnam in the first place rose steadily throughout the war, 77 percent of those questioned favored escalation to either withdrawal or a continuation of wherever the current level of military operations stood. "There is a tendency," Schwartz concludes, "for war to become absolute." Anger at having gotten into the war in Vietnam (or Korea, for which the figures are similar) was massive; but there was also a great desire to "finish it once and for all." However, it might be more interesting to consider the traceable shifts in opinion as government policy changed. Thus, in 1965–1966, when Hanoi and Haiphong were off limits as bombing targets, only 30 percent of those polled thought they should be bombed; when they were bombed in July 1966, 85 percent thought it was an excellent thing to have done. There are similar statistics on support for seeking negotiations through bombing halts. Support for such a policy, which stood at 37 percent in September 1967, rose to a remarkable 64 percent once Johnson had decided on just such a halt.[5]

But the statistics do not tell us enough. By the numbers, in the absence of other information, Korea was a more unpopular war than Vietnam. If popularity ended wars, the Korean War should have been over before it began. "The data suggest," public opinion analyst John E. Mueller concluded in an essay comparing popular support for the two wars, "that while *the opposition to the war in Vietnam may have been more vocal than that in Korea, it was not more extensive.*" The voice of the opposition, Mueller argues, was that of an emergent group of leftist intellectuals with "political, though not necessarily electoral, impact" whose roots lay in the anti-McCarthy, ban-the-bomb campaigns of the mid to late 50s, nourished by the civil rights movement of the early 1960s. The new left, Mueller concludes, was the "*old left with new methods of expression, of vocalism.*"[6] A vocal opposition may not be the same as a mass movement, but an opposition in full public voice means that attention, on the part of the press, politicians, and pundits, has to be paid. And once attention is paid, questions can be asked, questions that may lead to the unraveling of some, though hardly all, of the dominant ideology of the day. Senator William J. Fulbright, who had shepherded the Gulf of Tonkin Resolution through the Senate only a year or so earlier, by 1966 was ready to hold public hearings on the war. The hearings, in turn, provided the antiwar movement with an abundance of information and an evident respectability.

Rhodri Jeffrey-Jones, in his book *Peace Now!* argues that the serial nature of the movement made it more effective, as it expanded from student groups to include churches, civil rights leaders, and the nascent women's movement, and made modest gains in the ranks of organized labor. "The protests had a cumulative effect that sapped the resistance power of the policymakers."[7] A 1967 Central Intelligence Agency (CIA) assessment, while silent on the power of policymakers to resist, draws a remarkably similar picture of the movement itself:

"The American peace 'movement' is not one but many movements; and the groups involved are as varied as they are numerous. The most striking single characteristic of the peace front is its diversity." In a rolling set of paired opposites, some of which antiwar organizers might have used to describe themselves, the CIA report unfurled a "peace umbrella" under which it said could be found "pacifists and fighters, idealists and materialists, internationalists and isolationists, democrats and totalitarians, conservatives and revolutionaries, capitalists and socialists, patriots and subversives, lawyers and anarchists, Stalinists and Trotskyites, Muscovites and Pekingese, racists and universalists, zealots and nonbelievers, puritans and hippies, do-gooders and evildoers, nonviolent and very violent." Indeed, "anti-war sentiment has taken root in separate sectors of society having little else in common. In addition to the professional pacifists, activists come from the student world, from militant elements of the Negro and other minority communities, from the labor movement, and from the intellectual sphere." The degree of diversity, the CIA noted, brought with it "confusion and more than a little disagreement." After all, the analysts observed, not unsympathetically, the task of "coordinating a program of joint action, first within the US and then internationally, is an enormous one." And yet, despite the "strains and complications," the coordinators had done an "impressive" job. Moreover, "we see no significant evidence that would prove Communist control or direction of the US peace movement or its leaders."[8] The longer the war lasted, the more diverse the opposition, until by the early 1970s it embraced significant numbers of the House, the Senate, the business community, the federal bureaucracy, family members of high government officials, and the Democratic Party, which in 1972 nominated a peace candidate, George McGovern, for president.

It is useful to recall the sheer variety of activity in which those opposed to the war expressed their views: draft counseling, draft-card burning; sit-ins at draft centers; draft resistance; nonviolent demonstrations (local, regional, national); demonstrations with violence against property; teach-ins; movements to remove ROTC and war research from university campuses; barring and/or removing from campuses recruiters for Dow Chemical and other war-related industries; sanctuary and support for military deserters at home and abroad; antiwar coffeehouses near army bases; support for the movement against the war inside the military; and so on. The protests, historian Gabriel Kolko has observed, "fixed to the war an unprecedented social price."[9] A recent critical assessment of the antiwar movement by Edward Morgan comes to a similar conclusion: For all its weaknesses, "movement militance and the ensuing social chaos may have forced the Nixon administration's hand, helping to bring the war to an end on terms that fell somewhat short of the total destruction of Indochina."[10] In short, it increased the price to the government of continued prosecution of the war.

Part of that price was paid by the army. "The morale, discipline and battleworthiness of the U.S. Armed Forces are, with a few salient exceptions, lower than at any time in this century and possibly in the history of the United States," Colonel Robert D. Heinl wrote in 1971. "By every conceivable indicator," his article for the *Armed Forces Journal* warned, "our army that now remains in Vietnam is in a state approaching collapse, with individual units avoiding or having refused combat, murdering their officers and noncommissioned officers, drug-ridden, and dispirited where not near-mutinous." As he tolled the woes of the military, Heinl's prose turned apocalyptic: the Armed Forces reflected the country, with its "agonizing divisions and social trauma," and disclosed the depths of society's problems in an awful litany of sedition, disaffection, desertion, race, drugs, breakdown of authority, abandonment of discipline, and, as a cumulative result, the lowest state of military morale "in the history of the Untied States."[11]

Between 1968 and 1971, desertion rates had doubled and stood at twice the peak rate for Korea; there were 788 confirmed cases of fragging for the period 1969 to 1972, 252 chargeable acts of insubordination in 1968 and double that number in 1971; and often violent racial conflict. In addition, there was organized protest within the military, including between 141 and 245 underground newspapers; underground radio stations (more difficult to quantify); 14 dissident GI organizations—2 of them made up of officers; and 6 antiwar veterans' groups. Heinl was especially concerned about the connections that had been forged with the civilian antiwar movement. Three organizations of lawyers specialized in aiding GIs in antiwar trouble, including one that operated in Vietnam itself, set up in Saigon in 1970 to offer free legal services for dissident soldiers being court-martialed.[12] Vietnam Veterans Against the War (VVAW) and similar dissenting groups were never large, but their existence, along with more informal acts of protest in all three services, indicated a state of crisis in the military establishment.[13] The antiwar movement did not demoralize the armed forces, the war did. The movement did aid and abet antiwar soldiers and veterans when it could, but more important, the existence of visible, vocal protest at home normalized the act of protest itself, making it available to soldiers as to all citizens.

Most historians who have studied the antiwar movement conclude that, at minimum, "the continuous decline of support for the war among the general population was, in part, a result of the well-organized campaigns that countered the line from Washington."[14] President Johnson's bombing halts and the opening of peace talks in Paris were the result of a combination of domestic pressure at home, international pressure abroad, and military pressure in the field. Richard Nixon, like Lyndon Johnson before him, was extremely sensitive to the antiwar movement and monitored it closely. "Realizes," H. R. Haldeman noted in his diary for September 29, 1969, referring to the president, that "war support is more tenuous every day and knows we have to maintain it somehow." Fearful of the coming October moratorium, Nixon considered scheduling a press conference that would "preempt coverage of the day's activities." The point, Haldeman told his diary, was to "try to make the innocents see they are being used. . . . Hard to do much because momentum is tremendous and broad based." The November moratorium disturbed Nixon even more. He thought hard about it and had "helpful ideas like using helicopters to blow their candles out. . . ." Much in the style of his superior's later observation of the Great Wall of China, that it was a great wall, Haldeman noted that "the big march turned out to be huge."[15] In a compliment to the power of the antiwar movement, both Johnson and Nixon thought it sufficiently threatening to warrant major covert efforts to infiltrate and disrupt its activities.[16]

The marches were to grow larger. When their initial effort to detail U.S. war crimes in Vietnam received little public attention, VVAW organized a weeklong "limited incursion into the country of Congress," from April 19 to April 23, 1971. Over 1, 000 veterans set up camp in Potomac Park, performed guerrilla theater, lobbied Congress, and marched. But VVAW owed its most dramatic moment to the misguided security effort of the Nixon administration. Foiled in their effort to return their medals and battle ribbons to Congress, the veterans stood one by one before a microphone, announced their names and their citations, and then tossed them over the high fence protecting the Capitol Building. Inside, a navy veteran, John Kerry, testified before the Senate Committee on Foreign Relations: "In our opinion and from our experience, there is nothing in South Vietnam which could happen that realistically threatens the United States of America. And to attempt to justify the loss of one American life in Vietnam, Cambodia or Laos by linking such loss to the preservation of freedom . . . is to us the height of criminal hypocrisy, and it is that kind of hypocrisy which we feel has torn this country apart."[17] On April 24 the veterans were joined by over 500,000 protesters for the largest single demonstration of the war.

Joan Hoff, a historian of the Nixon administration, has argued that "Nixon never changed his attitudes or policies on Vietnam because of protests," although she concedes that "the bombing of North Vietnam was ruled out by the administration in February and March 1969, possibly due in part to concern about general public opinion."[18] I have already addressed the artificial distinction between the "general public" and the antiwar movement, but putting that aside, Hoff's conclusion is too grudging. Other historians are far less tentative and describe a firm link between public protest and White House policy. At issue in 1969 was not just bombing North Vietnam but radically escalating the war through an all-out offensive against Hanoi (Operation Duck Hook). Nixon was dissuaded by numerous advisors who predicted a dire public response both at home and abroad. "Put cynically," Stephen Ambrose has written, "after having proclaimed that he would not let policy be made in the streets, Nixon let policy be made in the streets."[19] Larry Berman's massively documented account of Nixon's war reaches the same conclusion: the major demonstration planned for October 15, 1969,

> played an important role in the cancellation of Duck Hook. With hundreds of thousands of demonstrators taking to the streets of Washington, D.C., it was apparent that Nixon's attack would face a groundswell of opposition. In the end, Nixon cancelled Duck Hook because it would have been very difficult to pursue an open military solution while the country was ostensibly beginning its disengagement from Vietnam. In short, American public opinion already had him over a barrel, and he knew it. . . . [20]

The really huge marches were not limited to the United States. Demonstrations across the world against U.S. policy merged with broader efforts for social equity and justice in France, Mexico, Japan, West Germany, Great Britain, Scandinavia, Italy, the Netherlands, Canada, and Australia. In 1968, when the forces of the National Liberation Front and Hanoi launched the series of attacks that have been summarized by the single word for the Vietnamese New Year Tet, it seemed as if the streets of the capital cities of the globe were themselves exploding in sympathy. In many countries there was, as well, direct aid to deserters and draft evaders, which constituted a defiant challenge to the U.S. effort in Vietnam. The movements in Europe and elsewhere were both local and international, joining domestic issues to an anti-imperialist passion that strengthened the U.S. movement. When demonstrators arrested at the Democratic National Convention in Chicago in 1968 claimed that the whole world was watching, they were just being accurate.[21] The effort of the Nixon administration in particular to isolate the movement and lead a putative "silent majority" to reject not his policies but those who demonstrated against them foundered on the sense of a wider, sympathetic audience.

Did the antiwar movement aid and comfort the enemy, as Johnson and Nixon both charged? The force of the accusation was sufficient to discourage the Reverend Dr. Martin Luther King Jr. from traveling to Paris to meet with North Vietnamese representatives.[22] And certainly Hanoi and the National Liberation Front were convinced that the American and international antiwar movement could make a contribution to their victory. But given the history of Vietnamese nationalism and resistance, it is an act of supreme arrogance to imagine that without the antiwar movement, the Vietnamese would have fought less hard or less long. Throughout the war, Hanoi hosted delegations of sympathetic Americans, released prisoners of war directly to representatives of the antiwar movement, sent delegates to international conferences, and with the help of the alternative news media publicized their diplomatic initiatives.[23] The effort was to inform and persuade the American public of Hanoi's war aims and its desire for peace, and the antiwar movement played an important role in this endeavor. Although their resources were minuscule in comparison to those available to the U.S. government, publications like, *Ramparts, Viet Report,* and *Liberation* disputed the government's account of the origins and progress of the war and disseminated Vietnamese peace proposals in the face of the silence or, worse, distortion of the mainstream press. Through Third World newsreel, documentaries filmed in both South and North Vietnam were distributed in the United States and became a regular feature of college teach-ins. And the antiwar movement benefited from the work of the U.S. press corps. Reporters too raised questions about the veracity of government spokesmen and the reliability of government reports; the *New York Times* printed secret documents leaked by analyst Daniel Ellsberg and congressional aide Anthony Russo; and photojournalists took pictures that gained iconic status—the burning Buddhist monk in 1963, the execution of an unarmed guerrilla in the streets of Saigon in 1968, the flaming body of a child racing down a road in 1971—their power enhanced by their publication in the *Times* rather than *Ramparts.* These documents and images showed that the antiwar movement was not making it up.

The antiwar movement has become a footnote in essays, documentaries, novels, and films that focus on that amorphous proper noun, the Sixties. In contrast to Nixon, Haldeman, and the CIA, who recognized the power and broad base of the political movement that annually deposited tens of thousands of citizens on their doorstep, the latter-day media and popular historical treatment of the 1960s, trivialize and depoliticize them, representing the decade largely in terms of styles of consumption. The war, insofar as it has any presence at all in these renderings, is reduced to a peace sign displayed by preference in multicolored ink on the flat belly of a topless young woman swaying to the music at an endless Woodstock festival. More generous critics, themselves often veterans of the era, suggest that the 1960s were best characterized by utopian politics that died of their own excesses: factionalism, romantic revolutionary violence, and blind anti-Americanism. Their only legacy was the identity politics, individualism, and consumerist greed of the decades that followed.

The separation between political and cultural movements these analyses insist on distorts the history of the period. The two movements overlapped in terms of personnel, practices, anticapitalist yearnings, and occasional tactics; they were mutually reinforcing. Skepticism about constituted authority—medical, governmental, philosophic, historical, political, pedagogical—marked both the counterculture and such political groups as Students for a Democratic Society (SDS) or, more broadly, the New Left. The source of this skepticism lay in the political and cultural movements of the late 1950s and early 1960s that preceded the antiwar movement and continued after the war had ended. One of the most interesting interpretations of post-1945 American history is sociologist Tom Engelhardt's *End of Victory Culture.* Engelhardt argues that the great mobilizer of American national consciousness has been the war story—victorious, of course, and always just. In 1945 the United States had won the war (as Americans liked to put it to themselves), and yet over the next five years the world had become an ever less safe place: fear of domestic depression was widespread; young men were being recalled to service; the news was full of reports of unprecedented military defeats in Korea, rapidly escalating casualties, and savage tactics; and the unthinkable, but obsessively thought about, likelihood of nuclear world war.[24] The possibility of an alternative foreign or domestic policy had been decisively defeated in 1948. The collapse of the Progressive Party and the successful representation of its remnants as communist dupes meant that the language of protest was tainted. The mildest expression of doubt about the Korean War was subject to sharp criticism, even repression. Cultural repression went hand in hand with political repression, as the recent literature on the dreary history of 1950s' gender, sexual, and familial constrictions, which paralleled and supported America's policy of containment abroad, has made abundantly clear.

For conservative groups in the United States, the stalemate truce in Korea was not a satisfactory substitute for victory, and in its aftermath there remained a herd of scapegoats who could be blamed: the press; the cowardly and/or treasonous Democratic administration; the cowardly and/or treasonous behavior of American prisoners of war; the failure of a generation of soft, coddled young men; communist spies. There was a strong sense of an enemy within, not only Karl Marx's old mole, but more problematic forces born of America's very success. David Riesman, in his best-selling *The Lonely Crowd,* described the United States in 1950 as a society in a "phase of incipient decline" due to the eclipse of the sort of American who had made the country great, the 19th-century "inner directed" individualist, and his replacement by conformist, peer-pleasing "other directed" men.[25]

For students and young people in general, there was no political language in which to challenge the status quo directly. Movements for civil rights and against racial intolerance (as it was then called) were couched in the rhetoric of the Cold War and containment. The vision of the Founding Fathers, eternally renewed, endowed the country with the capacity to change course and reform itself without raising any systemic questions.

Yet by 1957 the activist-poet Allen Ginsberg decried the fate of the best minds of his generation and suggested that something fundamental was wrong with the country. The music, drugs, styles of consumption, anti-Protestant work ethic, contempt for capitalism and its values, and polymorphously perverse sexuality of the late 1950s received a media name (and temporal restriction): the Beat Generation. The Beats marked the beginning of the 1960s, offering their readers the language in which to question the world of Mamie and Ike and Lawrence Welk. At about the same time, the civil rights movement was beginning to introduce the country to a set of tactics and the images that went with them that raised connected but different questions. What was the nature of the federal government's commitment to universal suffrage? Would it use federal troops to enforce equal rights for all its citizens? Questions about contemporary racial arrangements led inevitably to historical ones and an uneasy recognition of the contradictory nature of the vision of slave holding Founding Fathers.

Another strand in the rope from which the standard American national narrative would later be hanged in effigy were the different responses of the government and of significant sectors of the population to the revolution in Cuba.[26] Fidel Castro addressing thousands of people at Soldier's Field in Cambridge, Massachusetts, eating fried chicken in the Hotel Teresa, and speaking the language of a noncommunist political, social, and cultural revolution could not be dismissed as another Soviet clone. In addition, there was the more sedate movement, also with international connections, to end nuclear testing, with its implicit suggestion that a foreign policy of global anticommunist containment was no longer self-evidently justifiable. In both the civil rights movement and the test ban movement, the efficacy of an older American tradition of protest and nonviolent civil disobedience was rediscovered. The word "communist" might still be flung as an epithet, but its power to wound, to humiliate, to threaten one's job, was spent. Among the last people in America to believe in its incantatory power was Lyndon Johnson, who asked the Federal Bureau of Investigation (FBI) and the CIA to investigate the peace movement in hopes of connecting antiwar protesters to shadowy purveyors of Moscow gold.[27]

The civil rights movement is the best, if most complicated, example of the coming together of a social movement that predated the war with the movement that arose to protest it. Some elements of the civil rights movement made the connection very early. Malcolm X, for example, denounced the war in December 1964, and before the year was out, he was joined by James Forman, executive secretary of the Student Non-Violent Coordinating Committee (SNCC). In 1965 the McComb, Mississippi, branch of the Freedom Democratic Party explicitly called for draft resistance:

> No one has a right to ask us to risk our lives and kill other Colored People in . . . Vietnam so that the White American can get richer. We will be looked upon as traitors to the Colored People of the world if Negro people continue to fight and die without a cause. . . . We can write our sons and ask if they know what they are fighting for. If he answers Freedom, tell him that's what we are fighting for here in Mississippi. And if he says Democracy tell him the truth—we don't know anything about Communism, socialism, and all that, but we do know that Negroes have caught hell under this American democracy.[28]

Chicano draftees, like African Americans, with far fewer options than their white counterparts, nevertheless joined the ranks of resisters. The first was Ernesto Vigil, who refused to fight against his "brown brothers in Vietnam."[29]

By 1967 white America's favorite civil rights leader, Martin Luther King Jr., had not only endorsed draft resistance but expressed an unexpected empathy for the "desperate, rejected and angry young men" who had set ghettos from Watts to Washington, DC on fire:

> As I have walked among [them] I have told them that Molotov cocktails and rifles would not solve their problems. . . . But they asked—and rightly so—what about Vietnam? . . . Their questions hit home, and I knew that I could never again raise my voice against the violence of the oppressed in the ghettos without having first spoken clearly to the greatest purveyor of violence in the world today—my own government. . . .[30]

A May 1967 FBI report on the potential for racial violence in the summer of that year noted the link between the civil rights movement and Vietnam with considerable alarm: "King has now joined [Stokely] Carmichael, [Floyd] McKissick, and other civil rights extremists in embracing the communist tactic of linking the civil rights movement with the anti-Vietnam-war protest movement. . . . King's exhortation to boycott the draft and refuse to fight could lead eventually to dangerous displays of civil disobedience and near-seditious activities by Negroes and whites alike."[31] The assassinations of King and Malcolm X short-circuited what might have been a powerful, united movement against the war and for fundamental social change. Thereafter, the antiwar movement swallowed the protests of the preceding decade. For the overwhelming majority of the antiwar movement, it was enough to try to end the slaughter.

Finally, Ho Chi Minh did win. His colleagues and heirs had defeated the world's preeminent military power. And the antiwar movement had succeeded as well, if not in ending then at least in limiting the destruction done to Indochina. It took over a decade to achieve this modest good, but the legacies of the antiwar movement, like the legacies of the war itself, linger. The mantra of every administration since Nixon has been the necessity for broad public support of any military intervention abroad, treating such support as a thing in itself, separable from the goal of the intervention itself. As if recognizing the difficulty, these administrations also have labored to make their wars exceedingly brief, over almost before they have begun. Yet they seem still to look over their shoulders nervously: Is that a chant in the distance?

## Notes

1. There is another position, also attractive to both left and right, to which the role of the peace movement is irrelevant: North Vietnam did not win the war at all, the United States did. Noam Chomsky, contemplating the destruction of the semi-autonomous insurgency in South Vietnam along with the rural society out of which it grew, the illustration the war provided to rebel movements elsewhere in the world of the costs of defying the United States, and the acquiescence of postwar Vietnam to the exigencies of global capitalism, has concluded that it is hard to describe the end of the war as a victory for Hanoi. General William Westmoreland agrees, for the same reasons. See Edward S. Herman and Noam Chomsky, *Manufacturing Consent: The Political Economy of the Mass Media* (New York: Pantheon, 1988), 246–247. See also Chomsky, "Visions of Righteousness," *Cultural Critique* 3 (1986): 30.
2. Adam Garfinkle, *Telltale Hearts: The Origins and Impact of the Vietnam Antiwar Movement* (New York: St. Martin's Press, 1995), 18–19.
3. Ibid., 26–27.
4. McNamara's remarks were directed at this writer on October 16, 2001 at Dartmouth College.
5. For the RAND polling statistics, see Benjamin Schwartz, "Casualties, Public Opinion and US Military Intervention" (Santa Monica, CA: RAND Corporation, 1994).
6. Italics in original. John E. Mueller: "Trends in Popular Support for the Wars in Korea and Vietnam, "*American Political Science Review,* 65 (June 1971): 358–375.
7. Rhodi Jeffrey-Jones, *Peace Now! American Society and the Ending of the Vietnam War* (New Haven, CT: Yale University Press, 1999), 224. See also Tom Wells, *The War Within: America's Battle Over Vietnam* (Berkeley: University of California Press, 1994); Todd Gitlin, *The Sixties: Years of Hope, Days of Rage* (New York: Bantam, 1993); and Paul Berman, *Tale of Two Utopias: The Political Journey of the Generation of 1968* (New York: Norton, 1996).
8. I am grateful to Marc Gilbert for bringing the document to my attention. The summary section of the forty-six-page report was analyzed and reprinted in Charles DeBenedetti, "A CIA Analysis of the Anti-Vietnam War Movement: October, 1967," *Peace and Social Change* 9, no. 1 (Spring 1983): 31–41.
9. Gabriel Kolko, *Vietnam: Anatomy of War* (New York: Pantheon, 1985), 174.
10. See Edward Morgan, "From Virtual Community to Virtual History: Mass Media and the American Antiwar Movement of the 1960s," *Radical History Review* forum, no. 78 (Fall 2000).

11. Colonel Robert D. Heinl Jr., "The Collapse of the Armed Forces," *Armed Forces Journal,* June 7, 1971. Reprinted in *Vietnam and America: A Documented History,* Marvin E. Gettleman, et al, eds., (New York: Grove Press, 2nd rev. edition, 1995), 327.
12. Ibid., 330.
13. See Gerald Nicosia, *Home to War: A History of the Vietnam Veterans' Movement* (New York: Crown, 2001); Richard Moser, *The New Winter Soldiers: GI and Veteran Dissent During the Vietnam Era* (New Brunswick, NJ: Rutgers University Press, 1996); Richard Stacewicz, *Winter Soldiers: An Oral History of the Vietnam Veterans Against the War* (New York: Twayne Publishers, 1997); and Andrew E. Hunt, *The Turning: A History of Vietnam Veterans Against the War* (New York: New York University Press, 1999).
14. Melvin Small, "The Impact of the Antiwar Movement on Lyndon Johnson, 1965–1968: A Preliminary Report," *Peace and Change,* 10, no. 1 (Spring 1984): 2.
15. H. R. Haldeman, *The Haldeman Diaries: Inside the Nixon White House* (New York: Berkley Books, 1995), 110, 129.
16. Operation CHAOS was initiated by the CIA on Johnson's orders in 1967. Its mandate was to infiltrate the movement and uncover connections between the antiwar movement and foreign, especially communist, governments. CHAOS violated the CIA charter and was terminated in 1972. Operation COINTELPRO (Counter-intelligence program), instituted by the FBI in 1967 and expanded under Nixon, also sought to link the protest movement to communists, domestic and foreign. Its undercover agents acted as agents provocateurs, while regular FBI agents engaged in more traditional acts of intimidation by photographing participants in demonstrations.
17. John Kerry, testimony before the U.S. Senate Foreign Relations Committee, April 22, 1971, reprinted in Gettleman et al., *Vietnam and America,* 458.
18. Joan Hoff, "Richard Nixon, Vietnam, and the American Home Front," Dennis Showalter and John G. Albert, *An American Dilemma: Vietnam, 1964–1973* (Chicago: Imprint Publications, 1993), 197.
19. Stephen Ambrose, "Nixon and Vietnam: Vietnam and Electoral Politics," Third Dwight David Eisenhower Lecture on War and Peace, April 19, 2001, Kansas State University, online at www.ksu.edu/history/specialevents/Eisenhowerlecture/eisenhower3.htm.
20. Larry Berman, *No Peace, No Honor: Nixon, Kissinger, and Betrayal in Vietnam* (New York: Free Press, 2001), 57.
21. See, for example, *1968: A Student Generation in Revolt,* Ronald Fraser, ed. (New York: Pantheon, 1988) but also Todd Gitlin, *The Whole World Is Watching: Mass Media in the Making and Unmaking of the New Left* (Berkeley: University of California Press, 1980).
22. See Cable, FBI (Hoover) to President, cc to Secretary of State, CIA, May 13, 1967, Declassified Documents CD-Rom ID#1986030100866/fiche #1986–76. The cable states that an informant close to Stanley Levinson reported a conversation in which King expressed concern that he would lend

force to the notion that Hanoi based its policy toward negotiations on an assessment of the strength of the peace movement in the U.S. He was certain, he said, that "The United States would revoke his passport if he decided to make a trip to Paris, therefore he could not take a chance on that."

23. See Robert Brigham, *Guerilla Diplomacy: The NLF's Foreign Relations and the Vietnam War* (Ithaca, NY: Cornell University Press, 1999), 90–91.
24. Tom Engelhardt, *The End of Victory Culture: Cold War America and the Disillusioning of a Generation* (New York: Basic Books, 1995).
25. David Riesman, with Nathan Glazer and Reuel Denney, *The Lonely Crowd: A Study of the Changing American Character* (New Haven, CT: Yale University Press, 1950).
26. See Van Gosse, *Where the Boys Are: Cuba, Cold War America, and the Making of the New Left* (London: Verso, 1993).
27. See, for example, the 1967 CIA report to Johnson cited above.
28. Joanne Grant, ed., *Black Protest, History, Documents and Analysis, 1619-Present* (New York: Fawcett World Library, 1969), 415–416.
29. Ramon Ruiz, "Another Defector from the Gringo World," *The New Republic,* July 27, 1968, 11. See also early issues of the Chicano journal *La Raza.* See also George Mariscal, *Aztlan and Vietnam: Chicano and Chicana Experiences of the War* (Berkeley: University of California Press, 1999).
30. James Melvin, ed., *I Have a Dream: Writings and Speeches that Changed the World* (New York: HarperCollins, 1992), 135–152.
31. Federal Bureau of Investigation, May 23, 1967, "Racial Violence Potential in the US This summer," 71 pages, Declassified September 14, 1988, www.*ddrs.psmedia.com.*

CHAPTER NINE

# HALL OF MIRRORS

## LLOYD GARDNER

In his second term as prime minister, Winston Churchill was as determined to make peace with Russia as he had once been to prosecute the war against Nazi Germany. Stalin's death, he believed, had opened a window. The new Soviet leadership had raised hopes for negotiations on a series of issues. The shooting had come to an end in Korea. Surely this was the moment to explore the possibilities for a settlement of Cold War issues, particularly in Europe. But when a close advisor brought back news from the 1954 Geneva Conference which suggested to Churchill that the meeting's outcome might spur an American anticommunist crusade in Vietnam, the old man exploded. Vietnam, he said; I have lived seventy years without ever hearing about such places. Why, now, must I be plagued with Vietnam?

The Geneva Conference had opened at virtually the same time that the Vietminh stormed into the Dien Bien Phu fortress, ending 100 years of French rule. Churchill's presentment that the United States would now decide to make a new stand in Southeast Asia turned out to be all too accurate. The standoff in the Korean War had left a bitter taste across the nation but also a heightened sensitivity in Washington to the need to create a "healthy" environment for Japan's reentry into the world economy. Communist China now loomed as a bigger problem than anyone had imagined before Korea. Flushed with revolutionary zeal and supposedly with endless human resources behind him, Mao offered a challenge no less menacing than Stalin's had been—perhaps, indeed, greater because of China's cultural advantages in Asia. Or so, at least, thought Secretary of State John Foster Dulles, who led the American delegation to Geneva and who made it plain he had no use for a face-saving defeat in Indochina. Thus it was that the Korean War provided the essential background for American involvement in Indochina, even as American military leaders feared the idea of another land war on the Asian continent.

The issue of American "credibility," so much a part of the later rationale for staying the course in Vietnam, evolved out of the need to ensure Japan's loyalty to the West. And the only way that could be done, American policymakers understood, was to offer the newly reconstructed island country decent opportunities to participate in the free world's markets. Cut off from Chinese outlets, not welcome in Korea, there were not too many options left. Eisenhower himself said as much in his famous description of the domino game in Asia, describing Japan as the ultimate objective of the players. And so began the fateful American commitment to rescuing Vietnam from the ruins of the French empire.

Churchill, of course, had himself sounded an early warning about Moscow's global ambitions in his influential Iron Curtain speech of 1946 thereby providing one of the foundation stones for Washington's view of the world. But he thought that Eisenhower would now listen to him the way he supposed Roosevelt had listened earlier; he thought that "Ike" understood that with Stalin's death, it was time to test the new leadership in the Kremlin to see if the hints about a more reasonable approach were anything more than a lulling maneuver. Hence his reaction to the news about the American resistance to the Geneva "settlement," which was, as everyone knew, about the only way for France to get out of Indochina. And why shouldn't they? What was more important, a few French planters in Southeast Asia, or the future of Europe?

But Eisenhower—and his successors in the White House—took such attitudes as simply the last vestiges of an outdated imperial mentality, a feeble swipe of the lion's paw. The British had appeased Hitler in hopes of saving the empire, and now Churchill seemed willing to appease China to save Hong Kong and to gain a few pounds in trade with the communists. The old man still imagined himself sitting on some cloud with FDR, Eisenhower complained, handing down decisions for the rest of the world. Well, he was mistaken. The Cold War was no longer a European affair. It was a struggle to keep communism from coming to power in crucial areas under the guise of revolutionary nationalism. Much later, Secretary of State Dean Rusk would similarly chide the North Atlantic Treaty Organization (NATO) allies for their lack of support in Vietnam. If you like what we are doing in Europe, he said, then do not turn your backs on us in Asia. To be sure, the stakes were different then, involving attitudes about the consequences of abandoning an increasingly abstract commitment to a creation of the American imagination. Yet, as George Herring points out in chapter 2, at times Rusk was reduced to uninspiring sarcasm, as when he suggested that if Russia invaded Sussex, the British should not come crying to America for help.

Solving Japan's specific reentry problems soon became an obsolete issue. Rusk and other policymakers had to explain the war in abstract terms. For a time the appeal continued to resonate, and to stir the national consciousness. America's assumption that it had a special mission in Asia that European "imperialists" could not understand long antedated the Cold War, after all. At the time of the Boxer Rebellion in China at the turn of the twentieth century, Washington refused to join in a punitive campaign against the Chinese after the besieged legations had been rescued. And when the Chinese were forced to pay a humiliating indemnity, the United States used its share to set up scholarships for Chinese students at American universities. In 1916 it promised the Philippines independence and made good on that promise immediately after World War II. It put pressure on the colonial powers, especially the Dutch, to hasten independence for the East Indies. Finally, it prided itself on its anticolonial reputation.

With the Cold War spreading to Asia, however, Americans found themselves in something of a quandary. It was all very well and good to say that colonialism was a dying system, and good riddance, too. The French in Indochina had been a problem for American objectives in Asia from the moment they yielded control to the Japanese occupation in 1941—an event that triggered the final sequence to Pearl Harbor. Now, waiting outside the door were the communists, whose cunning ploys knew no limit. Imperial Japan had trumpeted its Greater East Asian Co-Prosperity Sphere as promising a better life for Asians once the white man had been driven out of ancient lands. The reality was entirely different—a colonial regime worse in many ways than French rule. But the Japanese had achieved one of their goals, destruction of the myth of Western invincibility.

Ho Chi Minh's clever use of Jeffersonian-style rhetoric in his August 1945 "Declaration of Independence" was designed to appeal to the "Spirit of '76," the American Revolutionary tradition. Ho's letters to Harry Truman made the appeal even more explicit. They failed to elicit any response, as William Duiker points out in chapter 1. But so did his letters to Stalin. Truman was preoccupied with issues of much larger import—at the time—than the fate of Vietnam. He and his advisors worried about French blindness to the real situation that faced them in attempting to reconquer their lost colony and regain their lost pride after the humiliating defeat in 1940. But there was little to do except hope for great wisdom in Paris.

There was another reason, however, for the White House's silence. What little was known about Ho Chi Minh did not encourage a favorable reception to his overtures. There was a parallel here with Chinese revolutionary leader Sun Yat-sen's appeals to Woodrow Wilson before World War I. Wilson suspected that Sun had taken money from the Japanese, and might indeed be their "agent" in China. So, too, was Ho thought to be an "agent" of a rival system, disguising himself as an admirer of Thomas Jefferson and the American Revolution. Claims to be the trustee of the one "true" revolution shaped policymakers' thinking about the wars in Vietnam in a variety of ways. Certainly the French could not provide either spiritual or material leadership to satisfy the demands of Vietnamese nationalists. But the communists were worse, because they hid their ultimate purpose to make Vietnam into a subservient part of the Soviet empire, destined to do Moscow's bidding to spread the false revolution to the rest of the world.

When Senator Frank Church (D-Idaho) queried Secretary of State Rusk about the U.S. military response to the Vietnamese revolution, he got a sharp response that what Hanoi was attempting to foist on South Vietnam was imported from China. It had nothing to do with the American Revolution, nothing at all. Church's point, on the other hand, was that most revolutionaries accept—indeed are compelled to accept—foreign aid from where they find it. On another occasion, while talking privately with General Maxwell Taylor, Rusk pondered whether it would be possible to prove once and for all the illegitimacy of the so-called Vietnamese revolution. As he went over these matters with Taylor, Rusk mused about an idea he had. Would it be possible to explore with South Vietnamese leaders, "whether there was any possibility of the RVN's talking to Front leaders and persuading a couple of them to defect. Such defectors, who say publicly the whole Front was a fraud and a sham, would be worth a great deal—perhaps several mission [million] dollars in Switzerland."[1]

General Taylor once complained that while he was ambassador to South Vietnam, he was inundated with specialists from Washington, eager to take over the tasks of democratizing the country along approved liberal lines. General Taylor once quipped sourly about the "reformist" nature of this effort that American pioneers had long ago realized it was not safe to plant corn outside the stockade until the Indians had been driven away. But the impulse to prove American worthiness showed itself in Vietnam in a variety of ways, as Marc Gilbert illustrates in chapter 6, by exploring the "other war" for the hearts and minds of the Vietnamese. The fate of the members of the International Voluntary Service (IVS) as they collided with the need to cooperate with Saigon's war effort pointed up the dilemma. The larger the number of American troops in Vietnam, the more the possibility of victory in the other war faded. As Gilbert points out, the Americanization of the war strengthened the belief in the DRV that Saigon had no hope of "winning the hearts and minds of the Vietnamese people" and convinced many Vietnamese on both sides of the war in the south that the RVN continued to exist only because of the presence of foreign military forces.

While the Soviets and Chinese resented Ho's ability to manipulate their ideological rivalry within the communist "world," there was very little they could do about it. The rivalry was a great boon to the enemy forces, of course, but probably not crucial. The "agent" theory of revolution posits that revolutions (and counterrevolutions) occur because of subversion and outside agitation. In Dean Rusk's confrontations with Senator Church and other war critics on the issue of whether Vietnam was a case of outside aggression or a civil war, he always fell back on the agent theory of revolution. Accordingly, this interpretation argued that Hanoi, after Geneva, had left behind agents throughout South Vietnam, who waited for a proper moment to exploit the aftermath of colonialism and the French war to suit their purposes. Behind them were men in the northern capital who pulled the strings; behind those men were the men who sent orders from Beijing; and behind them were the shadowy figures in the Kremlin who had started all this trouble for the world in the first place with the Bolshevik Revolution.

Given this interpretation of the Vietnam War, it is indeed difficult to see how American leaders could disengage very easily. As Robert Brigham points out in chapter 4, however, to ask the question "Why did the North Win the Vietnam War?" denies the Vietnamese much of a role in their own history. It suggests a variation on the agent theory of revolution. Consequently, the authors in this collection are at some pains to demonstrate instead how the war arose out of Vietnamese history and conditions. Brigham demonstrates that southerners ultimately dominated the Politburo debates over decisions to launch military initiatives and that after Geneva both the Soviets and the Chinese were loath to encourage another American military intervention in Southeast Asia. The war worked almost the opposite from the way the "agent" theory said it had. To say this, however, does not mean that Moscow and Beijing were disinterested in the outcome or were unhappy at America's defeat. Again, it is George Herring who reminds us of the careful and cautious policies pursued by both the Soviet Union and China until the American escalation of the war changed dramatically to its disadvantage. "In ways the United States appears not to have anticipated," he writes, "its own escalation of the war forced the Soviet Union and China to assist North Vietnam in ways that undercut U.S. military pressure." The Soviet Union, of course, then took away exactly the wrong lesson from Vietnam, when it engaged in a lengthy attempt to suppress an Afghan rebellion under the illusion that the victor in the former war was communism.

It may well be, as some argue, that the Soviet Union's revolutionary urges were rekindled after Stalin's death by the success of "revolutionary nationalism," first in China and then elsewhere. But the demonstrated higher priority Moscow placed on bilateral issues with the United States suggests a continuing ambiguity about Vietnamese communism. Recent discussions of the Vietnam War, moreover, as Marc Gilbert points out, have been much influenced by the end of the Cold War and the concomitant disappearance of the Soviet Union. Vietnam loses its place as a traumatizing era in American history and thereby becomes a badly planned war, politically and militarily, or a case of "liberal" faint-heartedness, or a tragic miscalculation. Former Secretary of Defense Robert McNamara has devoted himself in recent years to warning the nation—and the world—about the dangers of nuclear war. Miscalculation, obviously, increases the danger that a superpower will go to war and, ultimately, use nuclear weapons. To prove the case about miscalculation's dangers thus becomes an imperative for him in remembering the Vietnam War.

We were wrong, then, McNamara has argued, in imagining that the North Vietnamese were merely "agents" for the Soviet Union; but they were also wrong to imagine that we would never allow a reunification process to go forward. McNamara has had some difficulty in convincing former Vietnamese enemies that the war was a case of mistaken identity. Numerous commentators, including several serving in the government when the decisions were made, also have challenged his assertion that lack of expertise and historical perspective was the cause of the tragedy in Vietnam. In sections of a memo he sent President Johnson that he did not include in his memoirs, McNamara avers that the Chinese were attempting to construct a coalition in Asia against American interests:

> This understanding of a straightforward security threat is interwoven with another perception-namely, that we have our view of the way the U.S. should be moving and of the need for the majority of the rest of the world to be moving in the same direction if we are to achieve our national objectives. . . . Our ends cannot be achieved and our leadership role cannot be played if some powerful and virulent nation—whether Germany, Japan, Russia or China—is allowed to organize their part of the world according to a philosophy contrary to ours.[2]

McNamara seems to indicate a clear sense of what was assumed to be at stake here. If there was a miscalculation, authors in this collection suggest, it was in the thinking of both sides about the determination of the other to stay the course. Vietnamese decision makers thought they could offer Washington an honorable way out of the war. Their U.S. counterparts believed that when Hanoi realized that it risked destruction of the communist home base, it would call off the dogs of war. In chapter 3 Jeffrey Record notes that critics of the military believe that a failure to develop a strategy to achieve the latter purpose spelled defeat in Vietnam. While there was much to criticize in the Pentagon's performance, especially a parochial attitude by each of the services (and their chiefs), the real failure was in not warning civilian leaders that the war they imagined could not be won. John Prados, in chapter 5, notes the irony of the immense intelligence system the United States established in Vietnam to determine when the breaking point had arrived.

"American intelligence," he writes, "could operate within its most efficient parameters only as American power failed to defeat the insurgency."

The intelligence system, like the bombing and the use of high technology, was supposed to overwhelm the enemy simply by its magnitude. Instead, as Jeffrey Record points out, the weight of the American presence in Vietnam on one level, and the transitory nature of the units in battle on another, each worked in its own way to defeat the American cause. Ambassador Henry Cabot Lodge might look out his window high in the gleaming new embassy building in Saigon and see evidence of the growing might of America in Vietnam on the river and all across the city, and report home on the panoramic magnificence of what he saw, but it was the invisible Vietnamese who would determine the outcome. Likewise, Secretary Rusk thought he could demonstrate for his skeptical senior colleagues why America would inevitably succeed by placing his hands against a heavy oak table and pushing it a few inches across the floor from his position seated at the head of the table. When America decides to do something, he declared, it does it.

Andrew Rotter, in chapter 7, provides an answer to both Lodge and Rusk. The Vietnamese foe did not have to move polished oak tables to win the war, and their Vietnamese opponent could not absorb the overload that poured into South Vietnam from American ships and planes. The foe's "economic culture" required less to supply the enemy at the front, while the American way of war in Vietnam, that helped to create an economic boom at home in the United States, meant disaster for the Saigon regime. The effect of U.S. intervention was practically surreal. The Saigon sanitation system failed when its workers abandoned their posts for construction jobs on U.S. military bases, where the pay was much better than in the city. As Rotter notes, one day a Vietnamese scrawled on the pavement in front of a garbage pile, "This is the fruit of American aid."

Perhaps the antiwar movement in America is the most debated aspect of the Vietnam era. Perhaps not. But, as Marilyn Young points out in chapter 9, both the left and the right like to exaggerate its actual impact on the outcome of the war. For the right, it provides a way of criticizing not only Dr. Spock's spoiled babies but also the entire liberal agenda in the 1960s—demonstrating how close it brought the nation to total disaster. For the left, it provides an alternative "useful past" for organizing in the present. Her conclusion is that it helped to raise uncomfortable issues, that its goal to end the slaughter was a noble purpose and no less patriotic than opposition to the Mexican War a hundred years earlier.

Her account of the competing narrative sponsored by certain elements of the antiwar movement suggests again, almost in passing, a very important question about the American way of history. Complete with a vast array of new patriotic images, counterparades, counterflags, and a new set of founding fathers—Fidel Castro, Ho Chi Minh, Mao Zedong—the movement's extremists mimicked the very forces they opposed. Lyndon Johnson was deeply suspicious of the "Harvards," as he called them—yet he prided himself on having all those "action intellectuals" at his beck and call. Once, down at the ranch, LBJ introduced his under secretary of state, George Ball, to a foreign statesman as one of the leading eggheads in his administration. Ball remonstrated sharply. Mr. President, he said, don't ever do that again. Ball rejected being labeled as an intellectual, not because he thought intellectuals were elitists of the sort Johnson had always envied, but because they believed too much in the power of their theories. Vietnam discredited many theories, but, as Marc Gilbert points out in the introduction to this volume, an enduring legacy of the war has been the rise of historical interpretations across the ideological spectrum that disdain traditional forms and content of historical inquiry and that "privilege" theory over evidence as little more than competing texts.

What emerges with great clarity from these chapters is that the Vietnam War was really many wars, but only one that finally counted for the Vietnamese. Its victims were primarily the Vietnamese, and its victors were the Vietnamese. Fifty years on, historians will look at the Cold War and wonder why the Americans did not understand better the folly of their attempt at nation-building. Vietnamese infiltrators into the Saigon regime's innermost councils escaped detection, while the countryside was ruled by the enemy whenever there was not the actual presence of American troops. The reality of Vietnam was as elusive to American policymakers as the enemy forces were to the men they sent to this hall of mirrors. They saw only their own reflections, multiplied over and over.

## Notes

1. Memorandum for the Record, April 3, 1965, *Foreign Relations of the United States, 1964–1968, Volume II, January-June, 1965,* National Defense University, Taylor Papers, Cables 1965. Top Secret, no.237, www.state.gov/www/about_state/history/vol_ii/221_240.html.
2. Draft Memorandum, November 3, 1965, *Foreign Relations of the United States, 1964–1968, Volume III, January-June, 1965,* Washington National Records Center, RG 330, McNamara Files: FRC 71 A 3470, South Vietnam, Statements and Supporting Papers. Top Secret. no.189, *www.state.gov/www/about_state/history/vol_iii/180.html.*

# About the Authors

Robert Brigham

Robert K. Brigham is Associate Professor of History at Vassar College. He earned his Ph.D. with George C. Herring at the University of Kentucky and his Bachelor's degree at the State University of New York—Brockport. He is the author of numerous books and essays on the Vietnam War, including *Guerrilla Diplomacy: The National Liberation Front's Foreign Relations and the Vietnam War* (1998) and, along with Robert S. McNamara and James G. Blight, *Argument Without End: In Search of Answers to the Vietnam Tragedy* (1999).

William Duiker

William J. Duiker is Liberal Arts Professor Emeritus of East Asian Studies at the Pennsylvania State University. A former Foreign Service officer with posts in Taiwan and South Vietnam, he currently specializes in the history of modern China and Vietnam. He was awarded a Faculty Scholar Medal for Outstanding Achievement by Penn State in the spring of 1996 and retired from the History Department the following year. Professor Duiker has written several books and articles on subjects related to modern Vietnam. His *The Communist Road to Power in Vietnam* (1981) received a Choice Outstanding Book Award for 1982–1983 and a second award when it was republished in a new edition in 1996. Other recent books include *Sacred War: Nationalism and Revolution in a Divided Vietnam* (1995), *U.S. Containment Policy and the Conflict in Indochina* (1994) and *China and Vietnam: The Roots of Conflict* (1987). His biography of the Vietnamese revolutionary Ho Chi Minh, entitled *Ho Chi Minh: A Life,* was published in the fall of 2000. During his professional career at Penn State Professor Duiker received grants from the Social Science Research Council, the Ford Foundation, and the National Endowment for the Humanities. He has served as director of the East Asian Studies Program at Penn State, as well as director of International Programs in the College of Liberal Arts. In recent years he has developed a strong interest in world history and with colleague Jackson Spielvogel published a textbook entitled *World History* (3rd ed., 2000).

LLOYD C. GARDNER

Lloyd C. Gardner is Charles and Mary Beard Professor of History at Rutgers University, where he has taught since 1963. A graduate of Ohio Wesleyan University and the University of Wisconsin (Ph.D. 1960), Gardner is the author of more than a dozen books. His recent work has focused on the Vietnam War and includes, *Approaching Vietnam: From World War II to Dienbienphu* (1988) and *Pay Any Price: Lyndon Johnson and the Wars for Vietnam* (1995). Gardner has been the recipient of several fellowship awards, including two Fulbright professorships in Finland and England, and a Guggenheim Fellowship. He is a past president of the Society of Historians of American Foreign Relations and a fellow of the Society of American Historians.

MARC JASON GILBERT

Marc Jason Gilbert received his Ph.D. in History from the University of California—Los Angeles in 1978. He is a Professor of History at North Georgia College & State University, where he teaches courses in modern South and Southeast Asian history. He also serves as codirector of the University System of Georgia's programs in Vietnam. He has written widely on Vietnam's place in world history and on the impact of the Vietnam War on the United States. He also has lectured on Southeast Asian security at a variety of academic and government institutions, including the Center for Strategic and International Studies and the United States Air Force Special Operations Command School. He is the editor of *The Vietnam War: Teaching Approaches and Resources* (1991), *The Vietnam War on Campus: Other Voices, More Distant Drums* (2000), and coeditor, with William Head, of *The Tet Offensive* (1996). He cowrote and coproduced along with James Forscher and Lon Holmberg the award-winning documentary *Lost Warriors* (1999), an examination of the plight of homeless American Vietnam combat veterans. He is also a coauthor along with Peter Stearns, Michael Adas, and Stuart Schwartz, of *World Civilizations: The Global Experience* (3rd ed., 2000), a survey of world history that offers extensive coverage of both Vietnamese history and the Second Indochina War.

GEORGE C. HERRING

George C. Herring is Alumni Professor of History at the University of Kentucky. He is the author of numerous articles, essays, and books, including *The Secret Diplomacy of the Vietnam War: The Negotiating Volumes of the Pentagon Papers* (1983), *LBJ and Vietnam: A Different Kind of War* (1994) and *America's Longest War: The United States and Vietnam, 1950–1975* (3rd ed., 1996). He served as editor of the *Journal of Diplomatic History* from 1982 to 1986 and was president of the Society for Historians of American Foreign Relations in 1990. In 1991 he was a visiting Fulbright scholar at the University of Otago, New Zealand, and in 1993–1994 he was a visiting professor at the U.S. Military Academy, West Point.

JOHN PRADOS

John Prados received his Ph.D. in Political Science/International Relations from Columbia University in 1982. He is the director of the Vietnam Documentation Project of the National Security Archive in Washington, D.C., Prados has written and lectured widely on security, intelligence, and military affairs. He is author of several books on the Vietnam War, including *The Sky Would Fall* (1983), *Hidden History of the Vietnam War* (1995), and *The Blood Road: The Ho Chi Minh Trail and the Vietnam War* (1999). His fresh history of the Dien Bien Phu crisis, *Operation Vulture,* will appear later this year and a biography of William E. Colby is in press. He is coauthor (with Ray W. Stubbe) of the definitive history of the siege of Khe Sanh, *Valley of Decision* (1991).

JEFFREY RECORD

Jeffrey Record is Professor of International Security Studies at the U.S. Air Force's Air War College in Montgomery, Alabama. He received his doctorate at the Johns Hopkins School of Advanced International Studies. During the Vietnam War, he served as an Assistant Province Advisor in the Mekong Delta. He has been a Rockefeller Younger Scholar on the Brookings Institution's Defense Analysis Staff and Senior Fellow at the Institute for Foreign Policy Analysis, the Hudson Institute, and at the BDM International Corporation. He also has served as Legislative Assistant for National Security Affairs to Senators Sam Nunn and Lloyd Bentsen and later as a Professional Staff Member of the Senate Armed Services Committee. Record is the author of four books and a dozen monographs, including: *Revising US Military Strategy, Tailoring Means to Ends* (1984); *Beyond Military Reform: American Defense Dilemmas* (1988); *Hollow Victory: A Contrary View of the Gulf War* (1993); *The Wrong War: Why We Lost in Vietnam* (1998); *Perils of Reasoning by Historical Analogy: Munich, Vietnam and American Use of Force Since 1945 (1998);* and *Failed States and Casualty Phobia (*2000*).*

ANDREW J. ROTTER

Andrew J. Rotter is Professor of History at Colgate University. He received his Ph.D. in History from Stanford University in 1981. He is author of *The Path to Vietnam: Origins of the U.S. Commitment to Southeast Asia* (1987); *Comrades at Odds: The United States and India, 1947–1964* (2000); and articles in *Diplomatic History,* the *Journal of American History,* and the *American Historical Review.* He is also editor of *Light at the End of the Tunnel: A Vietnam War Anthology* (rev. ed., 1999).

EARL H. TILFORD, JR.
Earl H. Tilford Jr. is Professor of History at Grove City College, in Grove City, Pennsylvania. He received his B.A. and M.A. in American history at the University of Alabama and his Ph.D. in American and European military history at George Washington University. During the Vietnam War, he served as an intelligence officer working on air operations in Laos. During his subsequent career in the United States Air Force, he taught history at the Air Force Academy and was the editor of the *Air University Review,* formerly the professional journal of the air force. Tilford is the author of numerous articles and books on Vietnam, the latest being *Crosswinds: The Air Force's Setup in Vietnam* (1993).

MARILYN YOUNG
Marilyn Young received her Ph.D. from Harvard University in 1963. She is Professor in, and a former Chair, of the Department of History at New York University. Young teaches courses on the history of U.S. foreign policy, with particular reference to Asia, as well as courses on the history of modern China, the history and culture of Vietnam, and social change and gender. Her publications include *Rhetoric of Empire: American China Policy, 1895–1901* (1969); *Transforming Russia and China: Revolutionary Struggle in the 20th Century* (with William Rosenberg) (1980); and *The Vietnam Wars, 1945–1990* (1991). She has also edited and coedited several anthologies, including *Women in China: Essays on Social Change and Feminism* (1973); *Promissory Notes: Women and the Transition to Socialism* (with Rayna Rapp and Sonia Kruks) (1983); and *Vietnam and America* (with Marvin Gettleman, Jane Franklin, and Bruce Franklin) (1995). Young has twice been awarded a Golden Dozen Teaching Award. She is currently a recipient of a Guggenheim Fellowship and a fellowship from the American Council of Learned Societies awarded in support of her research on the Korean War.

# INDEX